# ACCESS YOUR ONLINE RESOURCES

T0341225

*Sex Ed for Grown-Ups* is accompanied by a number of printable online materials, designed to ensure this resource best supports your professional needs.

Activate your online resources:

Go to www.routledge.com/cw/speechmark and click on the cover of this book.

Click the 'Sign in or Request Access' button and follow the instructions in order to access the resources.

Jonny Hunt knows his stuff. For years he's given dynamic sex-education lessons to children and young people. Now, to bring adults up to speed, he has transcribed his down-to-earth approach into this informative, big-hearted, open-minded book. It puts sex and relationships topics into social, emotional and historical perspective with solid research, personal and professional anecdotes, empathy, humour and an insightful angle on how unequally girls and boys experience growing up. As parents, we have a lot to learn before we become more comfortable talking openly with our digital-native kids. *Sex Ed for Grown-Ups* points us in the right direction.

*Leah Jewett, Outspoken Sex Ed Director*

In this excellent book, Jonny Hunt explores the myths and challenges of speaking about sex and relationships, and offers much sensible and practical advice around the topic. A practitioner of considerable experience and expertise in working in both primary and secondary settings, Jonny brings a conversational and reassuring tone to tackle all aspects of relationships and sex education, from early conversations with very young children to the more mature areas such as pornography and teen sexting. It will give readers the confidence to engage with these issues in a fact-based and young person-focussed manner, and I would recommend it not only for parents but also teachers of relationships education and the wider children's workforce.

*Andy Phippen, Professor of Digital Rights,*
*Bournemouth University*

# SEX ED FOR GROWN-UPS

When it comes to talking to children and young people about sex and relationships, it is difficult to know what to say. How do you answer their questions? How much is too much? And what is age appropriate?

*Sex Ed for Grown-Ups* is an open and honest guide that empowers adults to talk to young people about all things sex and relationships.

Written by an independent relationships and sex education consultant, this light-hearted and accessible book encourages grown-ups to think and talk about the topics that scare them the most: from body parts, gender, puberty and first-time sex, to pornography, sexting and knowing what to do when things go wrong. Full of hints, tips and first-hand stories, it is a fun, compassionate and engaging exploration of relationships and sex, which will help adults to fully support young people as they develop a healthy view of both sex and themselves.

*Sex Ed for Grown-Ups* is essential reading for parents, teachers, youth workers, social workers and any adult who wants to have well-informed and positive conversations with the children and young people in their lives.

**Jonny Hunt** is an independent relationships and sex education (RSE) consultant. Jonny has spent his career working face to face with children and young people of various ages (from four years upwards), and training the professionals who work with them around all aspects of sex and relationships. Jonny specialises in delivering inclusive RSE, with a rights-based approach, encouraging both adults and young people to explore their values and attitudes to sex and relationships.

# SEX ED FOR GROWN-UPS

## How to Talk to Children and Young People about Sex and Relationships

JONNY HUNT

Routledge
Taylor & Francis Group

LONDON AND NEW YORK

First published 2022
by Routledge
2 Park Square, Milton Park, Abingdon, Oxon OX14 4RN

and by Routledge
605 Third Avenue, New York, NY 10158

*Routledge is an imprint of the Taylor & Francis Group, an informa business*

© 2022 Jonny Hunt

*British Library Cataloguing-in-Publication Data*
A catalogue record for this book is available from the British Library

*Library of Congress Cataloging-in-Publication Data*
Names: Hunt, Jonny, author.
Title: Sex ed for grown-ups : how to talk to children and young people about sex and relationships / Jonny Hunt.
Description: Abingdon, Oxon ; New York, NY : Routledge, 2022. |
Includes bibliographical references.
Identifiers: LCCN 2021011297 (print) | LCCN 2021011298 (ebook) |
ISBN 9780367641344 (hardback) | ISBN 9780367641337 (paperback) |
ISBN 9781003122296 (ebook)
Subjects: LCSH: Sex instruction. | Sex instruction for children. |
Sex instruction for youth. | Parenting.
Classification: LCC HQ57 .H86 2022 (print) |
LCC HQ57 (ebook) | DDC 649/.65–dc23
LC record available at https://lccn.loc.gov/2021011297
LC ebook record available at https://lccn.loc.gov/2021011298

ISBN: 978-0-367-64134-4 (hbk)
ISBN: 978-0-367-64133-7 (pbk)
ISBN: 978-1-003-12229-6 (ebk)

DOI: 10.4324/9781003122296

Typeset in Myriad Pro
by Newgen Publishing UK

Access the companion website: www.routledge.com/cw/speechmark

For

Gem and Izzy

and for my Dad...

I miss our conversations.

# CONTENTS

# ACKNOWLEDGEMENTS

*Remake* by Lunarbaboon is reproduced with kind permission from the artist Chris Grady.

Thank you to all the young people who have shaped my ideas over the years. You have challenged my understanding of relationship education and helped me to re-evaluate my values. You have made my job a pleasure.

Thank you to my wife Gemma, without whom there would be no book.

# TERMS AND ABBREVIATIONS

## Sex education

**CSE** comprehensive sexuality education (internationally used term – not to be confused with CSE as in child sexual exploitation)
**RSE** relationships and sex education
**SRE** sex and relationships education

## Gender identity and sexuality

**asexual** Someone who does not usually feel sexual attraction or sexual urge towards other people. Asexuality can work on a spectrum. Some will engage in sexual activity to please a partner, but often simply do not find sex interesting, fulfilling or important.
**bisexual** Sexual attraction towards people of the same and opposite genders. However, not all bisexual people will have romantic relationships with both.
**cis** Used to avoid using terms such as 'normal'. Means the gender assigned at birth matches their gender identity.
**gender queer** Umbrella term for someone who is non-binary.
**heterosexual** Attracted to the opposite gender M+F/F+M
**homosexual (gay/lesbian)** Attracted to the same gender, M+M/F+F.
**intersex** A person who is born with sex characteristics that do not wholly belong in either category of male or female.
**LGBTQA+** Lesbian, gay, bisexual, trans, questioning/queer, asexual + other sexual identities.
**non-binary** More often than not refers to gender identity and describes someone who identifies gender as a spectrum rather than solid binary categories such as male or female. Instead may sit somewhere in between or move along the spectrum.

**pansexual** A person who is sexually attracted to people of any gender. Attracted to the person's character as a whole regardless of their gender identity.

**queer** Umbrella term for sexual and gender identities that are not heterosexual and cisgender.

**trans** Someone whose true gender is different to the gender they were assigned at birth.

# At the clinic

**AIDS** Acquired Immune Deficiency Syndrome
**ART** antiretroviral treatment
**EHC** emergency hormonal contraceptive
**GUM** genito-urinary medicine
**HIV** Human Immunodeficiency Virus
**IUD** intrauterine device (coil)
**IUS** intrauterine system (hormonal – Mirena™ or Jaydess™)
**LARC** long-acting reversible contraception
**PEP** post-exposure prophylaxis
**PrEP** pre-exposure prophylaxis
**STD** sexually transmitted disease
**STI** sexually transmitted infection

# Miscellaneous

**AI** artificial intelligence
**AV** age verification
**PIV** penis in vagina (penetrative sex)

# INTRODUCTION: SO… WHAT WAS YOUR SEX EDUCATION LIKE?

**A**sking a group of adults about their own memories of sex education certainly opens up some interesting conversations. Regardless of whether I am delivering training for professionals or a meeting for parents, it is a great way to break the ice. The majority of adults I speak to have few positive things to say about the sex ed they received. For many, it was non-existent and, for the rest, they still shudder at the thought as they relive the embarrassment of the ordeal in their heads.

Possibly my favourite story I have ever been told in response to the question was shared during training I was delivering a few years ago, for a mixed group of professionals, consisting of social workers, youth workers, school nurses and teachers. I had asked each of the professionals to introduce themselves one by one and to give us a brief overview of their memories of sex education. We eventually came to the social worker in question, who explained in her thick accent that she grew up 'on the island of Ireland in the 1970s', where she attended a catholic convent school.

DOI: 10.4324/9781003122296-1

A natural storyteller, she explained that in her entire time at school she had only had one 'lesson' where the topic of sex was openly spoken of. The girls in her year were formally shuffled into the school hall by a particularly aged nun who was renowned for being strict and short of patience. The girls all sat in their chairs in a horse shoe shape around the old overhead projector that was in the middle of the room pointing at the screen.

The Holy Mother banged a ruler on the table to get everyone's attention, making the girls jump. Now she had the girls' attention, she gave a bit of a preamble about the sanctity of marriage and of motherhood. She then gave them a stern warning about how some *wicked boys* would try to corrupt them and told them that they must remain strong and chaste.

To emphasise her point, the Holy Mother flicked the switch on the overhead projector. On the screen was projected a huge black and white picture of a penis, which filled the entire wall.

*'This is man,' the nun bellowed at the girls, 'this is what he will put in you!'*

Whilst this story stands out for obvious reasons, it is certainly not the only horror story I have been told over the years. To be honest, it is not the horror stories that bother me, it is the consistent lack of information given to young people to help them navigate their teenage years.

(Y)

Me, I am the generation of kids where my first foray into the world of sex education came at around the age of 11. We were ushered into the school library, which was essentially a box room with a couple of bookcases pushed up against the walls with lots of little clay figures that past students had made some years before. They then wheeled in the TV – do you remember those huge TVs that were in a locked cabinet on massive legs with wheels, that took two of the older kids in school to manoeuvre?

It was then unlocked and unpacked – the cabinet unfolded to create a canopy to prevent glare off the screen. In those days, no teacher had ever been taught how to use a VCR so there was the usual faffing around on discovering the tape needed rewinding. This only added to the tension that was already building. Then, finally, they pressed play and the tape started… and we all watched a video that destroyed our entire childhood.

Half of the class sat looking porridge-faced and horrified, whilst the other half were bright red and desperately trying to hide their giggles!

A week or two later, all the boys were sent out on the field to have an extra hour of football. Meanwhile, all the girls were shepherded back into the library to have a secret chat with the school nurse about 'stuff'. When we all returned to the classroom all hot and sweaty from running around, we were met with the girls all acting rather strange; some were strutting round the room looking impressed with themselves, others were looking a bit peaky and petrified – but they were all hiding mysterious little packages in their bags and refusing to answer our questions.

For most children, that was it – a quick chat about puberty and *some of your bits aren't nice* – before being packed off on buses to high school where you were surrounded by kids who were up to 18 years old.

If you were lucky, a few years later when in high school, a very embarrassed teacher who had obviously drawn the short straw – or missed the meeting and had been volunteered in their absence – would show you how to roll a condom on a banana or a broom handle… and that was kind of it.

I have worked in Relationships and Sex Education (RSE) for the past 17 years. I would love to tell you that during that time things have improved… but unfortunately, for many children, this is still their reality when it comes to RSE.

However, this should all be about to change. Thursday 19 July 2019 saw the official release of the new guidance for RSE.[1] The draft guidance had been floating around on the periphery for over 12 months, causing ripples. It had been reviewed, rewritten and consulted on; but now we had the official document. The first official update to the national guidance in two decades. Yes, you heard me correctly, the first update in 20 years. Having worked in RSE for my entire adult life, this is a marked occasion – this is the first piece of national guidance that has been published during my entire professional career. Finally, all children of all ages, in every school, should have access to comprehensive and positive information around relationships and sex.

(.)(.)

But here comes the problem…

One thing I am always quick to point out when I am speaking to parents or training professionals is that we, as the adult now in charge of delivering that work – whether at home or school – have never been the children on the carpet. It is those same adults, whose only experience of sex ed was the TV on stilts, that are now expected to talk to today's children and equip them with all of the information they need to go on to have safe and mutually respectful relationships and sexual encounters. On top of which, they are also supposed to be experts in new technologies – such as mobile phones and the internet – and helping young people to navigate these safely. Is it any wonder why many feel a little out of their depth, with no idea where to begin?

It is difficult to impart helpful information to the children and young people around you if you have never been given the best information yourself – especially when things have changed so quickly. In many ways children are growing up in a world that we do not recognise as the same one we grew up in.

For example, when we were children, you would not be alone to admit that you may have sneaked to the back of the class to the bookcase and, feeling brave, in a fit of curiosity, taken a dictionary from the shelf and looked up naughty words like s-e-x (ahh!) or t-i-t and giggled with your mates at the three-line definition (*a small native bird to the UK*). I can still remember, carved into the old wooden benches in the Biology lab at secondary school were the numbers 348 – which just happened to correspond to the page number for human reproduction in the school textbooks. The fact is these behaviours haven't changed – children still do all the same things we did, as they have always done – the only difference, is children are not reaching for the junior dictionary these days. Instead, they are typing these things into google. With the internet, children have access to information like they have never had before.

Even things like the way we watch television has changed. The watershed is no longer a thing. Most people watch TV on catch-up or via streaming services rather than live – so it is increasingly difficult to shield children from shows that traditionally wouldn't have been on until after the kids were asleep.

The vast majority of parents want to have conversations with their children about sex and relationships. This corresponds with my own experience of spending time talking to both parents and professionals alike. The majority of parents I speak to want to do things differently for their own children. However, wanting to do something differently is one thing, but then follows the next big question – what are we actively doing to get there?

(*)

In 2017 Dr Claire Bennett compared parental attitudes in the Netherlands to those of English parents. Unsurprisingly, Bennett found that Dutch families enjoyed much greater openness than their English counterparts. Conversations around sex and relationships are commonplace in the Netherlands, supported by positive messages from the Dutch government (Bennet, 2017). Whilst the argument that discussion of sex education poses a threat to childhood innocence still dominates domestic discourse here in the UK, in the Netherlands this notion is not entertained. This is true even amongst more conservative parents with strong religious beliefs. As a result, not only are Dutch parents more confident, but there is an expectation that parents have conversations with their children from an early age, as a matter of course (ibid.).

In my experience, parents in the UK on the whole want to talk to their children more openly about relationships and sex, but do not know how best to do it. Instead, despite their good intentions, parents make excuses about their children *not being ready yet* (Bennet, 2017). It is curious that so many adults use the excuse that their child hasn't asked yet – so mustn't be ready. There is no other aspect of personal wellbeing or education that we treat in the same way. We do not wait for our children to ask before we stick them in the bath or try to feed them broccoli. We start to show them how to cross the road safely from before they can talk. No one has ever waited for a child to ask before they have taught them about fractions or fronted adverbials!

One question that is often overlooked and yet should be the starting point of any discussion as parents when thinking about our children's future is: What is it we hope for?

> When it comes to our child's intimate relationships and their first sexual experience what is it we want?

For me, this is an essential question. It may be some way off but in an ideal world, what do parents hope their child's first sexual encounters will look like? If we could write the script, how would it go? Where would it happen?

What would the circumstances be? How would they feel afterwards? Why do we find this such an uncomfortable concept to think about? But most importantly, what can we be doing now to make that wish a reality?

Children who have access to open conversations around sex and relationships education (SRE) tend to have their first sexual experience later; when they do become sexually active, they are more likely to take precaution and practise safe sex; and they are less likely to regret their experience (UNESCO, 2018). So what is stopping us? Especially compared with studies of abstinence-only education whose outcomes are either non-existent or largely negative, with young people reporting higher cases of unsafe sex and being more likely to regret sex happening (Cocoran et al., 2019). This is hardly surprising when you consider it is difficult to plan for something that you have promised to abstain from.

In my experience, one of the biggest barriers to adults – parents especially – having positive conversations with children is feeling unsure and out of their depth themselves. Many parents know they should start young and make sex, bodies and relationships an open topic in their home, but they are unsure of what to say – how much is too much? And where should they start?

I know it can be scary. And I know for many of us this pushes us way out of our comfort zones. For example, it is now fairly common practice for children from Reception upwards to be taught the correct names for their private parts as part of safeguarding messages around safe and appropriate touching. This is great news – I regularly talk with small children who can use the proper names for their private parts quite happily, without a blush in sight. Meanwhile, however, the teaching assistant in the corner is bright red and trying not to giggle. In reality, the majority of adults have never used the word vulva in a sentence before – assuming they know what a vulva is (don't worry, we will discuss anatomy in detail in Chapter 2).

What's more, our generation of children are the first to grow up immersed in a world of digital technology. A world built on mobile phone and wi-fi connections. This has added an entirely new level of panic and worry in the minds of parents, especially when there are few amongst us that sit comfortably as digital natives (Prensky, 2011).

Unfortunately, there is so much information in the media that highlights the dangers of mobile phones and the internet; it is understandable why many adults treat these things with suspicion and see them as a serious threat to childhood.

However, what is often missing from discussions is the recognition of how mobile phones or the internet might be used to help young people to negotiate sexual boundaries; provide a new platform for difficult conversations; or help to keep young people safe by providing needed lifelines for vulnerable children. This is especially important for those who identify as LGBTQA+, who may not yet be out to their family and can seek help and support safely and anonymously.

Indeed, at the time of writing, in between Covid-19 lock-downs, as the world is still not back to any sense of itself, we have seen how important mobile phones and the internet are in keeping young people connected to the world. Whether as the primary source of formal schooling, or as a means of resisting the creeping feelings of isolation, we have all been gifted the means to stay in touch with loved ones, be they near or far away. Technology has really been a key factor in keeping us all connected and sane.

However, the negative and suspicious approach that adults have generally taken when tackling these topics not only risks shaming young people, but can actually push them away from asking us for help when they get in trouble. Let me explain: when I talk openly to young people about mobile phones, sexting and what they get up to online, when I ask: 'If you got in trouble on your mobile phone – if someone was bullying you, harassing you, you felt pressured or some was coercing you to send pictures – would you tell your parents or a teacher at school?' The unanimous answer is 'No!'.

So what is stopping our children talking to the safe adults around them when they need help?

because they will take
my phone off me…

I am very lucky in my job that I spend a lot of my time talking to children and young people of all ages about these topics – often this is the stuff that parents don't get to hear. Indeed, the majority of the training I deliver is based around passing on what young people tell me in our conversations.

As a parent, knowing this information can help you to make better decisions as to how to manage situations at home. There is no point continuing to take phones off our children as a response when things go wrong if all it does as a consequence is push children further away from our support.

My ethos has always aimed to open doors between young people and the safe adults around them. This involves changing the conversation and our approach.

And this is where this book fits in.

(())

In this book I will attempt to cover all of the topics that come up regularly when I talk to young people; from body parts; puberty; consent, sexuality, gender, mobile phones, sexting, pornography, first time sex, contraception and, importantly, what to do when things go wrong.

My intention in this book is not to tell you how to parent your children. I know for some of you, a lot of what I'll cover in this book may be uncomfortable. When you are discussing sex and relationships, we are cutting down to the foundations of our beliefs, our values, and how we see the world. Sex has always been political. But I am not here to try to convince you of anything.

And I don't pretend that I have all the answers.

I always say as part of setting the ground rules when I teach: 'This is not a maths lesson.' Now no offence to maths teachers, but in maths there tends to be a right answer. If we all show our working and remember to carry the 1 we should all come to the same conclusion. But that is not how *this stuff* works. The majority of the things I discuss are focused on our own values, our beliefs, our past experiences, and ultimately, how you feel. When you are talking about feelings, no one can tell you that you are wrong.

For me, it is more about exploring a topic rather than saying something is right or wrong. But that means we need to be mindful and respectful when we don't all agree. And that is ok. I am not setting out to dictate how you should feel about some of the more challenging debates or what you should tell your children – that choice is firmly yours. But what I am offering are the tools to make those conversations easier.

My intention in this book is to make sure that you are better informed, of not only the issues and research in each topic but, most importantly, you get to hear the voice of young people and what they say when the adults are not around.

Each chapter will tackle a different topic. We will explore the current debates, research evidence, practice experience, why it's important, and how it fits in with young people's lives today. But like all good sex education it should also be fun. Along the way I will share lots of anecdotes, conversations with young people, their parents and the professionals who work with them. There will be small exercises, activities and thought experiments to keep you busy along the way. There will be lots of references to popular culture and how we can use the TV shows and films we watch, the music on the radio and news feeds on social media to instigate conversations without feeling the need to sit children down to have 'the talk'.

Regardless of whether the children in your life are teens or toddlers, the information in the following chapters will be relevant. As the safe adults we can be modelling good behaviour and showing our children that we are available regardless of their age. If we want our children to talk to us we need to build the foundations first and show them that the door is open.

Whilst I have lots of experience of talking to young people of all ages, I also work on the other side – supporting professionals and parents to breach these topics with the young people in their lives. I am aware of the barriers and fears and have lots of tips and exercises that can help start a conversation. However, in order to feel comfortable integrating these conversations into daily life, we first need to feel comfortable with the topics.

So let this be the sex education you wish you had when you were young…

# Note

1  The Relationships Education, Relationships and Sex Education and Health Education (England) Regulations 2019 (DfE, 2019), made under sections 34 and

35 of the Children and Social Work Act 2017, make Relationships Education compulsory for all pupils receiving primary education and RSE compulsory for all pupils receiving secondary education. They also make Health Education compulsory in all schools except independent schools. Personal, Social, Health and Economic Education (PSHE) continues to be compulsory in independent schools.

# References

Bennet, C. (2017). Parental approaches to teaching children about puberty, relationships and reproduction in the Netherlands. Available at: www.wcmt.org.uk/sites/default/files/report-documents/Bennett%20C%20Report%202017%20Final.pdf.

Corcoran, J.L., Patrician, P.A., Childs, G.D. and Shirey, M.R. (2019). What do we really know about adolescent sexual health education: A dimensional concept analysis, *American Journal of Sexuality Education*, 14(3), 342–57.

DfE (2019). Relationships education, relationship and sex education (RSE) and health education: Guidance for governing bodies, proprietors, head teachers, principals, senior leadership teams, teachers.

Prensky, M. (2011). Digital natives, digital immigrants, *On the Horizon*, 9(5), 1–5. Available at: www.marcprensky.com/writing/prensky%20-%20Digital%20Natives,%20Digital%20Imigrants%20-%20Part1.pdf.

UNESCO. (2018). International technical guidance on sexuality education: An evidenced-informed approach.

# PART I

# BEFORE WE GET STARTED

# CHAPTER 1

# THE ISSUE WITH 'NICE'

**B**efore we get to the main event, it is probably worth taking some time to reflect.

When I am delivering training one of the first things I always try to do is start off by giving people time to explore their own attitudes and values. It can be a really helpful place to begin. I am aware that thinking about some of the issues we are going to cover in this book can be uncomfortable. Many of the topics we are going to unpick, on the surface, are things we often take for granted and accept as set in stone. In fact, as we will discuss in the following chapters, many of the assumptions we make about sex are based on falsehoods. As a result, we may simply be repeating the messages we were given as children without ever reflecting and wondering whether what we are saying actually helps.

In my experience, if we dive straight in to talking about private parts, abortion, sexting or pornography, people tend to react instinctively – they get their backs up and merely repeat the messages they have read in the media, with little thought. Instead, we are going to take a moment and mess with your head just a little bit…

So, let's start at the beginning. As I mentioned in the introduction, the obvious starting point for any discussion about what we tell our children is this: what are we hoping for?

**When it comes to our child's intimate relationships and their first sexual experience what is it we want for them?**

DOI: 10.4324/9781003122296-2

I know I raised this earlier, but we didn't really have time to answer the question. Now I want you to properly think about it. Yes, it may feel a bit uncomfortable, especially if your child(ren) are still in primary school and have not yet started puberty. But this is the perfect time to start thinking about all this as you will have more time to make your answers a reality.

In an ideal world, what do you hope your child's first sexual encounters will look like? This will probably bring back your own memories of your first encounter or the encounters in between. Unfortunately, odds are there will be a lot of people reading these sentences for whom memories of their first encounters will not be pleasant. For many of us that may simply be due to embarrassment or regret, or lack of knowledge, bodily control or what was spoken about in the hushed tones of rumours in the corridors at school the following Monday.

However, there will be some of you (too many of you) for whom thinking back to your own first intimate experience will not just be uncomfortable, it may be traumatic. It will be something that happened to you – something you will have spent a long time working through and getting over. For that, I am truly sorry. My intention is not to make you dredge up your demons. But the question remains: what can we all be doing to make sure that in the future there will be less people who feel this way? What can we say to our kids that will make sure they not only grow up with the tools and the knowledge to keep themselves safe but equally that they grow up not to be the person who harms someone else. We often forget that they were someone's child too.

So, grab a pen and a piece of paper and write some things down. What do you hope for? Whether you are thinking about your son or daughter, or the kids in your class, or the young people you work with? If it could be all sunshine and rainbows, what do you hope their first experience will be like? Who will it be with? What will they be like? How old will they both be? What will their relationship be like? Where will it happen? How will they feel afterwards? What about protection?

If you have a partner, or if there are other adults who share care for the child you have in mind, ask them to write things down too. Compare notes. Are they the same?

Obviously I am not psychic and certainly can't read what you have written, or whether you have even bothered to pick up a pencil or have simply carried on reading after ignoring everything I just said… But, if you did

- respect each other

- with someone they trust

- by choice, (consent) – not pressured

- safe

- they are ready

- care about each other

- be in love

- no regrets or pregnancy or infections!

**Figure I.I**

bother, it is more than likely you've included some of the words listed in Figure I.I.

Typically, people tend to focus on wanting their child to be safe. They focus on the things that could go wrong, such as unwanted pregnancy or catching an STI. I am pretty sure you included items around them not feeling pressured and that the encounter is consensual. Depending on your values and your personal beliefs, you may have written down that they should be in a committed relationship, or even that they are married.

Quick question: how many of you automatically imagined that your child would be with someone of the opposite sex? Just a thought.

More on that later…

However, back to the discussion at hand. One item that is, more often than not, conspicuous by its absence is the word PLEASURE.

(o)(o)

A few years ago, I was asked if I could attend a last minute parents' briefing at one of the many primary schools I had been supporting that summer. A handful of the parents had read some of the supportive information that had been sent home and not been very happy. They had been calling the school, angry and upset at what they thought was 'inappropriate content' in the programme. I had already delivered a parent information evening at the school, where I had covered all the content of the programme, but the parents in question had failed to attend. The school called and asked if I would be able to help support them to talk to the parents and answer their questions.

In fact, I can be very specific – it was June 2015. I know, as I was supposed to be at Wembley watching the Foo Fighters, but unfortunately Dave Grohl had fallen off the stage in Sweden the week before and broken his leg – instead, I was stood in a very different mosh-pit in a school hall, in a somewhat heated meeting with a group of unhappy parents.

The programme the school was delivering was designed to be delivered intensively over a week. Children in every class from reception to year six would take part in a lesson each day. It was a spiral curriculum, with messages drip-fed over the years, slowly giving the children more information. It was a comprehensive programme, meaning it explored different types of families, emotional literacy, friendships, body privacy, safe and appropriate touching, how to ask for help and puberty for the older year groups.

The parents all had children in year 4. The lesson in question was an explanation of how babies are made. For some parents, naturally, this can be a contentious subject. However, the session was very nicely put together, and simply covered where babies live before they are born; how they grow; and how they are born. Sex education at this time was (and still is) optional. Parents had the right to opt their child out of the lesson – however, very few parents ever choose to. Usually, if parents are uncomfortable with this lesson it is because they have more conservative beliefs and they feel the topic itself is inappropriate. What was interesting in this case, was not that the parents had particular religious or cultural beliefs; the point of contention was not around the topic itself but around a single word.

After much talking, it became clear that the parents were happy for their children to receive the lesson. They thought it was important that the children understood how babies were made – they liked the explanation of 'mummies and daddies bodies fitting together like two pieces of a jigsaw puzzle' (Rutgers, 2014). The issue was the word 'nice'.

As part of the explanation the lesson plan says that sex is something that grown-ups do, 'it is the closest that two grown-ups can get' and that it can 'feel nice'. And this was the issue. The parents were uncomfortable with telling children that sex is something that should be enjoyable and worried that this may encourage the children to have sex.

I acknowledged their concerns and was in the middle of explaining that there is absolutely no evidence that would be the case. In fact, evidence suggests that children who receive these kinds of lessons actually have sex later (UNESCO, 2018). I explained that, in reality, their children were more likely to be disgusted by the idea rather than encouraged – in a 'EWW! Why would you even want to kiss a girl! URGHH!' – sort of way. That, in truth, they really would not be focused on the idea of it feeling nice.

Understandably, they questioned why, if that was the case, it was even included.

I tried to explain that for many children, this may be the only conversation they ever have with a safe adult about what sex actually is. The word *nice* is a little seed planted for years later… for many young people who are having their first experience, sex isn't all that great. It is a disappointment at best. Sex is often something that happens to people – especially girls. If no one has ever told you it *should* feel good, then you are left with the feeling 'maybe this is it' – and assume that sex is supposed to be like that.

Equally, it is important for the small number of children in class who may have been abused. It is important they understand that what has happened to them was abuse and not sex. It is a small note of separation. I know this isn't a very comfortable thought or very easy to talk about but that is one of the reasons we do this work – to help all children.

As I was slowly and calmly trying to explain the nuance of the inclusion, one of the dads had had enough. He banged his fists on the table and shouted: 'I don't care what you say – I don't want my daughter to know that she should enjoy sex!'

It just burst out of him – to be fair, I think he was as shocked as everyone else in the room. And then he stopped. He had just realised what *he* had said.

Why would you not want your daughter to know that sex is something she should enjoy? What is the alternative? Would we rather that sex is something she does out of duty to please her partner? That sex is something that others do to her? Something she endures…

No. As a dad, and I am the dad of a daughter, that thought is horrifying.

As the dad of a daughter, I hope that when she is ready to have sex, it is something she enjoys. I hope she does it because it makes her feel good. That she fancies her partner, that she wants her partner. That she already understands her body and is brave enough to tell her partner what she likes and what she wants – as scary as that sounds, it is far less scary to me than the alternative.

Have you noticed that the worry always seems to be about girls? In my experience, there are very few parents of boys that share the same worries… but we will talk more about that later.

In my opinion, pleasure should be something we are talking to children and young people about. Yes, risk and safety are important too – but 'at a public swimming pool we have gates, put up signs, have lifeguards and shallow ends, but we also teach children how to swim' (Byron, 2008). By talking about pleasure, you can cover the risks too; sex is not pleasurable if it is pressured. Sex is not pleasurable if you are worried about pregnancy or sexually transmitted infections (STIs)… but equally, sex is not pleasurable if you feel used afterwards. Conversations about pleasure allow discussion about how we should treat people kindly and the emotions of sex rather than duty. Focusing only on risk is like teaching a cooking class and only talking about salmonella and food poisoning.

Unfortunately, there is a void of any 'sex positive' messages in the new Department for Education (DfE) RSE guidance.[1] The word 'pleasure' is not used once in the entire document, despite the growing evidence of the benefits of a positive rather than a risk-centred approach to RSE (UNESCO, 2018; IPPF, 2016). Furthermore, young people themselves have called for information about pleasure and enjoying sex (SEF, 2016; Barnardo's, 2018; THT, 2016).

These calls echo my own experience of talking with young people. The question remains, if we are not the ones to talk to young people about sexual pleasure and how to make sex a positive experience – for *both* parties – then young people will continue to seek information from other sources. In all likelihood, by other sources we mean either friends or online pornography. Pornhub is many things but sex education, it isn't. Unfortunately, *Pornhub, Redtube, Xhamster* (the list of free tube sites goes on) will be the first port of call for many of our youngsters, in search of the information we omit.

In my experience, for many young people I talk to, sex is still something men *do* to women, sex is something that happens to girls (Orenstein, 2016). When working with young people, it is clear they are rarely told information that includes any discussion around pleasure. This is especially true for girls.

Interestingly, a recent US study of college-age students' sexual attitudes and behaviours reported heterosexual young women defined their sexual encounters as more fulfilling than their male counterparts (Orenstein, 2016). This sounds like we are finally making some progress. However, when you dig into the detail it is heart-breaking. When you unpick the data, it becomes clear that the young men and the young women in the study hold very different criteria for what makes a sexual encounter fulfilling. For guys, it was very simple: they had sex! Woo! It was pleasurable, they enjoyed themselves. For girls, the story was somewhat different…

The top three were: it wasn't painful; they were not left humiliated; and their partner enjoyed *him*self. This is a very low bar for sexual fulfilment and doesn't even come close to taking into consideration their own pleasure.

The thought of talking to young people about pleasure may be horrifying to some people, including some reading this, but I honestly believe it is key to bringing about sexual equality and keeping young people safe. But equally I am also the dad who, when the time is right, will let my daughter's partners stay over. Why? Because I honestly hope that when the time comes, she has her first experience here under our roof… when we are at home.

Oh, I can feel the cringes and horrified looks from here! But seriously, what is the alternative? Drunk at some party? Sneaking into her partner's house when their folks aren't around… I don't want us to be in the house so I can overhear (what is wrong with you?!). I want us to be in the house because, if things go too far, if things feel uncomfortable, all she has to do is say stop. I want her to feel safe. For sex to be on her terms. For her to have fun and enjoy the sex she chooses to have – that is my idea of sunshine and rainbows.

Look back at your list. Compare it with the other care takers in your children's life and talk about what you can be doing to make it a reality. It won't be easy. It may be uncomfortable, but also think of the alternative.

# Note

1 The Department for Education (DfE) has released new guidance for all schools – from primary to secondary – for the delivery of relationships education, health education and relationships and sex education at secondary school. This is the first updated guidance since 2000. The new guidance came into effect in September 2020 (although due to the pandemic, schools have been given more time to implement the new curriculum).

# References

Barnardo's (2018). Involve us, respect us: Engaging young people in relationships and sex education.

Byron (2008). *Safer Children in a Digital World*. HMSO.

IPPF (2016). *Putting Sexuality back into Comprehensive Sexuality Education: Making the case for rights-based, sex-positive approach*.

Orenstein, P. (2016). *Girls and Sex: Navigating the complicated new landscape*, Oneworld Publications, New York.

Rutgers (2014). *Spring Fever: Relationships and sexual health education year 3 and 4 Pack*, Translated by E.P. Thomson Vertalingen and K. de Kruijf-Bassett, Warwickshire County Council.

Sex Education Forum (2016). *Heads or Tails: What young people are telling us about RSE*. National Children's Bureau.

THT (2016). Shh… no talking: LGBT-inclusive sex and relationships education in the UK. Available at: www.tht.org.uk/endthesilence.

UNESCO (2018). *International Technical Guidance on Sexuality Education, An evidence-informed approach, revised edition*.

# CHAPTER II

# BEING 'NORMAL'

**Is calling someone straight offensive?**

When it comes to talking about sex, language is important.

The words we use carry meaning; not only in what they convey but also by what they imply as a result. I love language – I love unpicking it, thinking about what words mean, their history, where they came from, why some words are seen as offensive whilst some are accepted despite their nuance.

So, what do you think? Is calling someone *straight* offensive?

Of course not. I am pretty sure that no one has ever felt personally offended by someone calling them straight. Many people use it happily, without issue. It certainly doesn't cause a fuss and I am not suggesting that it should. However, what is interesting is if we consider what it implies by default? If you are not straight, what are you? *Bent*.

Now, most people would agree that calling someone 'bent' is not very nice and no longer accepted. In fact, we would call it outright homophobic. So why are we still using the term 'straight' without a thought?

What does being straight even mean? You are straight down the line? Heading in the right direction? Or is it more an indication of what you are not? You are *not* bent, broken, damaged or a bit skew-iff!

Calling someone straight is not considered offensive because whether we care to admit it, being straight carries privilege. Being straight is the expectation… it is considered the norm.

DOI: 10.4324/9781003122296-3

## normal, *adj.* and *n.*

**A.** *adj.*
**I.** General uses.
**1.**
**a.** Constituting or conforming to a type or standard; regular, usual, typical; ordinary, conventional. (The usual sense.)

**b.** Of a person: physically and mentally sound; free from any disorder; healthy.

**2.** Having the function of prescribing a course of action or way of living; prescriptive. *Obsolete.*

**3.** Of, relating to, or intended for the training of teachers, esp. in Continental Europe and North America. Chiefly in **normal school.** Now *historical.*

**4.** Heterosexual. Cf. sense B. 6.

**Figure II.I** *Oxford English Dictionary* definition of 'normal'

Think back to the exercise in the previous chapter. How many of you assumed when you imagined your child's first partner that they would automatically be of the opposite sex?

But have you ever considered who gets to decide what is *normal*?

Figure II.I shows the OED definition of normal.

Again, heterosexuality or heterosexualism raises its head.

It is a little over 30 years since Margaret Thatcher's Conservative Government implemented the infamous Section 28 legislation.[1] In her notorious speech at the Tory Party Conference in 1987, Thatcher complained about *left* leaning schools overstepping their remit, teaching children 'anti-racist mathematics' and political activism; but the greatest fear was that: 'Children who need to be taught to respect traditional moral values are being taught that they have an inalienable right to be gay' (Thatcher,1987). Less than a year later Section 28 was passed.

Growing tension and fear had been rising since the decriminalisation of Homosexuality under the 1967 Sexual Offences Act. It is a commonly held myth that the 1967 Act legalised male homosexuality. In truth, it only partially decriminalised it. What this meant in practice, was that two consenting adults over the age of 21 (not 16 like heterosexual couples), could have sex in private – in their own home, behind lock and key, with the curtains firmly drawn – but only as long as there was no one else in the house to corrupt. Gay men could still not walk down the street holding hands or even showing any indication that they were a couple for fear of arrest and prosecution for gross indecency. In the years that followed decriminalisation on paper, gay sexuality was actually policed more aggressively in practice, by the state that was not completely sold on gay acceptance. There was an increase of prosecution for *unnatural offences* using archaic laws that still sat on the statue books (Tatchell, 2017).

There was a real fear that young people would be corrupted if *the gays* earned more rights and became more public. It would signal the end of the *normal* family unit.

Incidentally, it was fear over a children's book that put the final nail in the coffin for gay rights and allowed Thatcher's government to push through Section 28 and push gays back into the closet. *Jenny lives with Eric and Martin* was a paperback, illustrated booklet, translated from Swedish and published in the UK by the Gay Men's Press. It told the story of a little girl who lived with her divorced father and his male partner. It explored their lives together and the challenges they faced as a family.

This was too much for some, and Section 28 was the solution. The legislation banned the *promotion* of homosexuality by local authorities and this included schools. In practice, the clause meant that teachers were prohibited from even discussing the possibility of same-sex relationships with their pupils. Council libraries were forbidden from stocking literature or films that contained lesbian or gay themes, especially those that showed homosexuality as a 'pretended family relationship' (Local Government Act, 1988).

For an entire generation of young people who grew up under the shadow of Section 28, they were made to feel ashamed. Their existence was ignored. Their struggles were hidden from view and children were systematically bullied and broken. Is it any wonder why levels of anxiety, depression, self-harm and suicide are significantly higher for that generation of the LGBTQ+ community. Indeed, a 2018 YouGov study commissioned by Stonewall interviewed 5,000 LGTBQ+ individuals. They found that in the preceding year alone, half of LGTBQ+ people interviewed had experienced depression and three in five had suffered from anxiety – far exceeding estimates for the general population (YouGov/Stonewall, 2018).

You would be forgiven for thinking we have stepped into a time-warp as all this feels a bit familiar – even down to the racist mathematics. There is definitely a sense of déjà vu to all this. Thirty years later and we are still having the same conversations with the same insecurities being played out. Earlier this year, Parkfield Community School in Birmingham saw protests from angry parents, again protesting the inclusions of LGBTQ+ children's books such as *And Tango Makes Three*, or *Mommy Mama and Me* and *Julian is a Mermaid*[2] as part of the No Outsiders programme written by the deputy head Andrew Moffat. Three decades have passed but the arguments are still the same. The fear that children will lose their innocence and be corrupted by gay and transgender messages.

Times have changed but the arguments haven't.

Conversations around sex have always been political. In the 1980s sociologist Gayle Rubin designed the *charmed circle* to help explain the hierarchy of what is seen as acceptable or 'normal' when it comes to sexual behaviours and relationships and how these are policed by society (Figure II.II). The urgent desire to control and preserve the norm is central to societal panics around sexuality (Mulholland, 2013). And since the nineteenth century, protecting children has been the battleground.

The growth of sexology – the *science of sex* – in the late nineteenth century signalled a move away from the domination of the Church and religious thinking in discourse around sex. What was once characterised and controlled by the notion of sin, now were reclassified as illnesses and mental disorders. Sexual identities and practices took on new meanings as a result; masturbation or sodomy were no longer things one did but were now distinct identities that could be pathologised (Mulholland, 2013).

Looking back at Rubin's diagram, in the inner circle we have all those behaviours that were accepted by society as normal. The more a person's sexual relationships and practices fall within the inner circle, the more acceptable or natural they appear. When a person's behaviours fall on the outer circle, the more they risk sliding into oblivion. It is society's job to police the boundary.

Whilst the charmed circle may have shifted slightly, many of the key debates that exist today about sex are still seen through the lens of a moral argument rather than a reasoned one.

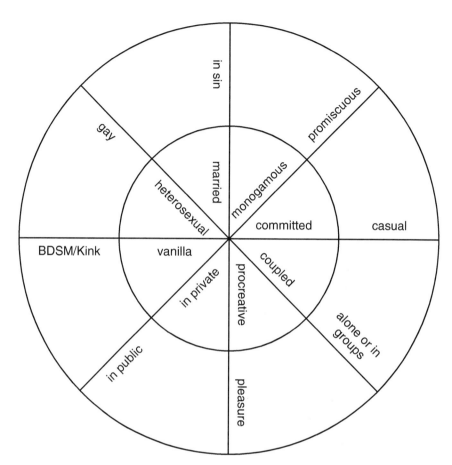

**Figure II.II** The Charmed Circle: adapted from Gale Rubins (1984), *Thinking Sex: Notes for a radical theory of politics of sexuality.*

Whether we are talking about porn, sexting, abortion, contraception, sexuality or gender identity, it is moral panics of potential harms (that may or may not exist) that grab the headlines, when the reality of many of the decisions that are taken in response to the panics are what actually cause the real harm – as we saw with Section 28. Unfortunately, it is often the most vulnerable in society that suffer the most.

You only have to look at the current discourse around the Gender Recognition Act (GRA),[3] which would allow trans folk to self-identify without a medical diagnosis. Whilst there have been column inches upon column inches written about toilets and changing rooms and accusations of women's spaces and safety being compromised – that womanhood is somehow at risk by the existence of trans-women. The same tired arguments we saw in the lead-up to the implementation of Section 28, of the corruption of children, promoting and encouraging children to identify as trans, toilets and changing rooms, dominate the headlines. It was nonsense then and it is nonsense still. What many of the transphobic authors fail to acknowledge is that trans women have been using these spaces every day for ten years without incident. Or the fact that a GRA was passed in Ireland five years ago[4] and there hasn't even been the whisper of such issues.

The problem is that conversation around sex, sexuality and identity are still dominated by moral panics and fear of anything outside the charmed circle of the normal. The irony being that our notions of normal are built on shifting sands. We accept some very odd things as normal and harmless with very little thought. It only takes a tiny bit of scrutiny to highlight the hypocrisy of our convictions.

Let me explain. There is a fantastic exercise I use during training with professionals, which I have adapted from Meg-John Barker's book *The Psychology of Everything: Sex* (2018). It is a really useful activity to help people consider what they deem as acceptable or not-acceptable when we think of sexual behaviours and practices – in other words, what we would call *normal*.

Read the statement cards in Figure II.III. Imagine there is a line drawn down the centre of the table in front of you. On one side is labelled: acceptable, normal, healthy, not concerning; the other side of the line is labelled the opposite: unacceptable, abnormal, harmful, worrying.

Have a think – imagine that a friend or an older teenager you know confided in you that they were taking part in one of these behaviours – how would it make you feel? Have a chat and see which side of the line each of the cards sit.

Are you done? Great... What is interesting to unpick, once people have gotten over the shock of some of the statements is to consider what influenced your decision? What made you decide that a particular behaviour was acceptable or harmful?

Perhaps, it was issues around consent or personal choice? Was capacity an issue? Or was it more to do with fear of actual or potential harm? Did it make a difference if the harm was only temporary or long term?

An individual gets a rush out of being put in terrifying situations that make them scream and cry out in fear. They engage other people to put them in a special device which will result in these effects. When their time in the device is up, their face will often be white, and they will have tears in their eyes and yet they beg to be allowed to go through it again.

A woman asks strangers to cause her extreme pain to her genital area. She does this regularly, as she feels better about herself following the painful session. Sometimes, she'll even do it to herself. If it is done correctly, no permanent harm results.

A small group of people arrange to meet in a private space in order to watch others role-playing scenes of being raped, humiliated and tortured. They find this as an enjoyable way of spending the evening.

A woman chooses items of clothing on which she has spent several hundreds/thousands of pounds, all of which painfully restrict parts of her body, forcing it into an unnatural shape and making it impossible for her to function normally. Over an extended period of time she knows this will damage her permanently. However, she experiences great pleasure, despite the pain.

Two people arrange to take part in a public scene. They spend a great deal of time preparing separately in advanced. On the night they dress in clothes made of satin. Watched by a gathering group of people they strike each other. The scene is considered a success if one of them briefly loses consciousness. The beatings are so severe they can result in permanent damage.

Figure II.III    Statement cards adapted from Meg-John Barker's book, *The Psychology of Everything: Sex* (2018).

One of the first questions I usually raise once everyone has had time to digest the activity and reflect, is to ask people: *Which is the statement that made you most uncomfortable?* And why? Most often, people tend to pick the card about 'role-playing scenes of rape' – for obvious reasons, it makes people uncomfortable. The very thought makes people skin crawl, as it does sound pretty horrific. Why would a *normal* person watch people pretending to sexually assault someone? What kind of person would get off on or enjoy seeing other people hurt?

This is where I usually point out that actually, that is something the majority of us do regularly – not only that, but we talk to our friends and colleagues about it openly, over cups of coffee. Have you never been to the cinema to watch a film like *Saw*, or any other violent horror movie? What about chatting through the latest episode of something like *Game of Thrones*? No?

Another statement that is usually high on the list is the statement about 'asking strangers to cause pain to a woman's genitals'. In people's heads they often imagine her walking down the street and just asking random men to perform some sort of horrific sex act on her in an alley somewhere...

Of course, the card merely describes her having a bikini wax.

You can guess where this is going, can't you? All of the cards describe a very *normal* behaviour, that is non-sexual. However, each scenario has been described as if it were a sex act. Suddenly, very acceptable behaviours, that you would talk about openly without any sense of shame, sound seedy and anything but *normal*.

Going on a rollercoaster at a theme park sounds like something out of a BDSM dungeon or fetish club. Taking part in a boxing match sounds like a kinky version of Fight Club. We've already mentioned watching the latest box-set and having a Brazilian.

The very normal can feel very scary when we judge it through the same prism that we view sex through.

Since the start of the Noughties, we have made huge strides forward when it comes to LGBTQA+ equality and the acknowledgement of a broader range of experience of sex and sexuality that is not merely confined to the inner charmed circle. This is especially true for women. There are many taboos, whether it is open discussion around fertility, periods or the meno-pause, or even people learning the difference between a vagina and a vulva, that are slowly being broken as the circle shifts.

However, whenever there is culturally any great change taking place there is pushback from corners of society who fear the change. This is where moral panics arise. Arguably, we are in the middle of the greatest shift in society since the nineteenth century and the Industrial Revolution; we are in our own digital revolution.

Whilst the influence of new technology, social media, mobile phones and the behaviours they bring can be scary, as parents we are programmed to see the dangers they possess – whether this is hardwired through our genetics or merely through the media, I don't know. But often in the midst of the moral panic and screams of 'think of the children', we often miss the potential they can also bring. Digital technologies present new freedoms, or lifelines for those at the margins, the most vulnerable. They can help us make connections or talk about things we were not brave enough to do face to face.

As you will see through the book, many of the arguments we think we are having for the first time are really not new. They just seem to mutate slightly. Unfortunately, history has shown us that often the more we try to vigorously enforce the boundaries, the more damage we do.

Now, I do not mean to suggest that society should not try to control or define rules for any aspect of sexuality. I am not suggesting a free for all, like a feast at Caligula's, with no rules or boundaries around sexuality or sexual expression. However, one thing I am sure of, using shame to police the boundaries only causes harm. Instead, I would suggest a rights-based approach. However scary it may be to us as adults, all children have the right to open and honest information about sex and sexuality.

Indeed, access to Comprehensive Sexuality Education (CSE)[5] has been recognised internationally by various human rights bodies as a funda-mental right for children. This is due to the fact that access to this infor-mation has been shown to help keep children safe from abuse.[6] The right to receive comprehensive sexuality education derives from a range of protected rights, such as the right to live free from violence and discrimin-ation, the right to the highest attainable standard of mental and physical health, but also the right to receive and impart information and the right to quality and inclusive education, including human rights education.

Whilst many of the current arguments surrounding what information is *age appropriate* for children to have has centred around the parents' right to choose what their child learns, the rights of the child to information (to keep themselves safe – both online and in the real world) is often neglected. It is curious that RSE seems to be the only area of recognised safeguarding practice where parents can opt their children out of the information designed to help protect them.

In my experience, there is very little you can't talk to children about, assuming you take the right approach. Children cope brilliantly, and relish the opportunity to talk about their bodies, their different families, their relationships and the world around them with an open mind. Adults, on the other hand, are often a different story! One thing I know: you will never protect children by keeping them in a bubble, however much we would like to shield them from the aspects of society we may find distasteful. Sadly, innocence and ignorance are not the same thing.

There seems to be so much confusion about what inclusive RSE looks like, especially at primary school, and what it may entail. There are no such thing as 'gay lessons' being delivered or being proposed. Instead, a typical lesson that most children at primary school will be asked to do on occasion is to draw their family (Figure II.IV).

All the children in the class will draw their own family. Some children will draw a stick house with a mummy and daddy and their brother or sister. Some children will draw lots of brother and sisters. Some may just live with mummy or just daddy. Some children may have to draw two houses because they share their time between their mummy and daddy, their new partners and step-brother or sisters… some children may live with

**Figure II.IV** Image of a family, as drawn by a small child. Includes dad, step-mum, child and cats.

grandparents or foster carers. Families come in all different shapes and sizes these days.

Now, imagine in this class we have a little boy who lives with his two mummies. For those who feel it is inappropriate to talk about same-sex families, what do they suggest we do? Are we saying, whilst all the other children get to draw their families, he has to make up a family that is more acceptable? Or perhaps he can draw his picture, but he is not allowed to show the rest of the class and certainly wouldn't be allowed to pin his picture up on the wall.

Or instead, do we use this as an opportunity to share the similarities and differences that make all of our families so special? The truth is, none of this is news to the children in class. They all pay attention – they see who picks who up in the playground after school; they play at each other's houses; and they talk to each other. We can use this as an opportunity to talk about difference and acceptance.

Just to be completely clear: small children who read stories about two gay penguins who adopt an egg and raise it as their own will not suddenly turn gay – they are more likely to pretend to be a penguin for the next half hour and waddle about.

Indeed, when we look past the obvious, it will not only be the little boy with same-sex parents who has two mummies. The little girl whose father has remarried has a step-mum too. The little boy who lives in care has a tummy mummy and a foster mummy. This is an opportunity to make all children feel accepted and welcome – no exceptions. Again, I ask what is the alternative we would prefer?

Perhaps it is time to admit that normal isn't so normal after all…

# Notes

1  Section 28 was enacted on 24 May 1988 as part of the Local Government Act 1988. It caused the addition of Section 2A to the Local Government Act 1986, which covered England, Wales and Scotland. The amendment stated that a local authority 'shall not intentionally promote homosexuality or publish material with the intention of promoting homosexuality'. This also covered maintained schools and the teaching of 'the acceptability of homosexuality as a pretended family relationship'. It was finally repealed in Scotland in 2000 by the passing of

the Ethical Standards in Public Life Act 2000, which was one of the first acts of the devolved Scottish Parliament. In England it was not repealed until the end of 2003 by Section 122 of the Local Government Act 2003.

2  *And Tango Makes Three*, by Justin Richardson and Peter Parnell, published by Little Simon. *Mommy Mama and Me*, by Lesléa Newman, published by Tricycle Press. *Julian is a Mermaid* by Jessica Love, published by Walker Books.

3  Whilst writing, the GRA was abandoned due to heavy criticism in the press and a minority of very vocal criticism. In the government's own consultation 80% of respondents were happy with the passing of the new legislation.

4  Irish Gender Recognition Act 2015, An Act to recognise change of gender; to provide for gender recognition certificates; to amend the Irish Nationality and Citizenship Act 1956, the Civil Registration Act 2004, the Passports Act 2008 and the Adoption Act 2010; and to provide for matters connected therewith.

5  This is where things can get a little bit confusing. Internationally, CSE often refers to Comprehensive Sexuality Education, what we in the UK refer to as Relationships and Sex Education (RSE). This can be further complicated by the fact that CSE in the UK more often refers to Child Sexual Exploitation.

6  These include the UN Convention on the Rights of the Child, the UN Convention on the Elimination of all Forms of Violence against Women, the International Covenant on Economic, Social and Cultural Rights and, at European level, the European Social Charter and the Lanzarote and Istanbul Conventions against child exploitation and abuse.

# References

Barker, M.J. (2018). *The Psychology of Everything: Sex*, Routledge, Abingdon.

Local Government Act (1988) HMSO, London.

Mulholland, M. (2013). *Young People and Pornography: Negotiating pornification*, Palgrave Macmillan, Basingstoke.

Oxford English Dictionary. 'Normal'. Available at: www.oed.com/viewdictionary entry/Entry/128269.

Rubins, G. (1984). 'Thinking sex: Notes for a radical theory of politics of sexuality', in *Pleasure and Danger: Exploring female sexuality*, edited by C. Vance, Routledge and Kegan Paul, Boston.

Tatchell, P. (2017). 'Don't fall for the myth that it's 50 years since we decriminalised homosexuality', *The Guardian*, 23 May. Available at: www.theguardian.com/commentisfree/2017/may/23/fifty-years-gay-liberation-uk-barely-four-1967-act.

Thatcher, M. (1987). Speech to the Conservative Party Conference, Winter Gardens, Blackpool in 1987 October 9. Thatcher Archive: CCOPR 664/87.

YouGov and Stonewall (2018) LGBT in Britain health report. Stonewall. Available at: www.stonewall.org.uk/system/files/lgbt_in_britain_health.pdf.

# CHAPTER III

# WHAT'S THE MESSAGE?

**I**n 2012, the then Coalition Government amended the definition of domestic violence to include young people under 18. Admittedly,
it only covered those who were 16 and 17 but it was a step in the right
direction. It was done in response to the British Crime Survey 2009/10
which found that 16–19 year olds were the group most likely to suffer
from abuse from a partner (HMO, 2010).

Even today when I pose the question:

### What age group are most likely to suffer from domestic abuse?

professionals are often surprised at the answer. The image most of us have
of domestic violence is something that young people may suffer through
their parents. This is why language is so important. When working with
young people around domestic abuse, we more often use the term 'relationship abuse' for this very reason – domestic abuse is something that
young people do not personally identify with, as it is what happens to
adults not teenagers.

This is just one example of how messages can get lost in translation if we
are not careful.

Around this time I was asked to run a number of young people's project
boards exploring young people's understanding of domestic abuse. The
aim of the project was not only to work with a group of young people

DOI: 10.4324/9781003122296-4

around the issues, but also with a view of gaining their insights as to how best to tackle the issue of intimate partner violence with other young people too. Basically, my job was to steal their ideas and turn them into campaigns and educational resources.

It was during one of these sessions that a member of the group said something that has stuck with me ever since.

We were watching one of the Home Office 'This is Abuse' TV adverts, 'If you could see yourself, would you stop yourself?' The one starring Georgia May Foote from *Coronation Street*.[1]

The advert does not make nice watching. In the clip, there's a teenage couple sat on the girl's bed watching TV. They are chatting about school, when he turns to her and asks if she 'wants to have a bit of fun before your mum gets back?'. When she turns him down, he turns aggressive, throwing her phone across the room before the intimidation escalates to physically grabbing her by the hair. The camera cuts to the same girl watching the scene from behind a glass wall, as she bangs on the glass telling herself to get out of the room.

As I say, the advert is pretty hard hitting and makes uncomfortable watching, especially when he takes his belt off unnecessarily as the advert cuts – its implication clear. There have been arguments in recent years that adverts like this actually serve little purpose – they are unnecessarily traumatic to watch and have little overall impact in behaviour change (Eaton, 2018). But that is not the point I want to make here.

The project board were unpicking the situation and what had happened in the clip. We had discussed the fact that the scene takes place in her bedroom. The lads in the group seemed to see this as an important point of mitigation: 'If there's no one else in the house, why don't they watch TV downstairs in the living room?' In their eyes, asking a boy up to your room was an invitation to much more, like a teen version of 'Do you want a cup of coffee…?'

The girls in the group quickly put them straight, explaining that in their eyes a girl's room is her safe-space; by inviting him into her room she is presenting him with a sign that she trusts him and is allowing him into her private world. In their eyes, this made his behaviour even worse – he had violated not only her but her sanctuary as well.

It was interesting to see how young men and young women (mis)read and interpret the signs so differently – there is definitely more work to be done there. But more of that later…

Anyway, the conversation moved on and I asked whether, if we put his behaviour to the side (we all agree that his behaviour is completely unacceptable and abusive), if we think about how he is feeling, can we understand why he behaves in such an abhorrent manner?

One of the lads, in typical helpful fashion, shouted out: 'Cause he got blue-balls inn'it mate, she's led him on and he's pissed!' The room erupted in right-eous anger as some of the other lads laughed and the girls (deservedly) threw things at him and cussed him.

Once things had calmed down, one of the girls spoke up and said: 'Nah, it's not that – it's because she don't love him and he's hurt…'

> *'How do you mean?'*
> 'Well, it's like you guys [adults] keep telling us, we should only have sex with people you love, so when she says no to sex, in his head, she's just blatantly told him she don't love him…'

(Wow! Moments like these are why I love spending so much time talking to young people.)

> *'Do you think that is true?'*
> 'Nah, it's not true – but that's what he's thinking – it ain't about sex, it's about his insecurities… he's like maybe she don't love me, or worse, she said they've already had sex before, so maybe he's thinking she thinks he's shit in bed… and when the phone goes, he's worried she's found someone else.'
> *'That's a lot going on in his head.'*
> 'Yeah, but he's insecure – and bullies lash out cause they're insecure don't they…'

To be clear, this is genuinely the conversation that took place – or as close to it as I can remember. And boy did she have a point. It stands to reason, if you only have sex with people you love, then if you don't want to have sex with me, it must mean you don't love me.

This conversation stuck with me for a long time and made me approach talking about healthy and unhealthy relationships very differently. In fact, one of the starting points I now use, following this discussion, is: *Does love make sex safe?*

This is a message we have been telling young people forever – you should only have sex with people you love. You need to be ~~married~~ 16 and make sure you really love each other first…

And I can see where this message comes from and why it makes sense. As adults, we are trying to highlight the fact that for many people, sex *means* something. It is *special* and should be treated as such. Whilst that may or may not be your point of view (in my experience, regardless of our own personal beliefs about sex, we often still get caught up in repeating *what we were told* as gospel, even if it isn't how we live our lives in practice), the issue is that simply being in love doesn't magically make sex safe. I would actually argue that it can put you more at risk in some instances.

However wonderful love might be, it doesn't offer much protection from the dangers we are always banging on about to young people. Being in love does not prevent an unwanted pregnancy, it is not a contraceptive. Being in love doesn't stop you catching chlamydia, syphilis or HIV. But, most importantly, being in love does not guarantee you that your partner will love you back or treat you respectfully.

Indeed, two of the topics I speak about most often in my work with young people in terms of relationships, are relationship abuse and Child Sexual Exploitation (CSE) – both of which often involve falling in love with the perpetrator. Love can be many things but protection is not one of them. Love is often used as an excuse for treating someone badly and can leave people stuck in a position where they are faced with the question: 'What's wrong? You would if you loved me…'

Now, contrary to the evidence above, I am actually a huge romantic but I can also see the damage that can be done if we aren't careful with our messages…

As we said earlier, it stands to reason, *if you only have sex with people you love – then if you say no – it means you don't love me.* This is clearly not the message we wanted to transmit but this is what young people may have heard.

Love is a many splendored thing – but just because you are loved, it doesn't mean you feel safe. This is certainly true when we talk to small children.

One of the messages I am a big advocate of when training primary school teachers is to ensure they focus on the message that family is the place we should feel safe not loved.

Imagine the scene: we have a group of small children, perhaps five year olds, and we are talking about families – how they spend their time together, what they look like, similarities and differences, whatever. Often as adults we give the message that one thing all our families have in common is that we feel loved. This may well be true but how that translates can mean very different things to different children.

In this particular class we have one child. In her family everything is perfect. They take windy walks together with their pet dog, have days out – eat ice cream, read bedtime stories, eat dinner together and talk about their days. This little girl nods when her teacher talks about families loving each other.

In the same class, however, we have a little boy. He lives in a house that looks very different. At night, he often hides in his room with his head buried under the covers on his bed to try and drown out the noise of his parents arguing. When things have quietened down and he has heard the front door slam shut, he counts to 20 (that is the biggest number he knows) and then creeps downstairs where he often finds his mum in tears. She spots him and waves him into her arms where he is told that his mummy loves him more than anything in the world.

When his teacher talks about families loving each other he nods too. He knows he is loved because mummy tells him… in fact, he is told he is loved more often than any other child in the class – and let's be fair he is loved – but I wonder if they would both still nod if we said families are where we should feel safe.

They say love is blind. Perhaps what they mean is that love can excuse all manner of sins. In the name of love, people can often behave in awful ways. Love can be intense and overpowering. Like the lad in the video clip we mentioned earlier, sometimes love can make us feel vulnerable and out of control. When we feel like that, sometimes people's response is to make others feel so small and frightened they are too scared to leave. In truth, it is the perpetrator that is scared. Scared to lose the one they love, but they simply do not have the emotional intelligence to control their feelings or their behaviour.

I am not making excuses. Love should not be an excuse for poor behaviour but we have all heard the line, 'it is only because I love you...' We need to be precise when we talk to children and young people; our messages need to be clear. I prefer to talk about healthy and unhealthy relationships.

It doesn't matter if you are talking about a long-term relationship, or a one-night-stand, you can still treat someone with respect. A hook-up or a booty-call can still have the hallmarks of a healthy relationship, just as a long-term, committed relationship can be unhealthy and abusive. The messages we give need to be clear and leave no room for (mis)translation.

This is no more true than when it comes to mobile phones...

A few years ago, I was involved in a small piece of research for Public Health. As part of their annual report Public Health wanted to get the views of young people from across the country about how they used social media. I was part of a team that ran a series of focus groups with children from year 7 to sixth form (11–18 year olds). During the sessions we discussed the apps they were using, the ones they were told they were not allowed to download, incidents of bullying or where people had got in trouble, but most importantly for the purposes of this conversation, how their parents managed their use. Regardless of the setting or the age of the group, the young people we spoke to all told us the same thing. When asked if they got into trouble on their mobile phones, if someone was being mean, if they were being bullied or teased, if someone was harassing them, or pressuring them to send pictures, would they tell their parents?

'No... because they will take my phone off me.'

I now ask the same question whenever I talk to students about mobile phones and time and time again, the answer comes back the same.

It gets worse. I was delivering inset training at a school. I spoke to various groups of teachers throughout the day but also had some time set aside to talk very informally with the pastoral care and safeguarding team. Similarly, we got on to the conversation about how they manage mobile phones. I told them the same story I have just told you and one of the team piped up in his lovely, broad Scottish accent, 'So what message are we givin' 'em? By the time they're in year 9, every single one of us here will have taken their mobile phone off 'em. How does that encourage 'em to come an-talk te-us?'

The policy in that school was, not seen and not heard or you lose it. I am sure we have heard that same message before... isn't that how we treated children, oh, they could be seen, but not heard.

If we want children to come and talk to us as safe adults, we need to make sure they are *seen and heard*. If mobile phones are only ever considered as the problem and an issue, why would they confide in us, when they know our response will be: 'Well, you shouldn't be on Instagram anyway!'

Online safety needs to involve more than telling young people which apps are and aren't appropriate. Unfortunately, the tools adults are using to try and manage young people's behaviours and keep them safe are the exact same thing shutting the door in their face. To be fair, the majority of adults say these things with the best of intentions – often we are simply repeating the same messages we were told when we were young, using the only tools we have.

Many of the messages we happily trot out to young people are not only simply untrue or unhelpful but, more importantly, can often lead to damaging consequences. Perhaps it is time to change the message.

## Note

1   To view the advert: www.youtube.com/watch?v=RzDr18UYO18&t=13s

## References

British Crime Survey 2009/10 (2010). HMO.
Eaton, J. (2018). Can I tell you what it feels like? Exploring the harm caused by CSE films, *VictimFocus*.
This is Abuse (2010). Abuse in relationships: Would you stop yourself? HMO. Available at: www.youtube.com/watch?v=RzDr18UYO18&t=13s.

# CHAPTER IV

# APPROACHING MENACE

**D**um, dum, dum, Dummm. Der-DUM!

Approaching menace is the theme tune to which classic quiz show?

The answer, of course, is *Mastermind*. The show where contestants make their way intrepidly to the black chair. Under spot-lights, in a darkened room they are quizzed on their specialist subject, which they have chosen and been able to meticulously prepare for. This is the contestants' chance to shine. Although we all know this only serves the purpose of lulling them into a false sense of security, before their world comes crashing down as they are grilled on their General Knowledge. The spotlights of stardom suddenly feel like the spotlight of an interrogation room.

It is easy to look smart when you can anticipate the questions and have time to prepare – a bit more tricky when faced with the approaching menace of the unknown from the shadowy reaches of a child's curiosity, the place where monsters still roam free.

In my experience, it is fear of the unknown that most puts adults off tackling conversations around bodies, sex and relationships with the children in their lives. The fear of what they might ask if given the opportunity, and worst of all fear of what we should say in response. But tackling conversations around RSE shouldn't be a quiz show – especially one with such a daunting theme tune.[1] But that's the point, isn't it? *Mastermind* is simply a two-round quiz show – nothing more – it is the music and the lights that makes the situation so intimidating. It doesn't need to be so scary.

DOI: 10.4324/9781003122296-5

I think this is how we similarly construct the notion of 'the talk'. We make it into a much bigger deal than it actually needs to be. Rather than waiting for the perfect moment to sit down and talk about the *Birds and the Bees* – waiting for your turn in the big black chair – I would suggest we bin the chair and bin the talk. Instead, look for those little *teachable* moments. Opportunities that present themselves without effort to start a conversation; point out something you can both see as you go about your day or just make a positive comment as you're watching TV together. It doesn't have to be a big thing.

And what's more, you can prepare and make this your specialist subject too. That is what this book is here to do. Do your revision… each chapter is broken down into a particular topic or issue, and as we go through I will do my best to point out where to look for those teachable moments.

With most things, the earlier you start the easier things are. Start young and you will notice that your days are filled with opportunities to point out different families or name body parts in the bath. Topics only become embarrassing if we teach children they should be. They don't need to be. Yes, this means balling up our own embarrassment and shame, and sitting on it – and very quickly, things will get easier for you as well.

Lessons can be fun too. Play games – how many different families can you find in the park? Make up stories as you sit on the park bench and guess how people might be feeling and why. What clues can you see?

> That man looks angry and worried. He overslept and burnt his toast this morning and is late for an important meeting… you can tell because he keeps checking his watch and trying to see if the bus is in sight yet…

> That girl on her phone is excited. You can tell because she is bouncing up and down like Tigger! Maybe someone has just phoned her to tell her she has got her dream job, or has got into University?

Often it is the things we say without thinking that can have the biggest impact. The off-hand comments, when our child overhears us gossiping with friends on the phone, making disparaging comments about what that person is dressed up like as they walk down the high street, or passing judgements on the characters in your favourite soaps. How we talk about others can be a mirror of how children think we will see them and their behaviours.

Calling the two teens who get pregnant in the latest Netflix drama 'stupid' and 'irresponsible' doesn't exactly scream 'I will be really supportive if you ever get in trouble' to your teenager. Instead, a throwaway comment of 'if only they had a mum/dad they could talk to… like you do' followed by a playful wink or poke in the ribs. Or, even better, ask them what they would do if they were in that situation. Now you have the chance to give advice without it sounding like you are giving advice. It is what we do in class – we call them distancing techniques.

Another I use regularly at home is we'll talk at the dinner table about other people's kids (whether real or imaginary) and the problems (whether real or imaginary) they may be having in front of our daughter Izzy to bring up the topic. We will then ask for our daughter's opinion – or what she has been told at school, and who she would talk to if she was in the same situation. Occasionally, we talk about some of the young people we come into contact with through work (my wife is a Social Work Lecturer). Sometimes we talk and Izzy watches reruns of *Friends* on Netflix and pretends to ignore us. That is OK too. The point is we talk about this stuff in front of her, whether in the house or in the car, and this simply sends the message that we can talk about these issues in our house.

Again, it is about opening the doors and making sure children know they have the green light to talk if they want to. But it is often easier to talk about other people, than it is to talk directly about your child. There is a lot of groundwork you can do without having a direct conversation. But if you want your child to talk to you, you need to earn that right.

Ultimately, you do not get to decide if and when your child talks to you or what they may or may not ask. All we can do is try and open as many doors as we can and, like any good boy-scout, be prepared.

Especially when it comes to small children, do not expect them to wait for the opportune moment; instead be prepared for them to blurt things out as they pop into their heads. Little ones tend not to do internal monologues; a bit like old ladies who wear purple, they tend to speak their minds without shame. However uncomfortable that may be in the moment, in the middle of the fruit and veg aisle in the supermarket, or when you're in your important zoom meeting… it is a wonderful thing.

There will come a time, in the not too distant future, where the questions will stop and instead you will be met with eye rolling, huffs, chuntered curses and slammed doors. I have a 13 year old. The more we can earn our stripes whilst they are still curious and the embarrassment of not having all the answers hasn't yet caught up with them, the wider we can throw those doors open and the more green lights we can shine.

The thing is, you do not need to have the perfect answer ready to trot out in retort. In fact, the answer isn't particularly important in the moment. The important thing is how you react.

We all know that moment when a toddler's legs can't keep up with their momentum and they stack it on the floor; all hands and grazed knees. And there is that moment, where the world holds its breath, as the toddler is completely still, as their brain processes how they went from waddling at 1,000 miles an hour to lying in the superman position on their belly. Silence. Then their head slowly turns to look at you, their safe adult, so they can decide how much it hurts by assessing the look on your face.

You have to act quick, poker face, big smiles and a whoops-a-daisy for good measure… but no, the barely audible gasp escaped your lips before you could swallow it. And we all know what that means. Tears and screams ensue, as all their spirit of adventure, confidence and bravery leaves their little body to accompany your traitorous gasp. That is, of course, unless it is your second child, by which time all your sympathy has been spent and instead, you merely tell them to blow on it and give it a rub even when there is bone showing. It's fine.

I digress. My point is that same moment exists when children ask a question. What we say or whatever well-thought-out answer we construct is not important. It is our reaction that children are looking for. If you turn beetroot red, and get embarrassed – or worse angry – then just as when they fall over, children learn how they should feel by our faces and our reaction.

Instead, if you can respond with, 'Wow, that's a brilliant question! I am so pleased you have asked me… but do you know what, that is such a good question, I need to have a think – because it deserves a good answer too… let me have a think and we can talk about it when we get home.' It is the Mastermind equivalent of whoops-a-daisy. Now, you have bought yourself some time but also your child knows that whatever they have asked is OK and that whatever it is, is something you can talk about together.

Yes, it will probably be a lie – you are most likely *not* pleased they have asked, especially in front of Mrs Simpkins from number 73, but it is no more of a lie than the poker face you pulled off as you picked gravel out of their skin.

Now you have time to have a think, phone a friend, to drink gin (you've earned it), or have a cry in the cupboard in the kitchen – whatever you need to do before you go back to their question when it is an opportune moment for you both. This round is not against the clock.

# Top tips for answering questions

- Children should be praised for asking questions. Say thank you and tell them what a fantastic question they have come up with. Encouragement is always a good thing.
- A great place to start is to ask the same question back to the child: 'That's a brilliant question – what do you think?' Not only will this give you a second to get your wits about you but more importantly it is a really simple way of keeping your answers age appropriate and doing an instant needs assessment. You can now find out what they have heard or what they already know – you can correct any bits that are wrong and then fill in the blanks. There is no point in putting the next brick in the wall if the one before isn't straight. It is important to ensure the foundations – the basics – are in place first.
- If you don't know the answer or don't know how to answer the question, then say so. There is no shame in not having all the answers. In fact, I think this is a really important lesson for children to learn: that no one has all the answers (especially when it comes to sex). But then you should go find the answer together.
- If you are not sure how best to answer a particularly tricky question, then delay. Praise, acknowledge the question, and their right to an answer and explain that you need time to think how best to answer… but be positive. '*Huff, Not now!*' is not considered a positive response.

# When it comes to older children and teens

As children get older, they often stop asking questions. If they do come to you, often it is not for answers, it is instead simply for an ear. A simple response of, 'Do you need me to just listen or do you want my advice or do you need me to intervene?' can be really useful for you both to help set the expectations. As adults, we often have the habit of trying to solve our children's problems. That is not our job. Most often, young people simply want you to listen. They want to make their own mistakes and work things out for themselves. There is nothing worse than an adult telling you what you should do. Especially as, when they ignore our advice as they are bound to do, we then get to tell them 'I told you so'.

Your job is to be the safe harbour – to repair the ship, resupply and send them back out into the world again. Whilst, a ship is safe in the harbour, and won't be battered by the storm, the beauty of a ship is its potential to explore the world.

Next contestant, please…

# Note

1  Well done Mr Neil Richardson who composed the theme.

# CHAPTER V

# QUIZ

**H**ave a go at this quiz and see how much you already know…

## General knowledge

1.  What is the current age of consent in UK?
    Heterosexual:
    Between men:
    Between women:
2.  How old do you have to be to access emergency hormonal contraceptives (EHC – more commonly known as the morning after pill)?
3.  At what age can a girl have an abortion without her parents' knowledge or consent?
4.  How old do you have to be to buy condoms?
5.  What is the average age for sexual debut in the UK?
6.  What percentage of girls under 20 years old give birth each year?
7.  What age group are most at risk of suffering from domestic abuse?
    16–19  20–25  26–30  31–35  36–40  40+
8.  What did Section 28 of the Local Government Act 1988 prohibit?
9.  In what year was Section 28 finally repealed?
10. How old do you have to be to send a 'sext'?
11. Figures from the Cervical Cancer Trust (2018) show that 38% of women chose not to attend their smear test due to what fear?
12. A picatrix was a type of Greek slave, but what was their job?

DOI: 10.4324/9781003122296-6

# PART II

# BODIES

# CHAPTER 1

# HEAD, SHOULDERS, KNEES AND TOES... MIND THE GAP

*Fairy, Mary, Twinkie, Dinkey, Wu ... Pee-Pee,* Nu-Nu, Minnie, *Flossy, Foof ... Todger, Tidler, Widgey, Winkie...* Whilst this may sound like the cast list of *In the Night Garden*, these are some of the many cutesy pet names we give our children's genitals.

Perhaps you prefer the old classic *Tuppence?* Or *Flower?* Or the all-encompassing *'front bottom'* or *'bits'.* Or the forever mouthed and whispered *'down there'.* Pardon the pun, but it can be a pretty big ballpark when a child says their 'private parts are sore'.

Unless you grew up in a house with a midwife for a parent, then in all like-lihood you have your own family favourites. But have you ever stopped to think why, as parents, we are often so uncomfortable using the real names? What's with all the weird and bizarre names? You don't call your hand your wave-wave or your foot your walkies?

It is odd that despite the practice of teaching children the correct name for their genitals being advocated by safeguarding professionals as early

DOI: 10.4324/9781003122296-7

as the seventies, it is still a stumbling block for many adults.[1] Many parents simply don't like the clinical sounding words of penis and vagina. There seems to be a feeling or a worry that by teaching children the correct names for their genitals we are somehow talking away a child's innocence. If genitals are ever mentioned, it is usually in the hushed tones of 'Get your hands out of your pants – they are dirty and not nice'.

There is this attitude that children simply do not need to know about such things. Which is really odd, especially with small children, as this seems the perfect time to focus on them – particularly as much of the early years is spent changing nappies, potty training and bathing your child. To be honest we need to be either deluded or naive to believe they haven't noticed they exist! Indeed, as I have said before, there is a huge difference between innocence and ignorance.

A number of years ago I was part of a fact-finding visit to Holland. We were sent to explore how the Dutch approached RSE, as they were seen as leaders in the field. At the time the Dutch had some of the best outcomes for young people, having the lowest rates of teenage pregnancy in Europe, and the lowest rates of STI amongst young people too; which is why we were so keen to learn and unpick the secrets behind their success and learn from their good practice. We had gone with the intention of trying to improve our approach and the outcomes for teenagers as, traditionally, it was always teenagers that were targeted and received the majority of RSE.

Whilst we were there we had a presentation by one of the project leaders at Rutgers, a non-government agency that promotes sexual and reproductive health. Elsbeth was the project leader for a programme called *Spring Fever*, which was aimed at primary school children from four years upwards. At the time, this was completely revolutionary to us. There was nothing like this in the UK; in fact, we were so impressed we ended up working with Rutgers to translate the programme and bring it back with us. I digress. Elsbeth said something during her presentation that stuck with me, and I have been using ever since. She had us all sing the children's rhyme: 'Head, Shoulders, Knees and toes…' OK, we are adult Brits, so *sing* is a very loose description. Think of the lack-lustre way we sing happy birthday and you will have a better picture of the scene.

Once we had sung the chorus, really simply, she stopped and gestured to her middle and said: 'But what about this bit in the middle?'

As I said, I have used this ever since. Whenever I am working in schools with small children, this is how I introduce the topic. There is a very big gap between your shoulders and knees. What's more, children love it. They love being given permission to talk about all the bits we miss out – often this leads to conversations about belly buttons, intestines and poo, which is not really where I was going with the introduction but fun nonetheless.

Naming something is an enormously powerful act; perhaps that is where the fear comes from of naming genitals... but equally, *not* naming something can send an even more powerful message. It shouts loudly, don't mention it. It's secret, taboo and not to be spoken of.

I remember vividly my daughter being 18 months or so old and sitting her on the table and playing with her, teaching her body parts. I'd ask, 'Where is your nose?' and get her to point and then poking it. 'Where are your ears?'... 'Where are your knees?' Belly button... even eyebrows and eye lashes. Most of us have done the same as parents but how many of us then skip over all the bits in the middle, just like the song. Whether through our own embarrassment, or shame, it is very easy to miss out naming a child's genitals correctly. At best we replace them with child-friendly, pet names. But by omitting them, all we do is pass on these negative feelings.

Through the very loud and clear silence as genital go unnamed, children learn that they are secret and shameful. This does not protect their innocence; it puts them at further risk as it makes it increasingly difficult for them to ask for help when they need it.

Giving children the correct words for their genitals is essential for a number of reasons – the most important being protection from abuse. Safeguarding organisations have long advocated teaching children the correct names for their body parts as this has been shown to be a protective factor when it comes to safeguarding children against sexual abuse or if abuse has already happened, it gives children the words to disclose and ask for help.

For my generation when we were at school, safeguarding messages amounted to little more than *Stranger-Danger*. This was a complete waste of time as we now know that the majority of abuse perpetrated against children is not done by a stranger but by someone known to the child;

they may be part of the family or a family friend (ONS, 2019). Abusers work hard to get into positions where they have access to children, especially in positions of care, and will often use secretive language to hide the 'games' they play with children.

The first child protection case I was ever involved in centred around a little girl who kept telling the professionals working with the family that she 'didn't like it when her uncle made her make cakes'. Reading that sentence now I am sure alarm bells are already ringing. But at the time, we didn't know better. This little girl didn't have the words to explain what was happening to her, because none of the safe adults around her had ever given them to her.

If, on the other hand, children are taught the correct terms, they are more likely to ask for help. There is no mistaking the sentence 'I don't like it when my uncle touches my vagina'. Unfortunately, if we don't give children the language to expose abuse, abusers will give them words to hide it from the protective adults around them.

As I said, there is a huge difference between innocence and ignorance. We teach children the correct names to keep them innocent. I know it is not nice to think about these things and we like to hope that it will never happen to our child.

Aside from protecting against abuse, there are other benefits too. All children at some time will feel sore or uncomfortable. Maybe they didn't wipe properly, or they may have been scratching, or have not washed properly. If a child is brought up to feel shame about their bodies, especially their private parts, they are less likely to speak up for fear of being told off or labelled as dirty.

Shame is a very powerful emotion that prevents people speaking out and seeking help. However, it is not only small children who benefit from us using our words properly and removing the taboo from our private parts. These attitudes are important to challenge as they lead to many further issues later on – especially for girls. A recent YouGov poll showed that almost half of women surveyed had failed to attend a cervical smear exam due to fears about whether their vulva looked or smelt normal.[2] When you consider that almost nine women in the UK are diagnosed with cervical cancer every day, this is literally putting women's lives at risk.

# Question: Do we treat girls and boys equally when it comes to RSE? Do we give them the same messages?

Little girls grow up in a very strange space when it comes to their genitals. Little girls are given messages from an early age that their private parts are both sacred and icky at the same time. There is no escaping the fact that we treat girls very differently, especially when it comes to their private parts.

For example, we know that most boys in the UK will start school knowing they have a penis. Surveys show that around about 70% of boys start infant school with a name for their private parts (Brown et al., 2006). Admittedly, most will have their own pet name for it: they may call it a willy, a winky, they may call it Dave – regardless, the majority know it is really called a penis. However, when we compare this with the fact that less than 35% of girls begin infants school with *any* name for their private parts, let alone know the correct name for their genitals (ibid.). This is made worse by the fact that 50% of the same girls know that boys have a penis….

And we wonder why sex is still something boys **do** to girls?!

To be fair to most parents, with boys it is easier. You can't actually miss it – it is there dangling about, flapping in the wind. When he looks down in the shower or sits on the toilet, there it is. He has something to grab, and to wave at anyone he chooses to. With little girls, it is all tucked away. When she looks down, there is nothing to see – unless she is very bendy or has a mirror. You can understand why parents may choose to allow the opportunity to pass and not mention them.

To add further insult to injury, even when we do make the effort to name female genitalia properly, we get it wrong. It is called a V-U-L-V-A, not a vagina. When a girl wipes after having a wee, she wipes her vulva. When she washes her private parts in the bath, she washes her vulva. Vulva not vagina.

The vagina is simply a potential space made of circular muscles that leads to all the funky baby-making kit inside. It is a stretchy tunnel, nothing more. The vulva on the other hand encompasses all the fantastic stuff on the outside. It is comprised of the labia major, labia minor, clitoris, vaginal vestibule, mons pubis and Bartholin's glands (Figure 1.1).

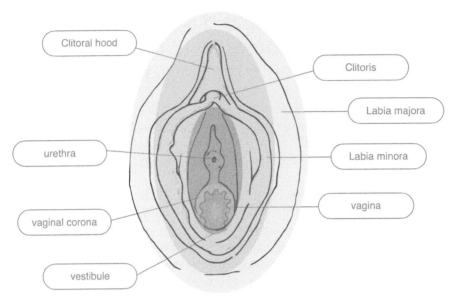

**Figure 1.1** Vulva diagram

I am well aware that this is the literal definition of mansplaining, if you happen to be a woman reading this, but unfortunately, it needs to be said. Nevertheless, it is really not uncommon for me to deliver training to rooms full of middle-aged women (professional women) who do not know the anatomy of their own body. To be clear, this is not a criticism of them but of the state of affairs we find ourselves in due to poor sex education. Indeed, in 2016 the Eve Appeal, a gynaecological cancer charity, asked women to label an anatomical diagram of female genitalia as part of an awareness campaign they were running; shockingly 44% of the women surveyed were unable to identify correctly the vagina on the diagram.[3] Worse still, 60% failed to correctly label the vulva.

This raises the question: how can a woman take control of her body, let alone her health, if she doesn't even know the basics of how it works or what it is called?

I do think it is telling that we choose to use the word vagina as the all-encompassing term for female genitalia. The word vagina was first used in medical textbooks in the seventeenth century and comes from the Latin term meaning scabbard. As historian Dr Kate Lister explains in her wonderful book *A Curious History of Sex*, the word vagina literally means the home for a sword. You can clearly tell early medical textbooks were written by men. For a long time now we have liked to reduce female sexuality to be centred around reproduction and penetrative sex (for men). By completely skipping the pleasure-packed theme park of the vulva, we are ostracising the notion of female pleasure. The vulva is literally the Voldemort of body parts – '*she-who-must-not-be-named.*'

Unfortunately, (mis)naming little girls' private parts is only the beginning. It doesn't get much better when we move on to the messages we give to girls when they get to the next step in sex education: the dreaded onset of puberty. As standard, most boys will be told about erections, producing sperm cells and ejaculation – essentially information explaining their sexual responses. They will be told about wet dreams and we may even go so far to mention masturbation – even if it is in a jokey *boys can't keep their hands out of their pants sort of way*…. But what do the girls get? Do they get to hear about their sexual responses? Do we tell them that they have wet dreams too? Of course not. What do they get…?

They get periods. Tampons, and advice about hot water bottles to manage their poor bloated bellies, assuming they happen to have a particularly empathetic teacher. It doesn't exactly feel fair does it? And yes, I did just say that girls have wet dreams too… don't worry, I will explain all about wet dreams in the next couple of chapters.

The question we need to ask is what are we so afraid of? What do we think will happen if we give girls the correct name for their body parts? As I have said countless times already, there is a huge difference between innocence and ignorance.

To be honest, if you are into words and etymology, the word vulva, isn't much better than vagina. Vulva dates to the late fourteenth century and again comes from the Latin, meaning womb. Baby making again. I am with Dr Lister as she instead champions the word cunt.[4] Arguably one of the most obscene and hated words in the English language, but it wasn't always so. Favoured by the likes of Shakespeare and Chaucer, cunt is the oldest term we have to refer to female genitalia, being several thousands of years old. The word is so old, we do not know for sure where it derives from, but we know that it has Proto-Indo-European roots and its meanings include, woman, knowledge, creator or queen (Lister, 2020). You couldn't get a word with a more powerful feminist history. It is interesting to note that a word of female power, is now used as a curse, an insult and is considered to be as offensive as the N-word... except in Scotland, where it is used as punctuation.

The history of swear words aside, it is essential that we are consistent with our messages to both boys and girls. Both have the right to understand their own bodies and be told, *your body belongs to you!* They should be told to enjoy and revel in their own skin – your body is the most fantastic machine, piece of technology or *thing* you will ever own. All children should be given messages of celebration not shame. And that starts with naming all of our body parts correctly.

Personally, I always advocate on teaching children both words: vagina and vulva, and most importantly the difference between the two. Think about a little girl who complains her privates are sore. What does she mean? Is it her bottom or is it something else? If she has the words to explain that her vulva is sore, we know straight away that it is the outside that is the issue and most likely will be something innocuous – maybe she didn't wipe properly or scratched when she got hot. We can put some cream on and we are done. If, however, she can tell us her vagina is sore, this may raise further questions. The vagina does not get sore without reason. Yes, it may not be anything scary – it may simply be something like thrush – but we know we need to investigate and take action.

Giving children the words is the first step... but now comes the stumbling block. You need to be comfortable enough to use these words yourself.

# Teachable moments

So, go walk to the nearest mirror... and repeat after me. Vul-va. Vulva. Vulva. It is a bit of an odd word, admittedly. The only other word I can think of with the repeated v-v consonant sound is Volvo... which are also well known for being sturdy, and able to fit a fair number of kids in the back. Vulva is an odd word to say – it can feel a bit strange in your mouth rolling around on your tongue (no pun intended – stop being rude!). Practice makes perfect. The more comfortable you are using the word, the more normal it will feel for children too. I promise, children manage perfectly. It is the adults that find it difficult.

I am not suggesting that you suddenly come down to breakfast in the morning and announce that boys have a penis and girls have a vulva to the breakfast table at large. Instead, we need to look for those teachable moments.

This is actually much easier with smaller children, but it is never too late to start. If your children are still small, then have a think and a discussion in advance with your partner or any other people who may be closely involved in care giving. Who will be there changing nappies? Who will be wiping bottoms, getting children dressed or helping at bath time. These are all fantastic opportunities to use the words in context naturally.

It is important to talk to other family members, child minders and anyone else you leave your child with. I have, on many occasions, seen small children chastised by the adults around them for using the correct names for their body parts. They are told not to use 'dirty words'. This tends to happen more with the older generations, for whom they were taught that these are naughty words – so be mindful, this is a big change for some people and goes against all the messages they have ever received. Take the time to explain; this may take a few awkward conversations – but we are supposed to be the grown-ups. In my experience, it is much easier to have a conversation upfront rather than waiting for an incident to take place before talking about it. No one likes to be told they did something wrong, plus this then removes the added issue of explaining to your child why grandma was wrong to tell them off.

I would also highly recommend talking to your child's school too. I work closely with so many schools and one of their biggest fears of implementing things like using the correct words in class – even though we know it is good practice – is fear that parents will complain or be upset. Please, show you are an ally; I will guarantee they will cuddle you! There is nothing better when delivering a parent meeting than one of the parents putting their hand up and asking in front of all the other parents there, 'I hope you will be teaching the children and using the correct names for private parts'. Suddenly you have given permission not only to the school but empowered other parents as well.

A word of warning: children do not always wait for these perfect teachable moments to ask their questions. It is just as likely that a child will ask in the middle of Tesco fruit and veg aisle, when you are busy and surrounded by old ladies, as they will take the perfect opportunity to ask when you are all calm at home. Children have a habit of loudly asking a question or telling you their penis is sore in public spaces – and naturally it will attract attention. This is where you earn your parent brownie points as you need to calmly turn to them and say: 'That is a brilliant question, but let think about it as I want to give you just as good an answer.' Or praise them for telling you they are sore or uncomfortable. The more you can model positive behaviours, the better.

If you cower and give in to the smirks and embarrassed looks around you, all you are doing is modelling shame to your child. Again, I promise the other adults in the supermarket will feel empowered and in awe of the way you handled it. Inside, you can quietly be dying and want to crawl into a hole – what do they say, fake it until you make it.

Set a good example yourself – try to be positive about your own body in front of your child. I know many families have open door policies when they have small children, and it is rare that you get to pee in peace – but again these are learning opportunities. Even for those of us that find nudity difficult, it is an opportunity to talk about privacy.

The key is as always to try to make the correct terms become as comfortable and natural as possible until penis, vulva, vagina, clitoris, testicles become as mundane as saying heads, shoulders, knees and toes! It all comes down to confidence. And confidence comes with knowledge. In the next couple of chapters I will take you on a guided tour of male and female genitals and a detailed exploration of puberty's, lumps, bumps and hairy bits.

# Notes

1 Protective Behaviours – 1970s USA Social Worker Peg West, Wisconsin, Australia 1980s, replace stranger danger – only 4% of abuse perpetuated by strangers… UK in 1990s Milton Keynes: www.protectivebehaviours.org/history-of-protective-behaviours (01 September 2020). Di Margetts (International Consultant Trainer).
2 Jo's Cervical Cancer Trust, 'Body shame Responsible for Young Women Not Attending Smear Test', Jo's Cervical Cancer Trust, 2018: www.jostrust.org.uk/node/1073042
3 For Gynaecological Cancer Awareness Month 2016, Eve Appeal undertook research that revealed a shockingly low understanding of the female genitalia, with 44% of women unable to identify the vagina on an anatomical diagram; with 60% also unable to identify a vulva on the same diagram. This demonstrated that many women simply do not know their bodies, with many not even calling the vagina by its real name but using a euphemism due to

embarrassment: https://eveappeal.org.uk/news-awareness/know-your-body/ (01 September 2020).

4   To be very clear I am not advocating teaching children to use the C-word – although you may be surprised to hear that it is not uncommon for children in primary school to shout out words such as fanny and minge when asked to name their genitals. The word vulva is fine – it's history may not be perfect, but at least it is inclusive of female pleasure and does not reduce female sexuality to only reproduction.

# References

Brown, K., Bayley, J., Newby, K., Wallace, L. and Dodd, L. (2006). What should we tell the children? Pilot evaluation of a theory and evidence based programme. Poster session presented at ninth Division of Health Psychology Conference, Colchester.

Lister, K. (2020). *A Curious History of Sex*, Unbound, London.

Office for National Statistics ONS (2019) Child sexual abuse in England and Wales: year ending March 2019. Available at: www.ons.gov.uk/ peoplepopulationandcommunity/crimeandjustice/articles/childsexualabus einenglandandwales/yearendingmarch2019#child-sexual-abuse-cases-that-come-to-the-attention-of-childrens-services.

# CHAPTER 2

# ALL ABOARD THE TOUR BUS

**B**efore we begin, let's see how you fair in anatomy class. In Figures 2.1 and 2.2 you will find two diagrams of both male and female genitals. Have a go and see if you can do better than the participants in the Eve Appeal study I mentioned in the previous chapter.

## Inequalities of anatomy

> *I change my tampon everytime I go to the loo, otherwise how would I be able to wee?*

> *But [girls] don't get turned on, do we?*

The two quotes above come from two separate young women. The first was a comment made by a young woman at a training provider for post-16s. She had come into the session late, all chaotic and loud. I liked her straight away. I was working with a small group of around ten; we were all sat around a table talking, when the girl in question burst into the room. Her first response when she saw me and all my kit spread across the table, 'Oh, I don't need none of this sex ed stuff, – it's too late… we all know it all anyway…'

DOI: 10.4324/9781003122296-8

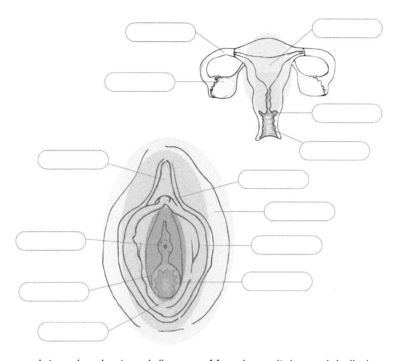

**Figure 2.1** Internal and external diagram of female genitals – unlabelled

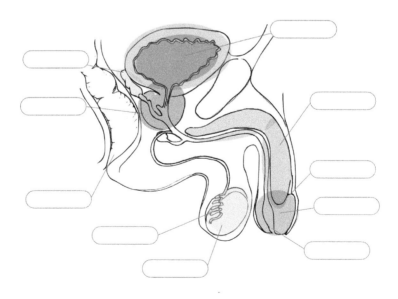

**Figure 2.2** Male genitals diagram – unlabelled

She settled down and got involved in the discussion despite her earlier protests, and was happy to talk openly about her own experiences. One of the other young women at the table asked a question about how the implant would affect her periods and the conversation developed until they were discussing how heavy their periods get and how often they change their tampons.

And that was when she butted in with this cracker of a quote: 'I change my tampon every time I go to the loo, otherwise how would I be able to wee?'

Here was a young woman who was sexually active and yet didn't know that she peed out of a different opening from where she puts her tampon. How on earth could she be in control of the sexual encounters she was taking part in if she didn't understand her own body? What was most scary was that her comment didn't raise unanimous protestation – the group were split on whether or not what she had said was accurate or not.

Perhaps even more heart-breaking is the second quote. I was in a standard comprehensive, talking to a class of year 11s. Again, they were old enough to know better; or you would hope so. I had been asked to deliver a session around what makes sex safe. This usually includes talking about STI transmission and explaining how this works (we will come to this in Chapter 9). Typically, I would explain that the majority of infections are passed on through sexual fluid and talk about how these are produced as part of natural sexual response.

I would ask the class, 'What happens when a guy gets turned on?' This is always met by a cacophony of raucous shouts of *'Bone-On!', 'Hard-On!', 'Stiffy!', 'Your nob gets hard!', 'Whooooop!'* or *'Boiiing!'* (obviously accompanied by some sort of hand gesture). I would then usually draw a huge penis on the whiteboard and we would talk through the fluids that males produce as part of their sexual responses.

This would then be followed by the obvious next question: 'So, what happens to women when they get turned on?' Interestingly, this question – in stark contrast – is often followed by silence. Tumble-weed style silence. And in that deafening quiet I heard one of the girls at the back of the class whisper to her friend, 'But we don't get turned on, do we…'

Is it just me that finds the fact a 16-year-old girl still has no idea of her own sexual responses, or even comprehends that this is something she is entitled to, heart-breaking. Sex should not be the sole domain of men in exclusion of women.

Unfortunately, I could go on telling stories and giving you examples to make my point. These incidents are not uncommon. I would argue that Figure 2.3 is in large the reason why. This picture is often the only image that girls (and boys) will be shown in school of what female genitalia looks like.

This is the perfect image if we want to explain the menstrual cycle or talk through sexual reproduction. But here lies the problem: sex education in school, whether in science or PSHE often doesn't focus on sex, it focuses on reproduction. It is all sperm and eggs and zygotes and embryos. There is no discussion of female sexual responses – these are skipped over, as non-essential information, to explain reproduction.

I mentioned earlier the difference in messages we give girls and boys and this is a key example.

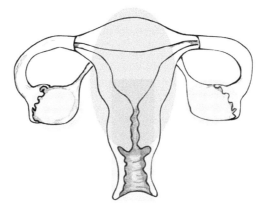

**Figure 2.3** Womb

Recently I was working with the Deputy Head and PSHE lead in a school, I had been asked to help them ensure their curriculum was ready for the new DfE guidance that has just come into effect. In secondary school one of the topics that is named in guidance is the law around 'So called Honour Based Violence', including Female Genital Mutilation (FGM).[1] Obviously this is not a particularly nice topic for discussion, but an important one nevertheless. We were discussing where FGM should fit into their programme of study. It was only when I highlighted, from looking at their curriculum, that they had at no point, including science, shown the children a picture of a healthy vulva in any capacity prior to the session that covered FGM.

Incidentally, many people who work in this area, myself included, would argue that placing FGM as a topic in Secondary school, as is done in the new DfE RSE guidance, is too late. We know that the most likely time that FGM will be performed is before puberty, often in the holidays between primary and secondary school. The reason being that it is more likely to go unnoticed by school staff as the child transitions between schools. Their new teachers will have no point of comparison to compare a change in the child's disposition. Indeed, FGM has been considered a form of child abuse in the UK since 1985. It was specifically highlighted in 2003 under the Female Genital Mutilation Act (England and Wales), which was later updated and amended in 2015 under the Serious Crime Act; however, it was only in 2019 that the first prosecution was secured against a mother who carried out the offence against her daughter when she was three years old. For this reason, waiting to raise the question of FGM until secondary school is far too late. Surely, we should be teaching girls (especially) and boys about healthy female anatomy before we teach them about mutilating it.

Without any more preamble, let us begin…

Unfortunately, I am going to undo all my previous ranting about how important it is to give vulvas the same priority the penis is privy to, by putting them to the side for a moment. Instead, we will give in to the attention-seeking penis. This is only because the plumbing of the penis is far simpler to explain to begin with, and it will give us a good platform to build from (there is definitely an erection joke in there somewhere!), before focusing all our attention on the neglected folds and mysteries of the vulva.

# Being a nob... the anatomy of the penis

The majority of people have a pretty good idea of what a penis looks like, and how the plumbing works. To be fair, when a graffitied line drawn of a cock and balls comes as standard issue on every high school desk and toilet door, is there any wonder? However, there are still some secrets hidden away, and many – *many* – misconceptions and general ignorance surrounding the penis and his two co-workers.

The penis (Figure 2.4) is a clever piece of anatomy, having two distinct functions. A penis is primarily an evolutionary solution to solve the issue of how to transfer sperm from one individual to another (Kelly, 2012). Its secondary function obviously is housing for the urinary waste tract. However, what is truly special about the penis is its ability to mechanically adapt from a flexible, easily to bend structure to suddenly becoming tumescent and rigid. As Dr Diane Kelly explains in her 2012 TED talk, the Penis functions as a hydrostatic Skelton, comprising a pressurised fluid (in this case blood), trapped with a reinforced wall to give it structure. However,

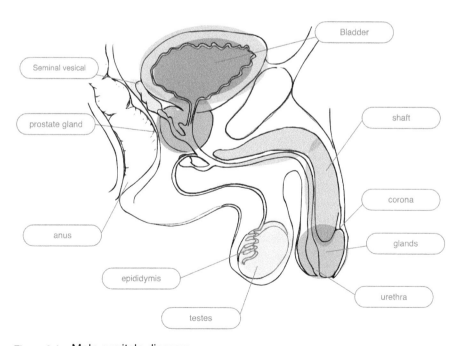

**Figure 2.4**  Male genitals diagram

unlike all other known hydrostatic skeletons in nature, the penis is unique in the way the collagen fibres are arranged at right angles (Kelly, 2012). This unique design is the reason why a penis can behave in a fashion to transform from floppy to erect.

Some quick points of interest that we should really deal with before we go any further. It is a common belief that erections magically appear during puberty. But as anyone who has changed a baby's nappy can attest, little ones get erections too. The penis is not some sleeping dragon that is magically awoken from its slumber when testosterone kicks in. In fact, we know that even inside the womb, tiny penises can become erect… we have the sonograms to prove it. This is equally true of little girls too. Physically, sexual responses are in place from day one; however, to be very clear, there are no conscious sexual drives until the onset of puberty. It is not uncommon for small children to enjoy having a fiddle – and they may even say that it feels nice – but this is a burly physical response, there is nothing *sexual* in this behaviour.

Regardless, this is another one of those things that no one talks about – and suddenly as a new parent – there it is! It is certainly not uncommon for parents to walk in on their little one and find them fascinated by this physical marvel, leaving the adults red faced and completely unprepared to manage their questions: 'Mummy… why has my dinkle gone all funny?'

Another important point to demystify is the notion of balls dropping. Whilst this may be a lovely phrase, and definitely a topic of discussion in the playground…

# On the ball…

I remember when I first went to high school; as was standard practice, we all had an appointment to see the school nurse during our first term. Everyone would be weighed and measured as part of basic health checks, which is still something we do today. As I attended an all-boys school, there was also lots of talk about the *cup-n'-cough* test. The story around school was that when we went to see the school nurse, they would also check to see if we had started puberty yet. Rumour had it, the nurse would ask you to take down your pants, cup your scrotum in their hand and ask you to cough.

I do wonder what conclusion the school nurse came to as to why every small boy that entered the room looked completely petrified by the thought of the imminent invasion of privacy they were expecting or why they all looked so hot and bothered. Obviously no cupping or coughing took place, because that would be inappropriate. Nevertheless, that was the myth that prevailed… in my school at least.

Even, today it comes up whenever I deliver puberty sessions. Someone always shouts out, 'boys' balls drop!' Which is not strictly true. Again, there is this notion that when your balls drop, your voice breaks. As if you pull down on your scrotum and somehow it is magically connected to your voice box! Or that men who wear tight jeans (that restrict the area) have high voices.

There is a lot of confusion and things we need to unpick with this narrative. In truth, doctors check baby boys to ensure their balls have dropped during their early post-natal check. Balls do not drop during puberty from inside the body; they should have dropped during early infancy, to be housed outside the body in the tight sack we call the scrotum; however, occasionally they get trapped in the pelvic cavity and may need to be rectified – but this would be checked during early infant checks.

During puberty the testes start to produce the hormone testosterone, switching on the sperm factory within. The perfect temperature for producing sperm is a few degrees cooler than body temperature, closer to 35°C; it is simply too hot inside the body, hence the reason testes hang in the sack behind the penis. What we really mean when we talk about *balls dropping* is actually the scrotum, the wrinkly sack just behind the penis which holds the testes, starts to hang a bit lower, away from the body. Basically allowing for a nice draught up their shorts, to keep them nice and cool!

In actual fact, the scrotum is a very clever bit of kit. It's the equivalent of having your very own meteorologist in your pants, a little Michael Fish if you will. On a cold day, when you are stood at the bus stop freezing your balls off, the scrotum reacts and shrivels up and goes all wrinkly; literally cuddling up to the body to absorb body heat. Alternatively, if it's a warm day, the opposite happens. The wrinkles disappear out of the sack allowing the testes to dangle a bit lower to keep them cool.

As we are talking about balls, you will notice that one tends to hang a little lower than the other. For the majority, the left will hang lower than the right. Kinsey believed this correlated with which was your dominant hand (right-handed people have a lower left testes); whilst this was what he noticed in his studies, there is no conclusive evidence that this is in fact the case. The reasons one hangs lower is again to do with temperature. It is easier to maintain the temperature in an individual testis as the other will not drain the heat energy away as they would if they were next to each other and directly touching. Equally, from a practice point of view, those that have a scrotum don't have wide hips and also have more muscular thighs as a secondary puberty characteristics, meaning their legs brush together as they walk. Having this difference in height between the testes means they are less likely to be crushed as boys walk or sit down. Handy.

Once the testes start to produce testosterone, sperm production begins. The average testes will produce over 1,000 sperm a second, closer to 90,000 sperm a minute, which is quite the production line. Sperm cells are the male gamete. They carry half the genetic information or instructions for producing a healthy embryo. However, there is no point in making all these tiny sperm cells without having a mechanism for sharing them and that is where the penis comes in.

**Did you know...**

Blue balls is actually a thing? However, it is probably not what you think...

We all know that the penis fills up with blood during sexual arousal, and grows in size as a result. However, did you know that the testicles expand too? They can double in size due to extra blood flow. This blood flow naturally subsides after ejaculation; however, if ejaculation doesn't take place it takes longer for this blood flow to subside, which is what causes the ache and discomfort. This is known in the medical world as Epididymal Hypertension (EH); doctors do not refer to it as blue balls – oh, and to be clear – this is not harmful in anyway.

# Balloon animals

So, we have come full circle, and are back to the penis as the solution evolution chose to solve the issue of how to transfer sperm from one individual to another (Kelly, 2012). The shaft of the penis is constructed with a pair of cylindrical chambers called the corpora cavernosa, which run along its length. These chambers are filled with smooth-muscle erectile tissue, full of tiny hollow spaces like a sponge (Roach, 2009). In response to sexual excitement, the brain triggers the release of an enzyme, which in turn causes the smooth-muscle to relax and expand as extra blood flows into the spaces, making this spongy material swell. Smooth muscle, unlike striated muscles that make up the majority of the body, are operated by the autonomic nervous system – which is why an erection cannot be consciously summoned or trained to make it stronger (Roach, 2009). Outside the chambers are the drainage veins for the penis. As the chambers swell with blood, the drainage veins become compressed between the expanding chambers and the reinforced wall of the penis. The resulting pressure closes off the veins and thus traps all the blood inside the penis, causing the penis to become and stay erect.

When I explain erections to young people, the way I have found to be most effective is this: imagine there's a clown making balloon animals (I know it sounds a bit random but stick with me). The clown takes the balloon, gives it a little tug and then blows into it; the balloon grows, getting longer and fatter, just likes a guy's penis.

If the clown holds on to the end of the balloon, it traps the air inside, keeping it rigid. When he lets go, the air flows out and the balloon immediately shrinks and becomes floppy again. A penis works in exactly the same way, except it is blood flow instead of air. Again, just like the clown grasping the end of the balloon, when this valve is released, the blood flow escapes and the penis will go floppy again – the only difference is a penis doesn't make the raspberry noise as it goes, which personally I think is a huge shame. Oh, and a word to the wise: whilst this is a useful analogy, I wouldn't suggest trying to twist a penis into a giraffe or poodle or something – it will most likely end badly.

As the penis becomes erect, the head of the penis swells with blood, and as it grows, the foreskin that covers the glands retracts. The head of the penis, just like the clitoris, is covered by a hood of skin for protection – just like your eyes and eyelids. The foreskin is attached by a thin, sensitive string of tissue called a frenulum (just like what anchors your tongue in place in your mouth). As the glands swell it becomes far more sensitive as it is packed full of nerve endings.

Whilst the penis is erect, a clear fluid is released from a pair of pea-sized glands called the Cowper's glands, located at the top of the urethra, below the prostate. This is known a pre-ejaculatory fluid or more commonly as pre-cum. Its function is to clear out any trace of urine, and neutralise it, as urine is acidic and can damage sperm. Don't forget, urine and semen exit the penis through the same tube. It is worth noting at this point – although we will discuss this in more detail in later chapters – if the penis owner has any sexually transmitted infections, they will be present in their pre-cum too; this is how STIs can be passed on even if they don't ejaculate.

Essentially there are two key sexual responses that both penis owners and vulva owners experience:

1. the erectile tissue in their genitals flood with blood causing them to engorge and swell;
2. their glands produce additional fluids.

If stimulated for long enough, whether using a hand, mouth or moving inside a partner's body during sex, it triggers a reaction which causes sperm to be released from his testes. More accurately, sperm are stored in the wiggly tube on the back of the testes called the epididymis.

 **Did you know...**

Foreskins and circumcision
Some penises are circumcised. This means the foreskin has been removed (most often when the child is an infant); this is usually done as part of religious or cultural practice.

Circumcision is often associated with the ideas of cleanliness, however its history, especially in Western cultures, has more to do with preventing masturbation. Perhaps this is where the idea of cleanliness comes from?

The sperm then travel along a tube, back into the body, past the prostate gland and the seminal vesicle, which produce the sticky liquid we call semen. Semen helps to protect the sperm cells from the conditions inside the vagina and is packed full of vitamins and nutrients, which act like an energy drink to keep the little swimmers swimming, as they attempt to travel the long distance to reach the egg cell – it's a long old way, after all. It's the equivalent of you swimming a hundred miles, when we consider the size of a tiny sperm cell.

As the sperm cells become mixed within the semen solution, they continue on their journey. As the muscles at the base of the penis contract making it twitch and propel the semen out of the opening at the end. This is what is referred to as ejaculation or more commonly as *cumming*. However, this in itself is another reason why language is so important. Referring to ejaculation as *cumming* is misleading as we also use the word *cumming* to mean orgasm – but orgasm and ejaculation are not the same thing.

Ejaculation is the physical act of releasing semen from the penis, caused by the rhythmical contractions of the pelvic floor muscles. Whilst this can be accompanied by orgasm, it isn't always. An orgasm is the release of neuromuscular tension built up through sexual arousal and stimulation as endorphins flood the body. Orgasms occur in the brain. This is often occupied by rhythmic contractions of the pelvic floor muscles that cause ejaculation – but you can separate the two. Some orgasms can be quite intense, others not so much. A lot depends on your state of mind. Unfortunately, ejaculating doesn't guarantee you an orgasm.

 **Did you know...**

By the early nineteenth century medical theories that the loss of semen caused serious harm had become well established (Lister, 2020). Men were warned to conserve their essence by avoiding masturbation (the recent 'NoFap' movement has echoes of this theory – which is complete nonsense from a scientific point of view) and saving themselves for sex within marriage. Indeed, Mr Kellogg of the golden cereal fame, was a huge anti-masturbation campaigner in his day. In fact, the reason he designed the cornflakes that still bear his name, was that he believed that a sparse, plain diet helped to suppress lust.

He not only advocated for circumcision to be performed (without anaesthetic) to help prevent boys from masturbating, but also recommended burning the clitoris with carbolic acid, 'allaying the abnormal excitement' in women too (Kellogg, 1887). Indeed, as Dr Lister explains, in her book *A Curious History of Sex*: 'It is no small part thanks to anti-masturbation crusaders, such as Kellogg, that circumcision is still so widespread in America' (Lister, 2020). Unfortunately, this is also the history of FGM too.

Indeed, the reason the penis has a foreskin (and the clitoris has a hood) is for protection. If you are circumcised, the head of your penis develops a thin layer of scar tissue to protect it from further damage, thus making it less sensitive. However, it will work fine and does exactly the same job.

For a time it was argued that a circumcised penis was cleaner and more hygienic as it didn't get a build-up of smegma, a white creamy discharge which collects under the foreskin which, when not washed away regularly, earns itself the lovely name of nob- cheese. However, smegma performs an important role as it allows the foreskin to peel back from the penis without sticking together; it's a kind of lubricant. As long as you wash properly, pulling back the foreskin and cleaning underneath and all around the glands of the penis regularly, there is no problem or hygiene issue.

There are a couple of medical conditions that may require a circumcision to solve. These include, phimosis, this is where the foreskins that do not retract below the glands of the penis. Equally, another issue can be when the foreskin is too tight and when the penis becomes erect, the foreskin can become trapped behind the glands – this is called paraphimosis. This can be painful and lead to issues if the blood flow becomes restricted.

# Penis problems

One of my jobs has been to work as an agony aunt on a website for teenagers. Young people would send in their questions anonymously, and I would answer them. Amongst the occasional people being daft, we would get many open and honest questions from young people of all ages. There were a few topics that came up time and time again… one of which, you will be unsurprised to hear, was penis size.

A lot of penis owners worry about the size of their penis – is theirs too small or does theirs bend slightly to one side? The truth is, size really isn't important. Just like any other part of the human body, everybody's comes in different shapes and sizes. The size of your penis has no correlation whatsoever to the size of the rest of your body either – no matter what you may have heard about hands, feet, fingers or noses. Unfortunately, the size of a penis has become wrapped up with the notion of being *good in bed*. This is a cis-het[2] male issue. Think about it – we even refer to a penis as your *manhood*. It is symptomatic of the male-centric notion of what sex should look like – as in penetration. Is there any wonder that young men feel insecure. In reality, penis size and penetration has very little to do with what makes sex pleasurable. Indeed, as I will discuss shortly, the female anatomy is not designed in a way that means penis size and pleasure have correlation to each other.

For many penis owners they catch a glimpse of other penises in the showers after sport or standing at the urinals, or even from watching well-hung guys in porn films, and worry that theirs doesn't quite measure up. The fact is, perspective is important. Geometrically speaking, a penis is cylindrical in shape. A cylinder will appear much large when viewed from the side, compared to looking down from above. So if two men are stood at the urinals and one takes a shifty look at his neighbour, his neighbour's penis will look far more impressive as it is viewed from the side, than he thinks it looks as he stares down at it… and vice-versa.

Another issue is due to the fact a penis is not a fixed solid structure – as we have discussed, it is a hydrostatic skeleton dependant on blood flow for its form. Therefore, a penis will change size and shape depending on the blood flow available at any given moment. This can vary due to blood pressure, exercise, temperature, stress, or how turned on you may be… meaning it is very difficult to measure a penis accurately consistently. Plus, where would you measure from and to? Do you measure across the top or along the bottom? Do you measure to your pubic hair or to the padded fleshy bit above. Or do you measure along the side… what if your penis has a slight curve in it? Do you measure to the tip or the end of your foreskin… some people have baggy foreskins? What if, by pulling your penis to measure, it starts to stir and swell… does it still count? Do you measure when the heating is pumping out or do you do it with the windows open?

You get the point. Equally, the size of your penis when it is flaccid has little to do with the size when erect. So I think we should put the measuring tape away…

Whenever I received a question about penis size, I always made sure I pointed out the fact that, regardless, worrying will not make it change, so what is the point? There is absolutely no point in getting worked up as there are no lotions or potions that will make it grow… so why worry? Instead, realise your body is amazing. Learn to love it and be patient with it. You do not need to compare it to anybody else's body. We need to unpick the way we think about sex and the notion that size and pleasure go hand in hand. Confidence and manliness has nothing to do with the size of your nob.

# Breaking taboos – the anatomy of the vulva

**Cunt...**
The three dots after the word are significant. That is the space where we instinctively draw breath in shock at what has been uttered. In the face of very little argument, cunt has become the single most offensive word in the English language. I suppose its only equal is the 'N' word… but this has a root in colonialism, slavery, torture and degradation. Cunt is simply a body part. It is interesting that a word, the very embodiment of feminine power, derived from the meaning: 'creator', 'knowledge' and 'queen' – that describes our doorway into the world, is deemed to be so offensive, and deemed to exist in the same sphere as a word steeped in hatred.

But let's not go over old ground. If you would like to explore the import-ance of the C word, I sincerely encourage you to watch Dr Kate Lister's TEDx talk 'The history of a 'nasty' word'[3] on the topic. We have already explored the importance of naming body parts correctly and our failure as a society to embrace talking about the vulva, especially with children and young people. The reason I bring this up again is that it is important for context. As Dr Jen Gunter, gynaecologist and twitter warrior,[4] attests, 'a lot of vulvar neglect is a result of patriarchal society's lack of investment in and fear of female sexual pleasure' (Gunter, 2019). If we exclude the vulva from conversations of sex education, we erase the organ responsible for female pleasure.

There is little mystery left when it comes to the penis. There it sits, front and centre. Having already photographed 100 penises for her project, *Manhood: the bare reality*, Laura Dodsworth contrasts the experience of turning her gaze and camera lens to the vulva, 'Penises are taboo, yes, but not hidden. For some women it was the first time they had seen their vulva' (Dodsworth, 2019). Part of the project is about exploring the visual range of what normal looks like. Dodsworth not only took pictures but also documented the stories of the vulvas she photographed.

Interestingly, Channel 4 followed her on her quest, and filmed eighteen of the hundred interviews Dodsworth conducted for a documentary which aired in February 2019. The documentary received three five-star reviews in the *Guardian*, *The Telegraph* and the *Independent*. The programme was titled *100 Vaginas…* which slightly undermines the point of the project.

The facts and functions of the vulva are shrouded in shame. Whether we are considering menstruation, virginity, pleasure, pain, discharge, vaginismus, childbirth, abortion, miscarriage… all of these topics are still not spoken about openly. The cosmetic and 'health' industry have created a monopoly built on insecurities about the smell, taste, or the look of the vulva. Indeed, it was in response to those who peddle snake oil and market products to 'purify', 'clean' and freshen the vulva that Gunter (2019) pulled together her *Vagina Bible* to counter the misinformation she encountered online.

To be clear, a vulva has no need of a jade egg. Intimate washes, wipes or vaginal deodorants are at best a waste of money, and in some cases harmful – as we will discuss shortly, the vagina is self-cleaning. There is no benefit to a vaginal sauna. Toothpaste will not firm up your vaginal walls and glitter should not come anywhere near the vaginal lips – this is not *Blue Peter* or *Art Attack*.

So, with no further ado, back to the tour bus.

# The basics – the three Vs

Let us keep things simple. The vulva is the outside. If it makes contact with your underwear it is part of the vulva. The vagina is simply the tunnel that leads to all the baby-making kit inside. The transition between the two is known as the vestibule.

The vulva consists of the mons, labia majora and minora (vaginal lips), the clitoris, clitoral hood, the vestibule, the opening of the urethra and the perineum (see Figure 2.5).

It may be worth pointing out that the organs that make up both male and female reproductive organs develop from the same origins. They are just moved around a bit. Consider there are two ovaries that hang from dangling tubes, not dissimilar to the two testicles that hang from dangly tubes. The head of the penis and clitoris develop from the same tissue, and both are covered by little flaps of skin to protect them – either a foreskin or clitoral hood. The labia contain the same erectile tissue as the shaft of the penis. Have you ever noticed that the scrotum has a subtle line down the middle – this is where the vaginal lips (or what could have been) fuse together during foetal development. As I have already mentioned, they

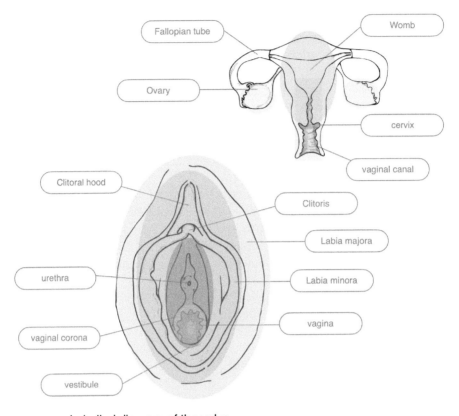

**Figure 2.5** Labelled diagram of the vulva

both display the same sexual responses too: they swell with blood and produce additional fluids.

The vulva is the ultimate multitasker (Gunter, 2019). It not only protects the vaginal opening – and is designed to manage the irritations caused by both urine and faecal waste matter – but is also designed to be ridiculously resilient and can birth a baby and heal itself after trauma. On top of which it is also the most important organ for sexual pleasure (Gunter, 2019).

Let us start at the top and work our way down. Above the pubic bone is the fatty pad of tissue known as the mons, which becomes covered in a natural thatch of pubic hair during puberty. This is designed as a protective barrier which leads down towards the labia. The outer labia or labia majora is often puffy and consist of fatty tissue. They offer protection as they form an outer ring around the inner labia or labia minora. The outer labia will become covered with hair during puberty. They house tiny glands that secrete a special type of oily sweat which contains trace elements of hormone and pheromones, which are believed to play some role in sexual attraction – similar to other mammals.

Pubic hair grows for a reason. It not only offers a layer of protection to our most sensitive of regions but also helps to keep us clean. It helps to trap microscopic dirt and debris, and helps to maintain humidity, which is essential as the skin of the vulva has a high moisture content (Gunter, 2019). It is a complete misconception that pubic hair removal is somehow cleaner. Indeed, studies have shown that those who remove their pubic hair completely are four times as likely to report history of STIs passed on through skin-to-skin contact, such as herpes and genital warts (Gunter, 2019).

## Hair today, gone tomorrow...

**Did you know...**

A picatrix was a Roman slave girl whose job was to style her mistress's pubic hair.

You may be forgiven for believing that pubic hair removal is a recent development. The trend for both men and women to shave or completely remove all of their pubic hair is certainly a contemporary cultural trend, with many people blaming pornography and TV shows like TOWIE for the fashion. However, we have evidence of human beings trimming their bushes and depilating dating all the way back to the ancient Egypt and Mesopotamia (Lister, 2020). There is plenty of evidence that both the ancient Greeks and Romans coiffured their pubic hair, which is unsurprising as they were public bathers. The bush came back into favour in the Middle Ages, in Europe at least, as a sign of good health. This was partly due to the rise in Syphilis, as being clean shaven became associated with ill health (Lister, 2020). One of the many awful, secondary-stage symptoms of Syphilis is hair loss, which was exacerbated by the common treatment of mercury at the time.

As with any trend, pubic hair has swung in and out of favour over the years. It was in the 1920s that shaving pubic hair again became the norm, which coincided with the shortening of skirt length and the new fashion for sleeveless dresses. There are rumours that the bush is currently making a come-back... ultimately, the arguments we are having around whether or not people (women especially) should feel pressured to remove their pubic hair are nothing new.

# Lip service

The inner labia or labia minora are hairless and made of erectile tissues, so become engorged during sexual stimulation. Where they meet at the top they divide into two folds, one forming the clitoral hood which hides the glands of the clitoris, the second fold creates a frenulum underneath the glands. The inner labia are packed full of sensitive nerve endings and are often one of the key sites of sexual pleasure.

As with all parts of the body, labia are not asymmetrical; each flap is slightly different and all come with unlimited variations – as depicted in Dodsworth's (2019) photo study, *Womanhood: laid bare*. The labia change during puberty, often growing and changing to a darker colour, which is often something we do not bother to mention when teaching puberty. We are happy to explain that penises grow, but as is so often the case, the vulva is neglected.

There is no such things as normal or typical labia. Studies show that there is great variety in length and breadth of size. One Swiss study measured 657 labia, with variations from 2 to 12cm, all of which are considered perfectly normal (Enright, 2019).

Where the labia minora meet at the top is where you will find the illusive clitoris, tucked away under their protective hood. Most people believe the clitoris to be a tiny pea-sized organ, but like an iceberg the clit has hidden depths. In Figure 2.6, you will see a picture of my clitoris (from my kit-bag), I take this out and about with me as I deliver sessions around anatomy, as so few people – adults included – have any idea of the size or structure of the clitoris.

The clitoris is the only organ in the human body whose sole purpose is sexual pleasure. Structurally, as you can see in Figure 2.6, the clitoris is wishbone shaped, like an inverted Y. The glands is the only part of the clitoris that is visible; the rest is hidden below the surface, its arms wrapping around the urethral opening (when urine is released), and down directly behind the vaginal lips.

All parts of the clitoris are sensitive to stimulation and are packed with nerve endings and erectile tissue. Like the head of the penis, the clitoris engorges with blood and swells as part of sexual response. The clitoris is the essential ingredient to orgasm. Even for the minority of vaginal owners

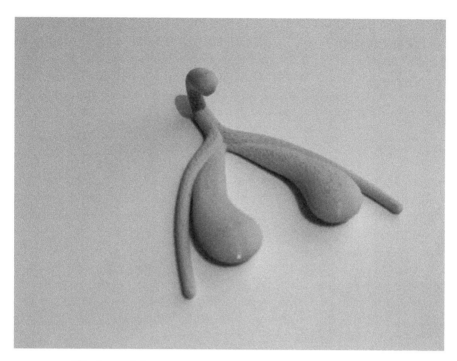

**Figure 2.6** Clitoris model

who can orgasm through vaginal penetration only, this will still be due to clitoral stimulation through the top of the vaginal wall.

# In we go...

As I mentioned briefly, unlike the penis, a vulva has two openings: the urethra – a tiny opening below the clitoris for urine extraction; and the vagina. The junction between inside and outside is known as the vestibule. Here you will find two sets of glands; the top pair are called the Skene's glands which are similar to the prostate, and the bottom pair are called the Bartholin's glands. Both contribute to vagina lubrication.

The vagina is not an open hole; it does not fill with water as it soaks in the bath. Instead the muscular walls are squeezed against each other like a closed fist (Enright, 2019). Like the penis, the vaginal walls are made of smooth muscle, which you will remember means they are not under voluntary control. You can no more will the vagina to open as you can will an erection into existence.

The internal muscular walls are covered in specialised skin called mucosa, arranged in folds and ridges called *rugae*. These folds allow the vagina to collapse on itself when at rest, with the walls touching, but also to expand and stretch to allow for penetration or childbirth (Gunter, 2019). Whilst we all seem impressed by the penis's ability to grow, it pales into insignificance when compared to the stretching abilities of the vagina.

This is a really important point…

The fact that the vagina opens up as part of natural sexual response. And then, when things have calmed down, just like an erection that subsides and allows the penis to return to its original flaccid state, when all is over, the vagina will close up again and return to its state of rest.

The reason I am at pains to stress this point is when I work with young people, one thing that comes up time and time again are the 'jokes' about 'bucket fannies'. There is this perpetuating belief that if a woman has lots of sexual partners, then somehow her vagina will expand and get bigger and baggier, like a wizard's sleeve or a clown's pocket. Forgive me, but these are the terms that are banded around young men's conversations… here I say young men – but it is not uncommon to hear men in their 20s and 30s make the same 'jokes'.

Not only is this complete nonsense and steeped in patriarchal and misogynistic tropes of purity, but what they seem to be unaware of as they throw their banter around the room is the fact that they are merely highlighting their own lack of sexual prowess and their understanding of basic sexual anatomy.

Indeed, I find it odd that these same men seem to believe the vagina is magic and can recognise the difference between *the one true penis* (theirs) and the penises of others… as seemingly this transformation occurs, not from the amount of sex one has, but due to the number of *different* penises that enter it… funny that?!

However, it is at this point I always enjoy highlighting their error as I explain, 'When you laugh and joke with your mate, and boast that *your "mrs" is dead tight…*', if we imagine there are subtitles below as you speak to translate what you have *actually* said, they would read: 'When I have sex with my Mrs, she is not remotely turned on, and not relaxed at all… indeed, sex is most likely uncomfortable for her and I would be surprised if she enjoys it at all – and I care so little about it, I tell all my mates.'

Harsh? Perhaps, but definitely fair.

The way we talk about sex is often not particularly nice or helpful. It perpetuates gendered stereotypes, as if sex is still something only for men. Sex is still something men *do* to women. On that point, let's talk about the hymen.

# Hymen and virginity myth

The notion one can tell the number of sexual partners a vagina has experienced is nonsense. The notion one can tell if a vagina has ever experienced a single partner is equally nonsense[5] (Brochmann and Dahl, 2017). And yet, we have all heard tales of breaking the hymen, popping the cherry, or deflowering the virgin. Ridiculously, medical science has been aware you can't examine the hymen to establish virginity status for over a century when Norwegian doctor Marie Jeancet examined a middle-aged sex worker in 1906 and compared her hymen with that of young maids and was unable to distinguish any difference.[6]

For most people, their understanding is that you lose your virginity through penetrative sex, when the hymen is ruptured by the invading penis, and this is why bloodstains are to be expected the first time. In my experience of discussing this very topic with young people and adults alike, the general consensus is that the vagina is covered by a thin, membrane-like structure, which is stretched across the entrance, like the skin of a drum. In their Ted talk 'The Virginity Fraud', Dr Nina Dølvik Brochmann and Dr Ellen Støkken Dahl demonstrate this notion with a hula-hoop wrapped in cling-film, which they proceed to break with a swift punch (2017). This typically seems to be the impression of how the hymen and losing one's virginity works in practice… sound familiar? But unfortunately, it is not remotely accurate.

The hymen is named after the (male) Greek god of marriage, Hymenaeus (or Hymen),[7] which gives you some impression of why the hymen was traditionally considered so important.

However, whilst the hymen does exist, it isn't what we have been led to believe. Think about it. If the vaginal opening was covered by a membrane, like the cling-film hula-hoop, how would menstrual blood escape each month? Surely you would just fill up with blood. Can you lose your virginity to a tampon?

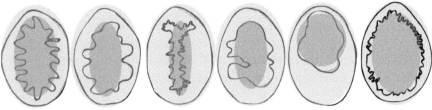

**Figure 2.7**  Examples of the vaginal corona

No. Because there is a bloody hole in the middle.

The vaginal corona, as the hymen is more accurately referred to, is located a centimetre or so just inside the vagina (Magnusson, 2009). As you can see from Figure 2.7, the corona comes in many variations, with a gap in the middle. The corona is not a brittle membrane, it is more often flexible – as Brochmann and Dahl helpfully demonstrate as they compare it to a scrunchy – and stays intact as an outer ring (Brochmann and Dahl, 2017). It doesn't break through horse riding, biking or performing gymnastics. The reason some women bleed the first time they have sex is more likely to do with sexual response rather than breaking the hymen. Occasionally, some hymens will cover the opening, but this is quite rare, and would need medical attention to deal with in childhood.

If the notion of breaking the hymen is not true, then it does beg the question what is virginity? And does it mean the same to everyone? We will cover this later, in another chapter. Now, back to the tour. For this next part you will need your helmet and head-lamp.

# The womb and baby-making kit

Imagine you are all really tiny and we are going caving. If we could walk inside the vagina, we would notice all the walls are moist. The cells of the vaginal wall contain less keratin, which allow a small amount of fluid from the ample network of blood vessels that surround the vagina (which is why it is so good at healing) to seep through, becoming part of vaginal discharge.

Vaginal discharge is essential to maintaining vaginal health. It is a combination of the moisture seeping through the walls and secretions from the cervix and from the Bartholin's and Skene's glands. This provide a perfect environment for its own eco-system of friendly bacteria that help to fight off infections and keep the vagina clean. Yes, the vagina is self-cleaning. This is why it is so important not to wash with soaps and perfumed products or to bother with intimate washes or wipes as you are more than likely going to damage the careful balance of bacteria that already do the job for you. Using vaginal products often does more harm than good.

As part of sexual response, the vagina will produce more discharge to help lubricate and protect the vaginal walls and to aid with penetration.

 **Did you know...**

The vagina is so good at self-cleaning, that within 24 hours after finishing menstruating, there will be no remnants of blood left anywhere inside the vagina. Talk about good housekeeping service!

If we carry on our journey, we will see that the vagina is a dead-end. There is no exit and nothing at the end of the tunnel. However, if we get out our torches and look up, we will see an opening above us – the cervix. The standard internal diagram we see in GCSE textbooks is misleading. It makes it look as if the vagina is a straight tube with the opening at one end and the cervix at the other, but in reality the womb is above the vagina. As part of sexual response, as the vaginal muscles begin to stretch, the womb is pulled upwards out of the way (for protection) in a move, un-erotically known as 'tenting'.

Now the question remains how we will make our way from the vagina into the womb. Helpfully, the cervix has this problem sorted. As hormone levels fluctuate as part of the menstrual cycle, this in turn effects the consistency of cervical mucus. When at their most fertile, the cervix produces excess of cervical mucus, dangling sticky rope ladders to allow ejaculated sperm (after sex) to make their way into the womb. Indeed, one of the ways in which hormonal contraceptives are effective is that they restrict the change in cervical mucus and make it more difficult for sperm to get into the womb in the first place.

The cervix can be felt with a (clean) finger. Often compared to the sensation of touching the end of your nose, essentially it is the neck and opening into the womb.

When it comes to the internal reproductive organs, most people's next mistake is overestimating the size of the womb. Everyone knows the uterus (as it is also known) is a very powerfully muscular stretchy sack, which can stretch large enough to fit a fully gestated foetus inside – however, it starts off quite tiny. Whilst it is the shape of a pear, it is much smaller, measuring only a couple of inches tall.

The lining of the uterus is covered with thick layers of blood and tissue called the endometrium. As part of the menstrual cycle the endometrium thickens, before being shed once a month as a period. The muscular walls of the womb rhythmically contract, helping to force the lining out of the cervix.

At the top of the womb we are faced with a dilemma. Do we take the left or right passage, as the womb splits into two arms known as the fallopian tubes. These in turn lead to the ovaries. Just as there are two gonads known as testicles dangling in the scrotum, there are also two gonads known as ovaries that are attached to the womb. However, unlike the testes, these do not produce egg cells. When a child is born with ovaries, they already contain all the eggs that child will ever have during their entire life.

Thus ends the tour. If you can return your tray tables and seats to their upright position before you depart.

I am guessing that some of the things I have discussed in this chapter you will have already known. But I am almost certain that there will also have been plenty you were never told in school. None of this should not be news to any of us... but unfortunately, biology class has never equipped penis or vagina owners with a decent user's guide. It is essential that we all learn about all parts of our bodies, not just the lungs and heart. It is especially important we start to break the taboo of talking about our genitals. The first step to being in control of your body and the sex you choose to have is to know how it (and your partner's body) works. How can you take care of your body, or enjoy it, if you do not know how it works?

If we are going to talk to children about puberty or where babies come from, these are the foundations that you will need to build your answers from. Yes, you will not use all this information in one go, but it will help you to shape your answers – ensuring you are not repeating half-truths, and the misinformation we were given. This is so important, especially for girls. We need to break the taboo of naming vulvas. They are amazing (all our bodies are!). As Dr Jen Gunter says, 'No woman [or man] has ever benefitted from learning less about her body.'[8] Now you have the information – your job is to pass it on.

# Notes

1 FGM involves the partial or complete removal of the external female genitalia for non-medical reasons. The WHO has classified FGM into four main types:
Type 1 clitoridectomy – removal of part or all of the clitoris.
Type 2 excision – removing part of all of the clitoris and cutting the inner and/or outer labia.
Type 3 infibulation – narrowing the vaginal opening by creating a covering seal by cutting and repositioning the inner or outer labia.
Type 4 other – all other procedures for non-medical reasons: this includes pricking, piercing, incising, scraping and cauterising.
This procedure is often performed by someone who is non-medically trained. In the UK, school staff, social workers and health care professionals have a duty of care (England and Wales) to report to the police if they have suspicion that a child has undergone FGM. http://nationalfgmcentre.org (accessed 7 September 2020)

2 Cis-het: Cis: used to describe someone who identifies as the gender given at birth (used as an alternative, to avoid using the term *normal* to describe someone who is not gender queer or trans.* het: short for heterosexual – attracted to the opposite gender.

3 www.youtube.com/watch?v=NveuGkSED1k&t=17s

4 Twitter: @DrJenGunter https://twitter.com/DrJenGunter

5 A point of clarification: if someone has been subjected to physical trauma from being raped or sexually assaulted or has experienced particularly rough sex, then yes, an examination would be able to recognise tears in the walls of the vagina, bruising and internal injuries. Although, often the body will do all it can to protect itself as best it can. It can be very confusing for rape victims, as they may find that they self-lubricated and became quite wet. This does not mean that 'subconsciously' they wanted it. It is merely a subconscious physical response to protect the body.

6 This century-old article is not available online, but these are the publication details: Kjølseth, M. (1906) 'Undersøgelser over deflorationens anatomiske tegn', Norsk Magazin for Lægevidenskaben.

7 Hymen was apparently the son of Dionysus and Aphrodite, although some stories claim he was instead the son of Apollo and a Muse. He is often depicted as a handsome youth, carrying a bridal torch and a garland. Taken from Chiron (2000), *The Chiron Dictionary of Greek and Roman Mythology*, 5th edition, Chiron Press, Wilmette, translated by E Burr.

8 Gunter, J. (2019), *The Vagina Bible: The vulva and the vagina – separating the myth from the medicine.*

# References

Brochmann, N.D. and Dahl, E.S. (2017). The Virginity Fraud TEDxOslo, May. Available at: www.ted.com/talks/nina_dolvik_brochmann_and_ellen_stokken_dahl_the_virginity_fraud/.

Dodsworth, L. (2019). *Womanhood: The Bare Reality*, Pinter & Martin, London.

Enright, L. (2019). *Vagina: A re-education*, Allen & Unwin, London.

Gunter, J. (2019). *The Vagina Bible: The vulva and the vagina* – separating the myth from the medicine, Piatkus, Little, Brown, London.

Kellogg, J.H. (1887). *Plain Facts for Old and Young*, I.F. Segner, Burlington.

Kelly, D. (2012). 'What we didn't know about penis anatomy', TEDMED.

Kjølseth, M. (1906). 'Undersøgelser over deflorationens anatomiske tegn', *Norsk Magazin for Lægevidenskaben*.

Lister, K. (2020). *A Curious History of Sex*. Unbound, London.

Magnusson, A.K. (2009). RFSU: Vaginal corona: myths surrounding virginity – your questions answered, Stockholm.

Roach, M. (2009). *Bonk: The curious coupling of sex and science*, Canongate books, Edinburgh.

# CHAPTER 3

# LUMPS, BUMPS AND HAIRY BITS

T oo little, too late.

Traditionally, in the final term of your final year at primary school, once SATs are out the way, you will have the puberty talk. Unfortunately, we know from studies and surveys,[1] for many children this is often too little, too late. In 2016 a study by the Sex Education Forum showed that 1 in 4 girls will have their period before any adult, either at home or school, talks to them about it. But it is hardly surprising, as parents, we are often guided by what happens at school, as we wait for the right moment, or an excuse to put things off (Bennett, 2017).

Nevertheless, whether we like it or not, puberty is starting earlier and earlier. It is not uncommon to have children in year 4 and certainly by year 5 already showing the early signs of puberty. To be fair to schools, many have started to react, and in the last couple of years as I visit various primary schools more and more have started to deliver their puberty lessons earlier. However, it is still often a one-off lesson. I always advocate that puberty should be on the agenda in years 4, 5 and 6. It should be something we return to again and again. This way, as children develop and grow they constantly have an opportunity to ask the questions that are on their mind. Not everyone is ready to ask questions at the same time. It may not have been relevant previously, but now it is.

Traditionally the class would have been split up. The boys in one room (which is better than it was in my day – we were sent out on the field to play football, whilst the girls had a secret chat with the school nurse

DOI: 10.4324/9781003122296-9

about… 'stuff'), and the girls in another one. The thinking being that it would be less embarrassing ~~for the girls~~, and that children ~~the girls~~ would feel more confident to ask questions without the ~~boys~~ others there.

This is still a point that comes up often in training with professionals, and in parent meetings. And it is always gendered as above. There is a real concern that girls will not speak up if the boys are there, that conversations about periods should be a boy-free zone. Boys won't cope and will spoil the session for the girls. My argument is that things will only change if we lead by example and make the change we want to see. I am a huge advocate for keeping lessons such as these mixed. That way children get to hear and learn from each other. We forget, some of our boys are growing up in houses full of women and will have knowledge and experiences that some of the girls will not. In my experience, it will be one of these boys that will ask the best questions or make the best points (it is easier for him, because he isn't anxious about getting a period – it's not happening to him!); not only will this help the girls, but also the other boys in the group – as they will see him be OK with periods and that boys can take interest. If we split the group, both the boys and the girls will suffer as a result. Indeed, it is up to us, the safe adults in the room, to create an environment that is accessible for everyone, regardless of whether they identify as male or female or as neither. In my opinion, the sooner we can get girls and boys talking openly and honestly about their bodies and relationships, the easier it becomes. It is hard to empathise with things you do not understand. And it is hard to understand things that you are excluded from.

I think we should be talking to girls and boys about what to expect from puberty for both girls and boys. However, we need to ensure that we are giving both girls and boys equal messages. This is still rare. We do not tell girls they have wet dreams too; we do not talk about their sexual responses. Instead boys get erections and ejaculations and girls get periods. This doesn't seem fair and is another weight on the scales, that gives the message sex is something for men not women.

In this chapter I will talk you through both the physical and emotional changes (because these are just as important – and are again, often excluded from the conversation) that take place to both girls and boys during puberty. This chapter will be a bit different, as I will explain everything the way I do if I was delivering a session in class, as I think this will be the most useful for you. When I was first starting out, I used to hate delivering puberty lessons. The children would just giggle and laugh every time you used the word penis or breasts – and I spent most of the lesson asking them to calm down. Then I realised that it was the way I was approaching the session that was the problem, not the kids in the class. Puberty is funny. It is the weirdest, oddest thing that ever happens. Mother nature certainly has a sense of humour. You have never been interested in anyone *that way* before, and as soon as you start to fancy people, your body explodes with grease, spots and hairs in places you had never even imagined. You become all gangly and awkward and desperate to fit in and be like everyone else – and instead some people in class are six feet tall with muscles or have breasts and curves, and other are still children. It is ridiculous, and not fair, and there is no rhyme or reason to it. Puberty is scary when you are left in the dark. Instead, what I found worked best was to not take it so seriously. To make children laugh at how silly it all is, and then they laugh with you and at you because you are highlighting the absurdity of it all, rather than laughing in embarrassment.

Quickly, puberty sessions became some of my favourites. If you get the tone right, children will open up, share their worries and stories and will ask the best questions – better than you could ever imagine. And I will try and cover the most common ones as we go too…

If you can get this right, whether you are coming at this topic as a parent, a teacher, an aunt, uncle, youth worker or carer, not only will it help set the children in your life for a much easier and less scary transition into puberty, but also it will help build the foundations for future honest and open talks. So let's bring on all the lumps, bumps and hairy bits…

# Why do we go through puberty?

Puberty is the process where a child's body begins changing into that of an adult's. You will be starting soon – in fact, you may have already have started. But don't worry, puberty doesn't just happen all in one go – it is a long, drawn-out process that won't be complete for some time. You are not fully developed until you are around 25 years old – so you have a long way to go.

Puberty can be a confusing time but is definitely nothing to panic about.

Puberty is the physical process where our bodies change size and shape as we grow – but there are also emotional changes that take place too, you will notice that you may start to feel different… You will become interested in different things and you may start to become attracted to people or think about having a girlfriend or a boyfriend, but also feel a bit more self-conscious too. In fact, puberty can be a bit of an emotional rollercoaster – where your moods go up and down. This is perfectly normal – but, remember, if you are feeling worried or confused you can talk to someone you trust.

The reason we go through puberty is simple – it is all to do with making babies. Puberty is all about getting you bodies ready for either making, carrying or looking after a baby once it is born. As you know, adults can have sex to make a baby. This does not mean that as soon as you start puberty you need to start thinking about sex – as we have said, puberty is something that takes a very long time.

You can't make a baby out of nothing – you need two key things: a sperm cell and an egg cell. Both carry half the information or instructions for making a baby. When you put them together you have all the genetic material you need to make a baby. But you also need somewhere for the baby to grow.

If you have testes, that is where sperm are made. If you have ovaries, then this is where egg cells are stored. One of the key changes that takes place during puberty is that you will either begin making sperm cells or releasing egg cells.

*So let's look at all the changes that are going to happen. Let's start at the top of the head and work our way down the body…*

The first thing we need to talk about is what happens in your brain… hormones.

Now, hormones are very important to puberty, as these are the clever chemicals which travel around the body and cause all the changes to take place during puberty. Hormones are responsible for many of the processes we have in our body; they help to control our sleep, stress levels, hunger, our heart rate, growth and when we start puberty – our sexual urges.

Puberty is triggered in the brain, in a special part called the hypothalamus. This sends hormones through the body to either the ovaries or testicles to wake up and start producing either oestrogen or testosterone. It is these two chemicals that cause all the other changes in the body to begin.

However, these chemicals – like any other chemicals we put in our bodies – can also affect how you feel and how you act. For example, when we eat too many sweets, the sugar can make us all excited and hyperactive and we bounce around the room like tigger! Or think about grown-ups – me, I drink a lot of coffee… before I have my first coffee I am all sleepy and feel slow and grumpy, but when I drink my coffee, I perk up and feel bright – because coffee has caffeine in it – and that is a stimulant.

If you have older brothers or sisters you may have noticed that sometimes they come home from school and they might be really tired. Other times they may be really moody and slam doors or sometimes they might get upset or feel down for no reason. This is all perfectly normal behaviour and is often just a side effect of those hormones working on their body. Puberty can be a bit of a rollercoaster ride for some people, with their moods going up and down all the time, but this will all eventually calm down.

One thing that is really important and can really help is to have people around you who you can talk to when you're feeling a bit confused and all over the place.

**Why do we get spots on our face during puberty?**
One of the side effects of those hormones we've been talking about is that they tend to make your skin and hair all greasy. Under your skin are little oil glands that help to lubricate our skin so it doesn't dry out. As we have this rush of hormones in our body, they cause these glands to work harder and produce more oil. If this grease isn't washed away regularly it can get trapped with dirt in our pores (the little holes in our skin) and cause spots and black heads. So, it's really important to start to wash your face every day, both morning and night, to make sure you get rid of all that grease. When you were little, you could get away without washing every day – now we need to take more care of our bodies and wash every day.

Unfortunately, whilst washing will help, it won't stop you getting any spots. Everyone will get spots as they go through puberty, and some will get more than others. Some people get acne, which is when those glands under your skin go into hyperdrive and become overactive. In this case, you would need to visit your doctor who can give you some special creams or even medication that will help slow them down and dry your skin out.

Another thing that can affect the amount of spots you get is what you eat. If you eat lots of greasy food, fried food, takeaways and fatty food, then this grease has got to find a way out of your body and one way is through your skin – and this can cause spots too. However, even if you wash every day and eat really healthily – you will still get spots. And not just on your face either; you might get spots on your back or shoulders too. They are just a natural part of growing up and happen to absolutely everyone.

On that point, one final thing to say about spots: it is really important that you look after and support all your friends and classmates too – and not just the people you like. Puberty can be stressful enough, without people being mean on top of everything. If someone in your class comes into school with a great big spot on the end of their nose, they will already be self-conscious and worried that everyone is looking – they don't need other people pointing and laughing or being mean too. ***This is an opportunity to highlight the importance of being kind – and not just to their friends but to everyone.***

### Facial hair, bum fluff moustaches and Gandalf beards

One of the side effects of testosterone, which is made in the testes, is that it encourages facial hair growth. For those with testicles, don't worry, you will not go to bed one night and suddenly wake up, with a massive Gandalf beard! Usually, especially those with darker hair will start to notice a dark shadow of fluffy hair over their top lip. After a while, it will grow coarser and more stubbly, and you will be able to shave it properly. This is usually followed by growing hair down the sides of your face which are called sideburns, then lastly under your chin and down your neck.

Some people will be able to grow nice twiddly moustaches, other might be able to grow big long Wizard beards that you can wrap around your head like a scarf. Other people might grow a nice face of stubble or a snazzy pair of pointy sideburns. Everyone is different. It is basically like choosing a haircut, but on your face! Some people have to shave every day; some people only have to shave once or twice a week – both are perfectly normal.

### Do girls get facial hair too?

Whilst growing facial hair is most often associated with boys, many girls will also experience some facial hair growth. This is perfectly normal, especially for those with dark hair. However, it will often be soft fuzzy hair, rather than coarse stubbly hair that you shave. It is usual for girls to get fuzzy hair over their top lip, or down the side of their face like sideburns.

Despite popular belief and what the adverts like to tell us, girls are hairy too. Both boys and girls will grow pubic hair during puberty. Again, this hair growth is stimulated by the increase of hormones flooding through the body. This is also the reason that old ladies quite often develop some facial hair later in life.

As women get older they go through what we call the menopause. This is where their bodies stop producing eggs and they stop having their period. This process is known as the menstrual cycle and again, is controlled by hormones. Once women stop their menstrual cycle, and stop having their periods, the levels of oestrogen, the hormones that helps control the cycle drop, meaning the naturally occurring testosterone in their bodies, is no longer in balance and causes coarse hair to grow.

### What does it mean when someone's voice breaks?
During puberty, everyone's voice gets a little bit deeper. However, for those with testes, another of the side effects of high levels of testosterone is that it cause your voice to break. We have already covered the fact that this is not because your balls have dropped but merely because testicles produce high levels of testosterone. This causes the voice box to develop and the Adam's apple to stick out. In the voice box we have vocal cords, and just like when we tune a guitar by tightening the strings, making the notes higher or lower, this is exactly the same as what is happening in the voice box.

The problem is this doesn't happen overnight. It can take months and months for your voice to completely change – and in the meantime, it does have the tendency to squeak – like someone playing a clarinet really badly. This is what we mean when we say someone's voice has broken. People might laugh when your voice squeaks unexpectedly – but try not to worry about this too much; they're not laughing at you because you've done something wrong, it is just unexpected and sounds funny. Try not to take it personally, and own it. Laugh along with everyone else and just put it down to a sign that you're growing up.

### Growing up and out – changing shape
One of the most notable changes that take place during puberty is that our bodies all grow much bigger and change shape. In fact, puberty is the time we grow the most of any time in life. We call this a growth spurt. This can lead to some very amusing class photos in the early years of puberty, taking on the look of a scene from the Fellowship of the Ring as some of the

class will look like hobbits next to their much taller classmates. This can be embarrassing for everyone – no one likes to be the odd one out, everyone looks at – that is equally true for those early bloomers and late developers.

Growth spurts are often accompanied by bouts of clumsiness. This is understandable as it simply takes a little while to get used to driving a bigger car. The external dimensions have changed, and it becomes a bit more challenging to park until you get used to it. This sudden growth can also lead to aches and pains as bones and joints grow quickly.

Before puberty, both girls and boys bodies look pretty similar in shape – in fact, you can hardly tell them apart, especially when fully clothed. We generally rely on superficial gender expressions, such as how long their hair is, or what clothes they are wearing, in order to guess whether a child is a boy or a girl. However, during puberty all this changes. Suddenly, bodies take on a less androgynous look as secondary sexual characteristics develop. This can be an especially traumatic time for those children that identify as either trans or non-binary.[2] For this reason some trans children who suffer strong and persistent gender dysphoria may be prescribed puberty delaying hormones or *puberty blockers* as they are more often referred (Giordano and Holm, 2020).

Currently there is much (negative) media attention given to the medical treatment and support offered to trans individuals, with particular emphasis on trans children. As is often the case, many of the arguments misrepresent the reality of support offered to trans children and completely ignores their experiences. However, now is not the time to unpack these issues; I only raise the topic here as it is important to recognise the difficulty that puberty can present to some trans children, as their body begins to change in ways that betray how they identify. The prescription of puberty blockers has been shown to not only reduce dysphoria (Kreukels and Cohen-Kettenis, 2011), but also reduce anxiety and suicidal intentions (Hembree, 2011; Kraeukels, Cohen-Kettenis, 2011; Murade et al., 2010). These are not experimental drugs and have been recommended for use by the Royal College of Psychiatrists since 1998 and are used worldwide as an effective temporary solution. Puberty is merely delayed to allow children more time to explore their gender without the added stress of their rapidly changing body.

For those with testes, their bodies take on a more masculine shape, as they develop muscle mass, especially across the shoulders and back, giving them a more triangular shape. Whereas those with ovaries will develop a curvier sort of shape, with breasts and wide hips, creating an hour-glass shape. Obviously, these are vast generalisations; we know that bodies come in all sort of shapes and sizes all of which are normal. It is not clear why those with testes develop more muscular bodies and what purpose this would serve. It has been suggested that it may be due to fighting over potential mates – or protecting their families – we simply don't know; however, we do know why those with ovaries develop wide hips and breast – and it is all to do with babies.

**The great bra stand-off**
This would be a typical question I would ask a class during a puberty session: *What are boobs for?* (typically accompanied by the universal sign language for breast – as someone who talks a lot with their hands it is unavoidable!) Often the reply has something to do with looking good, to get attention, or attraction, which is sad. In Western culture, breasts have become more associated with being seen as sexual rather than as dinner. This is no more obvious than in discussions around breastfeeding in public, and some people's outrage at the notion.

The fact remains that breasts are very simply designed to feed a baby. Children are always amazed and equally disgusted when I point out that the milk they pour on their cereal is essentially a cow's breast milk!

During puberty, as breasts first start to develop, you may notice a small bump called a breast bud grows under the nipple and areola – the darker circle area of skin around the nipple. The breasts get bigger and rounder as the fatty tissue and milk-producing glands inside the breasts continue to grow. The areola also gets bigger and darker and the nipples may stick out.

A quick point to raise – puberty doesn't come with its own set timetable. You'll probably notice that you and your friends grow in different ways. One person's breasts may develop earlier, whilst another may get their period earlier. Bodies tend not to develop in any set order and everyone's different. All you can do is sit back and be patient.

As the breast buds grow, it is not uncommon to notice tingling, aching or itching in the chest, and the nipples may swell or become tender. This is all perfectly normal and nothing to worry about.

Now, all breasts are different and unique – just like faces. Even the one hanging next to it will be slightly fuller or hang slightly lower. Our bodies are not symmetrical. It's common to worry about whether your breasts are normal. As I say, it's common and perfectly normal for one breast to be larger than the other, or for one to sit higher or lower than the other. Equally, nipples come in different shapes, sizes and colours too. They can point up or down; be dark or pale; large or small and again, are not perfectly symmetrical.

As breasts develop, now is a time to think about going bra shopping. For some people this can be a special and exciting moment, for others it is torturously embarrassing – both reactions are perfectly normal and understandable. At least these days there is much more choice and variety in styles available for those starting off in the world of bra shopping. But it is always worth starting off well. We have all heard the statistics about how many women are wearing the wrong-sized bra. A well-fitting bra, can make all the difference to your posture and prevent a sore back, especially for those on the larger side.

Developing breasts can be really embarrassing for some people – especially for those early developers. Suddenly you get all the attention from your classmates and even from strangers on the street. Yes, it can feel proper creepy, as the eyes of strangers suddenly start to notice, whether real or imagined due to feeling self-conscious, it can be uncomfortable.

When our daughter Izzy first started developing breasts we had a hell of a time trying to find underwear she was happy to wear under her school uniform. She simply refused to wear anything. No matter what she chose or what we bought, she wasn't having any of it. We ended up with drawers of different crop-tops and plain no fuss bras that were never worn. We have always been happy for Izzy to pick her own clothes and wanted her to be comfy in what she was wearing, but the problem was, because her school wore white blouses, it was getting to the point where you could see the dark circles of her developing breasts through the material. And whilst she didn't seem bothered, we were worried her classmates would point out the fact and be unkind as children can be. Nothing we said as we tried to explain made a difference. We had tears and we had tantrums – and our daughter wasn't much happier either…! In the end, her step-mum took the more visual approach. My wife took her bra off and pulled on (as best she could!) Izzy's tiny blouse, over one of her breasts and showed Izzy what it looked like…

Izzy's response: 'Well you're a woman, I'm just a kid…' which, to be fair was true enough. She was just a kid, whose body was developing faster than her emotions.

After, the no bra display by her step-mum, we thought we'd cracked it. We had no more tears or arguments. Izzy would get ready for school and come down wearing her cardie or jumper with no fuss. It would only be when she came home and threw her clothes in the dirty wash that we would realise she had not worn her crop-top style sports bras she had chosen.

Now I can be stubborn. Her mother can be really stubborn… but our daughter Izzy is the queen of stubborn! As was demonstrated the morning of the *Great Bra Stand-off*. Simply, I refused to take her to school until she was wearing one of her bras. We were 30 minutes late to school that day but I ended up having a very sympathetic and positive chat with the headteacher as I explained the situation. One of the issues of raising a child to be independent, have their own mind and to be confident in her own decisions is you are often on the wrong end of it!

To be honest, we were at a loss. We simply couldn't understand what the problem was. We had always been very body positive, had never made fun of her changing body and made sure she plenty of privacy and could pick the bras she was happy to wear. In the end, we finally got to the bottom of the issue. One of the other girls in class, who had developed breasts before any of the other girls, had come to school in her new bra – most likely feeling really proud and excited after going shopping with her mum and picking out the bra she thought was perfect – but one of the boys had spent breaktime twanging her straps and making fun of her. Rightly so, she had gotten upset. That was why our daughter didn't want to wear a bra to school… she didn't want to be next.

When we are talking to kids about puberty it is essential we talk about how to be kind and how to behave. We need to press home that personal boundaries are changing and how we touch each other changes too. Boys and girls need to know about how each other's bodies are developing, not just how their own is changing. Whilst boys twanging a girl's bra straps is nothing new – *boy will be boys after all…* – I'm sorry this no excuse. We know where that leads. It is not acceptable that a little girl should go home in tears because a boy doesn't understand that he needs to respect other people's boundaries. This is why talks about consent, and privacy need to come before children start puberty… and should be reiterated again and again as bodies and interests change.

No child's first experience of wearing their bra should be ruined because a boy can't keep his hands to himself.

It is not just the top half that starts to develop curves. During puberty, for those with ovaries, their hips will start to widen and tilt slightly forward. This is simply to help distribute the weight of a growing baby during pregnancy – and helps to make childbirth slightly easier as there is more room for the head to pass through. There is real strength in these foundations – we often underestimate the shear stress and endurance of carrying a growing foetus has on the human body. But, just as with dancing… it's all in the hips.

### A little topiary – pruning the bush

During puberty, it is perfectly normal for everyone to develop plenty of pubic hair. We don't seem to like to admit it, and try hard to hide the fact, but women are hairy creatures too! It is normal for the hair on your legs and arms to darken and thicken; but also for you to develop hair in completely new places too, such as in your armpit and around your genitals.

A side effect of high levels of testosterone in the body is an increase production in body hair. So, for those with testes, it is not unusual to also develop hairy chests, hairy backs, hairy feet and toes, and hairy bums – cracks and all!

 **Did you know…**

It is not strictly true to say that testosterone is the male hormone and oestrogen the female hormone. Both men and women produce both hormones. It is just that those with testes produce more testosterone, and those with ovaries produce more oestrogen. Sometimes these hormones can become unbalanced and cause unexpected side effects such as hair growth or breast development.

Some people may choose to trim, shave or wax their pubic hair. As we have already mentioned, this is not a new phenomenon. Pubic hair has been in and out of fashion throughout history (Lister, 2020) – at the end of the day, it is down to personal choice. Over recent years we have started to see more and more celebrities unapologetically sporting a bit of underarm hair on the red carpet, which can only be a positive step in relieving the pressure on people to fit a certain feminine stereotype, however unrealistic. Human beings are hairy, deal with it!

There is a notion that being hairy is not only considered to be non-feminine but also somehow unclean. This is simply not true. Hair is designed to wick moisture away from the skin to help keep you clean, which brings us nicely on to personal hygiene.

### Time for a shower

As all these changes are taking place it is understandable that our bodies will be working harder too… it is essential that young people start to wash and shower regularly. Before puberty, kids can get away with showering every few days or so. However, adult bodies sweat more. No longer can you get away with a bath once a week and the occasional splash of water on your face. In an ideal world we would all shower or bathe every day – especially if you have been doing any physical activity, otherwise we can start to get a little bit smelly, as we develop body odour. Sweat itself doesn't particularly smell – however, bacteria that naturally lives on our skin are happy to break down the sweat and this process creates the familiar pong associated with BO.

However, washing isn't enough. One mistake that many people make is that they may be good at showering regularly, but you also need to wash your clothes regularly too. Think about it: you sweat all day, take your school uniform off at the end of the day, hang it delicately in your carpet wardrobe by the radiator, where all the sweat that has soaked into the material festers away over night, and then you pick it up off the floor and throw it on for another wear… As teens go through puberty it is important that they change their clothes regularly too.

Equally, you may want to invest in some deodorant. Antiperspirant will reduce how much you sweat, and deodorant simply smells nice. The only difference between men and women's deodorants is that those marketed as men's are designed to be used on hairy arm-pits… that is all.

### Sperm and eggs

We have already done the basics anatomy of our genitals in the previous chapter. However, during puberty this is when we will become far more aware of our genitals. Suddenly, they are awake. Along with all the other changes we have discussed, now our bodies need to produce gametes – sex cells (either sperm or egg cells). This key change comes hand in hand with the arrival of our sex drives too.

As we know, sperms cells are produced in the testes, which hang in the dangly sack behind the penis. During puberty, the scrotum will grow and dangle a little lower and the penis will grow in size too. The surge in testosterone will have the slightly embarrassing side effect of causing spontaneous erections too. These are rarely noticeable to anyone other than the penis owner but can make them particularly self-conscious. Generally, like most things, if you ignore them, they will go away relatively quickly and no one will be any the wiser.

Equally, in the ovaries, eggs will start to mature; remember the egg cells have always been inside the ovaries since birth, however hormones will cause the menstrual cycle to begin, and an egg to mature and be released each month. Hormones will also effect the look of the vulva, as the vaginal lips will grow, swell and may even darken in colour.

Now before we get on to the topic of wet dreams and the menstrual cycle, one thing that is so often overlooked is vaginal discharge. Unfortunately, the amount of young women, who are confused and worry about the sudden appearance of whiteish stains in their underwear, and panic they have an infection or something is wrong, simply because we neglect to discuss discharge is frankly ridiculous and completely unacceptable in this day and age.

**Vaginal discharge**
Vaginal discharge serves the essential purpose of keeping the vagina clean and healthily regulated, sustaining a naturally acidic environment. It is made up of cervical fluid and natural lubrication that seeps through the thin vaginal membrane walls with added fluid from both the Skene's and Bartholin glands (Gunter, 2019a).

Generally, healthy discharge does not have a particularly strong or unpleasant smell, and can be white or clear, creamy, sticky or slippery and wet. Naturally vaginal discharge will change consistency due to hormone changes during the menstrual cycle. Discharge will leave stains in your underwear that are white or yellowish in colour. THIS IS COMPLETELY NORMAL, HEALTHY AND NOTHING TO BE ASHAMED ABOUT. At times you may have a heavy volume of discharge that can feel sticky or uncomfortable

**Did you know...**

In the English language, we don't have a specific term for vaginal fluid – unlike with male sexual fluids we call semen. We even have a name for the smelly discharge (Smegma) which collects under the foreskin if it isn't washed properly – but none for vaginal fluid...

The French use the term '*Cuprine*', to refer to vaginal fluid, which comes from Cyprus – the birthplace of Aphrodite, the goddess of love.

in your underwear, and you may need to nip to the bathroom and wipe it away. THIS IS PERFECTLY NORMAL TOO.

But remember, everybody is different and *every body* is different. The best thing to do is to pay attention and get to know what is normal for you. One of the key symptoms there is something wrong or out of place is when you have unusual discharge – but by that we mean unusual for you. You need to know what is usual, in order to notice a change.

The vagina is a doorway into the body – just like the mouth. Your mouth is moist and wet, and a fantastic environment for healthy bacteria to help keep it clean and healthy. You know how it feels when you fall asleep with your mouth open and your throat dries out, how sore and uncomfortable it is. Well, vaginal discharge is simply the equivalent – vaginal dribble, if you will.

This environment is perfect for sustaining the fine balance of healthy bacteria flora that fight off infection and keep the vagina clean. The friendly bacteria is like your own little cleaning ladies in there – in fact, after finishing bleeding during your period, within 24 hours there is no trace of blood anywhere inside the vagina – because those cleaning ladies keep a tidy house.

During the menstrual cycle it is perfectly normal for vaginal discharge to change consistency and volume. In the days before ovulation, which is usually around day 14 of the menstrual cycle, cervical mucus becomes sticky, white and creamy as oestrogen levels rise. (This plays an important part in fertilisation – the usual acidic environment of the vagina is not particularly hospitable to invading sperm cells, whereas this creamy discharge helps to protect any sperm that have been left in the vagina after sex, allowing them to survive for a few days as they wait for ovulation and the resulting egg cell.)

As we get closer to day 14 and ovulation, discharge will become more like uncooked egg white, that is clear, sticky and wet and there will usually be more of it. (This is the easiest discharge for sperm to swim through and allows them to move through the cervix as they swim along the dripping tendrils of mucus). After ovulation, oestrogen levels drop and progesterone rises, causing cervical fluid to become sticky and drier.

Final point: discharge is designed to keep your vaginal healthy and clean. YOU DO NOT NEED TO BUY SPECIAL WASHES AND YOU DO NOT NEED TO CLEAN INSIDE YOUR VAGINA.

**Wet dreams**

Most children have heard something about wet dreams, even if they are often a little confused of the details. Often they know it is something to do with waking up in a wet patch – but often the details are a bit skewed – and the body fluids involved vary in the telling. Indeed, during puberty lessons there is often a girl who gleefully tells the class all about it: 'Boys have dreams about girls they fancy and make a mess in the night as stuff squirts out their penis – and that's a wet dream!' Not strictly correct and trouble is, no one has told her that girls have wet dreams too… we seem to neglect to mention that fact.

Many adults I talk to are also surprised when I mention the fact girls have wet dreams too – not surprising really, when you realise a wet dream is simply your body practising your sexual responses – and we don't like talking about the female sexual responses, especially with young women.

You do not have to be having a 'sexy' dream, thinking about someone you fancy or even fantasising in any way – although sometimes these go hand in hand. Simply, two key things happen during a wet dream as your body goes through the motions of arousal. Blood is diverted to the genital region, engorging the erectile tissue in your genitals – be it the shaft of the penis or the vulva, in particular the clitoris and labia swell with blood. At the same time, fluid is released.

Obviously, this can be more noticeable for those with testes as they will be woken by the rhythmic contractions of the penis as they ejaculate semen into their pyjamas or whatever they sleep in. However, for vulva owners the same things occur. Some girls will experience contractions and will wake to find they feel particularly wet.

Be aware that for some young people, this can be quite a shocking experience, especially if no one has forewarned them of what to expect. Some children panic when they wake that they are bleeding or have wet the bed. There are so many messages to children that anything to do with their genitals is dirty. This can often lead to internalising feelings of shame as they try to clean themselves up secretly, thinking they have done something wrong. We can avoid all of this by simply explaining that this is perfectly normal and nothing to panic about. All they need to do is throw their PJs in the wash (or change the sheets), and not worry. It is just a sign they are growing up. Forewarned is forearmed.

Take the time to explain to your children, whether at home or in class, how their body gets ready for having sex and making babies.

Like any new skill, you need to practise. Your sexual responses (the things your body needs to do to get ready for having sex) are controlled by your subconscious brain – just like our heartbeat – we don't actually have to think about it – it just happens! So, your brain thinks a good time to practise is when you are fast asleep at night. Well, you wouldn't want it to happen in the middle of maths, would you?

So, your brain waits for you to fall asleep, and then sends blood to your genitals, making either your penis or vulva swell with blood. This makes everything feel much more sensitive as the nerves switch on. Next, your brain tells your glands to release more fluid and the muscles in your genitals may twitch. If you have a penis, you may ejaculate semen as the muscles spasm; whereas if you have a vulva, you may notice you feel damp between your legs as your vagina has produced more vaginal fluid. When you wake up, you may find a small wet patch on your pyjamas. This is nothing to worry about – it's just a sign you are growing up and nothing to feel embarrassed about. It happens to everyone.

But remember to tell the girls as well as the boys. Both have the right to understand what is happening to them, and not to feel ashamed because of it. At home, you may also want to start changing the sheets more often too.

**A visit from Aunty Flo**
One of the most significant events of puberty is periods. Half of the entire population of the earth have them and yet they are still surrounded in taboo. Even adverts that sell menstrual products to help manage the

situation use blue water as if we are talking about something that happens to Smurfs. Why, in this day and age, do we feel unable to talk about the very process that is instrumental in all of us being here?

Throughout history in various cultures (including our own) people have believed that periods are dirty and toxic. That a menstruating woman can cause crops to fail, can poison food or sour milk. We are still not rid of these myths, and periods are still used as a method to shame and disadvantage women. Whether it is the pressure to work or study through crippling pains or menstrual diarrhoea, or the fact that when it comes to taxation, until this year menstrual products were seen as luxury items. Unfortunately, for many young women growing up in poverty, menstrual products do become luxury items that they can ill afford. How, in one of the richest nations on earth have we got young girls missing school because they can't afford to manage their period each month?

There are some fantastic charities that have taken up the mantel, such as Bloody Good Period and Period Positive, who are tackling issues of taboo and poverty. We even now have a period emoji 🩸 ... look at us go.

Just as with wet dreams, the unknown can cause needless anxiety and shame. And guess what? Talking solves both. It is essential that everyone – not just those with ovaries – but girls and boys, mums and dads, learn about menstruation and the essentials of how it can be managed. So, let's start with the basics…

A period is part of the menstrual cycle which involves the development and release of an egg cell. The average cycle is taken as 28 days long, however they can be typically much longer or shorter and, unfortunately, some people suffer with irregular periods too.

The menstrual cycle is taken to start on day one of the period – the first day of bleeding. For most people they bleed for between three and seven days, some more heavily than others. In total, around 30–90ml of blood is released during a period although it can feel like much more (Gunter, 2019b). But the question remains, where does that blood come from?

The brain sends a signal to one of the ovaries to start maturing an egg cell. As a result, oestrogen is released which causes the lining of the womb to start building thick layers of blood and tissue, cell upon cell, like bricks (Gunter, 2019a). We call this the endometrium. When the egg is released (around day 14 – midway of a typical 28-day cycle), another hormone is released called progesterone, which acts like a mortar holding the lining in place and making it more hospitable for implantation of any zygote – fertilised egg cell (ibid.).

Each month, one of the ovaries will release an egg cell. They kind of take it in turn. It will slowly travel down the fallopian tubes, heading for the womb. If the egg isn't fertilised by a sperm cell deposited during sex, then it is simply flushed away by the body and discarded with the no longer needed lining of the womb. The sticky lining starts to break down and falls away… this is what we call a period or a menstrual bleed.

If you want to stop bleeding you put pressure on the wound; we all know that. However, how do you stop a period bleed? Again it is with pressure. This is what those menstrual cramps are as the muscles spasm to try and stem the flow of blood. Ridiculously, the amount of pressure recorded from menstrual cramps is the same as in the second stage of labour – the pushing stage! And yet we expect women to simply carry on with their day, to go to school and study? We tut and roll our eyes, wondering what all the fuss is about. However, we would never expect a women to carry on with her work during the second stage of labour!

Other than period pains, some people also suffer with menstrual diarrhoea, skin flare-ups of spots or acne, and some suffer with dramatic changes in moods caused by the fluctuating hormone levels that control the cycle. Some people get tearful, or simply feel down, whilst other people can suffer with actual depression. Unfortunately, some people really suffer awfully during their periods and have a really hard time of it. Others not so much. However, there are things that can help. If you suffer with severe period pains, heat pads or a good old-fashioned hot water bottle can really help; some people even use a TENS machine. There are also medications that are available – Naproxen, which is a non-steroid anti-inflammatory medication is often effective for those who need a little extra help to manage their painful cramps. It is available under numerous brand names and can be obtained both over the counter or on prescription. Another option is hormonal contraceptives. These are as often prescribed not only to prevent pregnancy but also to help manage painful, heavy or irregular periods.

**Menstrual products**
It is all well and good understanding what a period is and why they happen. Next thing we need to talk about is how to manage them. Luckily,

**Figure 3.1** Examples of menstrual products

these days there is much more choice than ever before, to suit not only your flow, and comfort but also your ethics and your pocket (Figure 3.1). It is estimated that the average British woman spends around £5,000 in her lifetime on menstrual products (Witton, 2019).

- **Disposable pads**: these absorbent pads are getting thinner and more and more discreet as absorbent technology improves. They are sticky on one side and attach to the gusset of your underwear. These come in lots of different absorbencies and shapes to fit various underwear.
- **Reusable pads**: a more environmentally friendly option. These cloth pads can be quite expensive upfront but are designed to be washed and reused. They often have little wings with press-studs to hold them in place. They come in many different colourful designs and patterns to suit your taste.
- **Tampons** come with or without an applicator for easy insertion. They are secured inside the vagina and expand as they soak up menstrual blood. They have a string running through their length to help remove them when they feel full. They are available in different sizes related to their absorbencies. Some people have concerns about using a tampon before they have lost their virginity – through fear of breaking

the hymen – but as we have discussed, this is not true. There is no reason why you can't use a tampon before you are sexually active.

- **Menstrual cup:** these are becoming more popular and are again designed to be a more environmentally friendly option as they are reused. These silicon cups are squeezed together and folded to form a 'c' shape before being inserted inside the vagina, where it will open and create a vacuum seal. The cup is then taken out and emptied. It is advised to have two, so one can be boil-washed whilst the other is in use.
- **Period pants** look like normal underwear, and come in different styles, including briefs, knickers, thongs and boxer-boy shorts. There is a built in absorbent lining in the gusset. They are designed to absorb your flow and then be washed. These are a great new comfortable addition for those who don't bleed too heavily, but they are expensive.

# Teachable moments

Next time you and your child are in the supermarket, take a detour and spend some time in the *feminine hygiene* section. Unfortunately, most supermarkets still use this awful term, which only perpetuates the notion of periods being dirty and unhygienic… but let's go with it for now. Spend some time looking at all the various products on display – these days, most big supermarkets will have a good variety of the products mentioned above. This is one of those ideal teachable moments where you can show that you aren't embarrassed and that it is a perfectly normal thing to discuss. Looking at the shelves should not be something that either of you ever feel embarrassed about. Periods shouldn't be a taboo in this day and age. This is a conversation that both girls and boys should have and it shouldn't just come from the mums either, Dads need to get involved too… because you can guarantee your daughter's first period will happen on his watch!

I was really lucky as I have a niece who is slightly older than my daughter. When Liv, my niece, was showing signs of starting puberty I was able to use her as an excuse to talk to my daughter Izzy about all the changes and to help prepare her for her future period.

As Liv spent quite a lot of time over at my house, I took my daughter to the supermarket and did exactly what I have suggested above. We looked at the shelves and Izzy helped me pick out the pads she thought Liv would like. *Lillette* do some nice looking pads especially for teens – they are packaged in a trendier way than the typical pads. I used this as an opportunity to talk about why Liv would need them and what might happen.

I explained to Izzy that some girls get embarrassed, and me being her uncle, Liv might not want to come and talk to me or ask for help if she got her period when she was at our house. Between us we came up with a plan of where to put them discreetly in the family bathroom. I showed her how to use them and we had a play with a few sticking them to spare knickers (and to the wall!) and pouring some of my coffee on them. Now she was in charge and had the information to help her cousin should things arise.

Obviously, I had ulterior motives in this little plan, I wasn't just thinking of my niece. It gave me the opportunity to talk to my daughter and prepare her ahead of time for her period, but without making it about her. This is a very simple distancing technique that just stops children from getting embarrassed as it wasn't about her (even though it kind of was!). She got to feel grown-up and empowered.

### Managing the school talk
Whilst you can be sure that your child's school will tackle puberty in class, don't rely on them to fill in all the blanks for your child. And as I mentioned way back at the beginning of this chapter, often these lessons come too late for some children.

I don't mean to be disparaging – I know plenty of schools that are brilliant but equally I am a realist too. Regardless, I don't believe that puberty should just be one lesson that we cover once and then never talk of again. No, it should be an ongoing conversation. The sooner you break the ice and start having those little conversations around buying deodorant or face wash, or having regular baths, you can start to drip-feed the information and show you are comfortable having these discussions.

Furthermore, if you and your child have already talked about puberty prior to any teaching that is done at school, it simply means they are in a position to get the most out of the session. Some children who are less prepared will naturally find the thought of discussing puberty embarrassing. Traditionally, it always has been and children internalise the messages of older peers and adults around them who still talk about the horror stories from their days. But it doesn't have to be that way.

When the school lessons come around, the night before or even better on the way to school, drop in to conversation, they will be learning about puberty in lessons. Explain that it should be fun, light-hearted and really interesting, and certainly nothing to worry about. Stress that it is all about growing up and that it happens to everyone. But most importantly, tell them that you would love to hear all about it when they get home. This two-minute conversation gives children the green light to listen in class and join in. It means they will ask the questions, and even better show off all the great things you have been discussing at home. But best of all, they are more likely to run out of the school gates at the end of the day and carry on the conversation.

Remember, don't just ask about what your child learnt at school. Ask about how the other children coped with the lesson, ask what made them giggle, talk about who felt embarrassed and why. These conversations are just as important as what new information they have.

# Teachers and youth workers – menstrual policy

I offer a lot of support to primary schools around delivering RSE. One thing I have noticed over the years: whilst the provision of support around puberty is improving, and the majority of schools do deliver fantastic sessions to their children, there is still a huge gap. I make a point of asking schools during training if they have a supply of menstrual products and spare underwear available in school, in case a child gets caught short on their watch. I am pleased to report, the majority of schools do have products on site. However, when I ask if they tell the children where they are kept, or if they take them out on school visits as part of their first aid kit, I am often met by blank faces.

It should not be a secret. And should be readily assessable for pupils in years 4 onwards. Puberty lessons in school should be an opportunity to help children manage situations when they are caught unawares by their period, without the need for them to be found crying in the toilets.

'Policy on menstruation' is an extract from my RSE policy template I devised for the school I support. As part of the policy, I added a good practice guide for managing menstruation in school – but it is also appropriate for other settings, such as youth clubs, too. It may have some points worth considering if you are a teacher or youth leader.

## Policy on menstruation

This does not need to be included – but it is an element that few schools have a policy for. This is good practice – (amend accordingly).

1.  We recognise that the onset of menstruation can be a confusing or distressing time for children if they are not prepared. As a school we acknowledge we have a responsibility to prepare children for menstruation and make adequate and sensitive arrangements to help children manage their period. Especially children whose family may not be able to afford or will not provide sanitary products.
2.  We recognise that period poverty exists in the UK and that some children are forced to avoid attending school if they are on their period, when they are unable to manage it sensitively. We do not want that to be the case in our school and will make every reasonable effort to support children to access their education and enjoy school.
3.  Puberty is occurring earlier than ever before, and it is now not uncommon for children to start their periods whilst in primary school even in year 4. For this reason we deliver puberty lessons to all children in year 3, 4 , 5 and 6.
4.  As part of these lessons all children will be told about menstruation and there will be discussion of what periods are, explanation of other symptoms associated with periods, how they can be managed hygienically and sensitively.
5.  Menstruation in a healthy biological function for 50% of our school. It should not be something that a person is made to feel embarrassed, shameful or be teased about. As a school we need to treat each other with respect and empathy and this includes changes that take place during puberty such as menstruation.
6.  During lessons where puberty and menstruation are discussed, we will take the opportunity to highlight the location of sanitary bins available in school, and how these are to be used.
7.  In school we have a menstruation kit available in year 4, 5 and 6 which contains sanitary products, spare underwear and plastic bags to wrap up underwear should there have been any accidents. Children will be made aware of where these are kept and how they can be accessed through designated members of staff, including lunchtime supervisors.
8.  When school trips or residential visits are arranged for years 4, 5 and 6 provisions to deal with a child's period needs to be considered and added to the risk assessment and planned for.

# Notes

1  Sex Education Forum (2008a) Key findings; Young people's survey on sex and relationships education. NCB; Sex Education Forum (2015) SRE – the evidence. NCB; THT (2016), Shh… No Talking: LGBT-inclusive Sex and Relationships Education in the UK www.tht.org.uk/endthesilence; OFSTED (2013) Not Yet Good Enough: PSHE Education in Schools; IPPF (2016), 'Putting sexuality back into comprehensive sexuality education: Making the case for rights-based, sex-positive approach'; Barnardo's (2018), Involve us, tespect us: Engaging young people in telationships and dex rducation; UNESCO. (2018), International Technical Guidance on Sexuality Education: An Evidenced -Informed approach.
2  Trans or transgender: a trans person is someone who feels that the sex or gender they were assigned at birth does not match or sit easily with their sense of self (their gender identity).
   Non-binary: being non-binary means not feeling that your gender identity fits naturally into the generic categories of male and female.

# References

Bennet, C. (2017). *Parental approaches to teaching children about puberty, relationships and reproduction in the Netherlands.* Available at: www.wcmt.org.uk/sites/default/files/report-documents/Bennett%20C%20Report%202017%20Final.pdf.

Giordano, S. and Holm, S. (2020). Is puberty delaying treatment 'experimental treatment'? *International Journal of Transgender Health*, 21(2): 113–21.

Gunter, J. (2019a). *The Vagina Bible: The vulva and the vagina – separating the myth from the medicine*, Piatkus, Little, Brown, London.

Gunter, J. (2019b). Why can't we talk about periods, TEDWomen. Available at: www.ted.com/talks/jen_gunter_why_can_t_we_talk_about_periods/transcript#t-142443.

Hembree, W.C. (2011). Guidelines for pubertal suspension and gender reassignment for transgender adolescents. *Child and Adolescent Psychiatric Clinics of North America*, 20(4), 725–32.

Kreukels, B.P. and Cohen-Kettenis, P.T. (2011). Puberty suppression in gender identity disorder: The Amsterdam experience, *Nature Reviews Endocrinology*, 7(8), 466–72.

Lister, K. (2020) *A Curious History of Sex*, Unbound, London.

Murad, M.H., Elamin, M.B., Garcia, M.Z., Mullan, R.J., Murad, A., Erwin, P.J. and Montori, V.M. (2010). Hormonal therapy and sex reassignment: A systematic review and meta-analysis of quality of life and psychosocial outcomes, *Clinical Endocrinology*, 72(2), 214–31.

Royal College of Psychiatrists. (1998). Gender identity disorders in children and adolescents, guidance for management, Council Report CR63, January.

Available at: www.spitjudms.ro/_files/pro-tocoale_terapeutice/psihiatrie/tulburari%20de%20identitate%20sex-uala%20la%20copil%20si%20adolescent.pdf.

Sex Education Forum (SEF) (2016). Heads or tails: What young people are telling us about RSE. National Children's Bureau.

Witton, H. (2019) *The Hormone Diaries: The bloody truth about our periods*. Wren and Rook, London.

# CHAPTER 4

# WHERE DO BABIES COME FROM?

**W**henever I work with primary schools I always encourage them to deliver a 'where do babies come from?' lesson as early as possible. I recommend year one when children are 5ish. Why so early? Well, the simple fact is, at that age you tend to spend a lot of time around pregnant people. Think about it: families tend to space their children a couple of years apart, so it is typical for children in infant school to be expecting a new baby brother or sister or cousin. At that age they have lots of questions. We can either take the initiative and use this as a teaching moment or take what feels like the easy option (it isn't) and let the opportunity pass us by.

Children become curious about sex well before they have any understanding of what it is. Children at this early age are interested in what is going on in that big pregnant belly – they want to poke it and feel it move. Often, children have questions but don't always feel able to ask them depending on how we – the adults – respond to their enquiries. Despite the fact that children will have little understanding that babies and sex are connected, they will undoubtably have heard the word banded about, in hushed voices by grown-ups, on TV shows they shouldn't be watching and to fits of giggles by older children. If, when questions are asked, the adults in the room go red, look flustered or get angry, children learn this is not something they can ask about.

DOI: 10.4324/9781003122296-10

Indeed, I can guarantee you remember when you were little and curiosity got the better of you, so you picked up the junior dictionary off the shelf when no one else was around. And daringly turned to 'S… E… X' to find out what it meant and giggled with your friends. Today's children are no different – except dictionaries are a thing of the past. Why would you ever need one when you can google it? Unfortunately, the answers that are likely to pop up (even on a safe search) are far more detailed than the couple of sentences you remember from your junior dictionary…

The truth is, children are far better off getting honest open answers from safe adults in their lives, rather than it being left to the internet or older children with a smartphone.

Tackling the topic in a matter-of-fact manner early, without embarrassment, means that we take the mystic allure out of the topic, making sex no longer the secret taboo you have to sneak around trying to find out about and instead something we can talk about at the dinner table. However uncomfortable a proposition that may be, it is far better than the alternative. For children, these questions are not rude; they are simply natural curiosity. The topic only needs to feel embarrassing for your child if *you* make it embarrassing by ignoring it.

Smaller children are more likely to have many questions that will pop out at any time. They tend to ask whatever is on their mind. However, at this early age children tend to be more interested in asking lots rather than listening to anything too detailed you might actually say in response! Often children are simply testing the waters to see if you will answer and if it is OK to ask.

My view is the best thing to do is to keep things short and simple, rather than going into long-winded explanations where children can become lost and confused. Remember, children's questions about babies are not sexual to them… at this age they will have no real understanding, expectations or notion of what sex is. It is innocent curiosity about where babies come from… nothing more. As adults, we have already opened Pandora's Box and know all of the secrets inside! Often we panic and assume the worst because we are coming from a very different perspective with all our own knowledge and baggage.

Whilst some parents prefer to defer the truth until later and will instead tell stories about storks, cabbage patches or ordering their child off eBay, I am a firm believer the truth is always better – however scary that may be. By drip-feeding the answers slowly, taking the opportunity to seize teachable moments, it creates a safe environment where children will keep coming back to you for an answer and with any worries they may have.

A great place to start is with family photos. Looking through old photographs is an ideal opportunity to talk about when they were a baby, to show how much they have grown, and to look at pictures before they were born during pregnancy of them inside mum's tum. Obviously, I am aware that some families will not have these photos for various reasons, and some children do not live with their birth parents. Even so, old photos of any family members – especially those during pregnancy or when people were babies, or of life before they were born, is a great place to start. Most children are fascinated by looking at how things used to be, and seeing themselves when they were little. Often, questions will come naturally – or can be coerced out of the situation.

If you prefer, there are lots of books you can use and read together about conception, birth and where babies come from – these days there are inclusive books that are aimed at same-sex families, or children that have been adopted. Regardless of what your family looks like or how it came to being, all children deserve to see families like theirs represented. And things are getting much better on this front.

Essentially, especially with small children, we are trying to create opportunities to stimulate a natural conversation that touches on babies, pregnancy and reproduction. These do not have to be big conversations; all we are trying to do is leave the door open – giving children the green light that this is something we can talk about without embarrassment, whenever they want. Embarrassment is learned not innate. However, if we can show a child that this is something it is ok to talk about without making them feel uncomfortable or feeling like they have spoken out of turn, we can create a situation where children feel safe to keep asking questions and coming to us for answers.

This is not only better for children, but like anything we put off as adults, waiting for the perfect moment – the longer you wait, the more moments slip by and the pressure continues to mount. It becomes a big deal for everyone involved, rather than a natural topic of conversation.

I have pulled together some common questions and answer suggestions – these are all examples from my experience of delivering lessons in a classroom full of children. They are based on what I have found to be useful when answering questions and trying to explain the ins-and-outs (no pun intended) of pregnancy and where babies come from.

Remember, with small children they are more interested in all the amazing things they can see and feel when it comes to pregnancy and babies. They have no concept of what sex is or looks like, so don't think for a second they will be looking for explanations about why your contraception failed or that you may have been a little bit drunk at the time… there are honest answers and too much information.

# Where do babies live before they are born – where do they come from?

*Before a baby is born it lives in a stretchy sack inside a mummy's tummy. This sack is called a womb. It is inside a woman's tummy just below her belly button. When she is pregnant the womb fills up with warm fluid to keep the growing baby nice and safe.*

# How do babies feed in mummy's tummy?

*Do you know why you have a belly button?* (Ask them to pull up their t-shirt and look at their belly button.) *That is how you were fed when you were in your mummy's tummy. You see a baby doesn't eat like we do… instead there is a special tube called the Umbilical cord, that attaches the baby to the walls of the mother's womb – and through this the baby gets all it needs to grow directly through the mother's body. When you are born, it is cut and you are left with a belly button.*

Yes, I would happily use the correct terms with small children such as *Umbilical cord.* Yes, it is a big word for a five year old to manage, but I would practise saying it with them – be silly and laugh about how it sounds as a word. Keep saying it in funny voices, make each other laugh – it is playful, and makes it far more fun an experience for both of you.

# How do you make a baby? How did it get into mummy's womb?

*Did you know it takes about 40 weeks – that's 9 months for a baby to grow. But you can't make a baby out of nothing – you need to start with something. Inside daddy's body he makes special cell called sperm cells. And inside mummy's body she makes special cells called egg cells. They each have half of the instructions for making a baby. You need a sperm cell from Daddy and an egg cell from mummy. When the sperm and egg cells meet, they join together to make something new.*

*Sometimes, nothing happens…*

*But sometimes, it starts to grow – just like you did – into a baby.*

*Thanks to all the food from the mother's body it slowly gets bigger and bigger and BIGGER AND BIGGER… it grows arms and legs and fingers and toes and a nose and eyes and starts to kick its feet and wriggle around (Figure 4.1).*

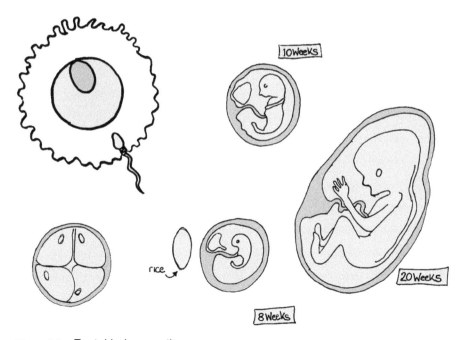

**Figure 4.1** Foetal baby growth

*You will be able to feel it if you put your hand on mummy's tummy and it will be able to hear you if you talk to it.*

# How do you make a baby for older children or children who have more questions or need more details

*You know that men and women's bodies are different because their private parts are different. Men have a penis and women have a vulva. But did you know that inside their bodies they also have one of the two special parts that make a baby – one each.*

*This is an egg. These grow here in the ovaries, just above the womb inside a woman's body (Figure 4.2). They have half of all the instructions for making a baby.*

*And this is a sperm. These grow here in a man's testicles – the dangly sack that hangs behind the penis. And just like the eggs, these have the other half of the instructions for making a baby (Figure 4.3).*

*You need a sperm cell from daddy and an egg cell from mummy in order to make a baby. The issue is, how do we get these two pieces together?*

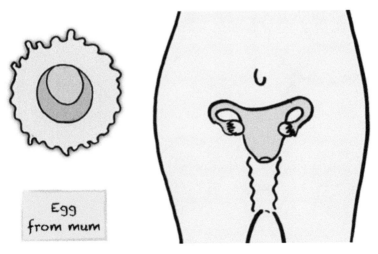

**Figure 4.2** Diagram of female reproductive organs (child-friendly)

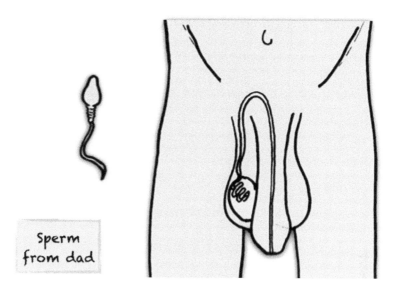

Sperm
from dad

**Figure 4.3** Diagram of male reproductive organs (child-friendly)

When grown-ups want to make a baby, they need to get a sperm from one body to an egg from another person's body.

*The best way for doing this is having sex, but a baby isn't made every time two adults have sex. A lot of it comes down to luck.*

*Sex is something that grown-ups do because it can feel nice\* and it is the closest two people can get to each other when they really like/love/fancy/care for each other* (pick your favourite).

*They might kiss and get undressed and stroke each other all over.*

*Grown-ups can fit together like two pieces of a jigsaw puzzle. The man's penis can fit inside the woman's vagina. If they are going to make a baby – this is when the sperm from the man's testicles swim through his penis and inside the woman's body. They will swim from her vagina up into her womb.*

*The tiny little sperm have a long way to go… they keep swimming and swimming and hopefully some of them will find the egg hiding high up in the tube joining the ovaries to the womb.*

*When the sperm and egg cells meet they join together to make something new… Sometimes, nothing happens…*

*But sometimes, it starts to grow – just like you did – into a baby.*

* This is what I was talking about earlier on the trouble with *nice*. This is the best way I have found for explaining what sex is in a simple way that makes sense – but also at the same time relays a number of key messages. I promise, saying this now will make answering questions easier later. Let me explain…

We start off by saying, 'Sex is something that grown-ups do…' This firmly puts the notion of sex in the future as an adult behaviour. Trust me, most children that hear any description of what sex is at this age think it sounds gross in a, '*Urgh! why would you even kiss a boy!*' sort of way.

I am well aware the mention that sex should feel *nice* is a notion that many adults are uncomfortable about telling children. The fear being it might foster the idea that sex is something they should try and make them want to have sex. To be very clear, there is absolutely no evidence that this is the case. In fact, the opposite is true. We know that clear, honest information early encourages children to keep talking to safe adults and actually delays sex (Bennet, 2017; UNESCO, 2018). However, I would argue that this is something we need to get over and I would suggest it is an essential piece of information to tell children. Do we not want them to think that sex is something intimate, caring and positive. A pleasure rather than a duty. Something to be enjoyed rather than endured. This is especially important as one of the most common questions I am asked by older primary school children is *does sex hurt – is that why people make noises because it's painful?* This makes perfect sense, if their only examples have been from glimpses in films and TV soaps – you can understand why they may come to this conclusion, especially when no one will talk openly about sex – we all tend to fear the worse.

Instead, by dropping the little word 'nice' into the explanation, we are setting up a light bulb moment for much later. It helps to promote an early concept that sex is something that is natural, normal and nice rather than something to feel guilty, ashamed or embarrassed about. We want young people to grow up with a positive attitude to sex and to feel able to talk to the safe adults around them when they have questions or worries – it is secrets that are dangerous, not the things we can talk about.

Equally, if children get the idea in their head that sex should feel good, then when they are having their first sexual relationship further down the line in years to come – and things don't feel quite right – rather than being left with the secret thought of *'this is it'* and accepting this is how it is supposed to be… BING! Our little light bulb can go off and spark the thought, it shouldn't be like this… If no one has ever told you that sex is something that should be enjoyed, how are you supposed to know?

I know it may feel uncomfortable, but the alternative is worse.

This explanation is also helpful when children ask about how two men or two women might have sex.

# How do two men/two women have sex?

The benefit of the explanation of sex as:

> *something that grown-ups do, because it can feel nice\* and it is the closest two people can get to each other when they really like/love/ fancy/care for each other* (pick your favourite). *They might kiss and get undressed and stroke each other all over.*

is that it makes answering the question around gay sex so much easier than if we have gone for the standard answer of: *sex is when a man puts his penis in a woman's vagina.* If that was our only explanation, we would now have to unpick what we had previously said, and then explain where everything may go. Which is kind of nonsense really anyway – there is no such thing as 'gay sex', but we will talk about that in more detail in Chapter 6.

Instead, we can simply say – *well it's exactly the same… Sex is the closest two people can get who really care for each other, They might kiss and get undressed and stroke each other all over, because it feels nice.* For most children that is enough for now.

# Simple explanations for other ways families have babies

*Not all couples can have babies by themselves. Sometimes things might go wrong or things might not work properly. This is why doctors might help or a couple might decide to adopt or foster a child and give them a loving and safe home if their birth parents are unable to care for them.*

*Some couples might need some extra help. Sometimes doctors can take the sperm from a daddy and put them together with the eggs from the mummy in a science lab. Once they have joined together they will then put them inside the mummy's womb to grow.*

*This can also be done if two men or two women who love each other want to have a baby too. Because remember, families come in all different shapes and sizes... and some have two daddies or two mummies.*

# How do babies get out of mummy's tummy?

*Some babies let their mother know they are ready and others may have to be helped out by a doctor. Sometimes it takes a long, long time and sometimes it is quite quick.*

*Most often babies are born by the mother pushing them out through the opening we call her vagina. The stretchy tunnel that leads from her womb to the outside – it is the opening hidden by her vulva that we have talked about. Sometimes this can hurt a lot as she will have to push and squeeze and her muscles will have to stretch.*

*Sometimes doctors will make a special opening just below the tummy and take the baby out this way and then close up the opening again. We call this a caesarean – and you might have seen a line like a smiley face on mummy's tummy where it has healed.*

## Birthing a ping-pong ball

If I am in class, this is where I would do my balloon and ping-pong ball demonstration. It is not what it sounds like – but actually it is exactly what it sounds like. This is the best way I have found to explain childbirth to children, and it doesn't leave them traumatised like the old birthing video that was standard issue where I grew up. I stole this from a midwife some years back...

Simply, you take a balloon, stretch the neck apart with your fingers and then drop a ping-pong ball inside. Blow the balloon up so it is the size of a pineapple – not too big, otherwise it will pop. Turn the balloon upside down (so the neck is point downwards), gravity will mean the ball falls to the neck and traps the air inside, so you don't need to tie the balloon. You now have a womb, similar shape, with a ping-pong baby inside.

I explain that when mum goes into labour the muscles in her womb contract and squeeze the womb. Slowly squeeze the balloon, moving your hands to the top. Now you can rhythmically contract the balloon womb. Don't worry, you can squeeze quite hard (just be careful if you have sharp nails!), and slowly you will force the ping-pong ball down the neck of the balloon.

As you squeeze, the children are all on tenterhooks waiting for the balloon to explode! As you keep rhythmically squeezing, talk about the contractions, and why it takes so much time and how much work it is giving birth – that is why we call it labour.

The ball will eventually crown. At this point I ask the children if they think it will be a boy or a girl. I often write boy/girl on my ping-pong balls too – just for fun. Eventually, after much effort the ball will pop out (bounce off a table and then roll across the floor) – just like a normal birth. Just make sure you point the womb downwards – not at anyone's face – you know the usual health and safety stuff, always point the womb away and never go back once it's lit.

Clearly, it is not exactly like childbirth – but it is a really fun demonstration to do with a bunch of eight year olds.

# What is sex? (An answer for older children)

When talking to older children I might include more than just the mechanics of sex and reproduction. Instead, I think it is important to explore our attitudes to sex as well. It is helpful to prepare children for the fact that some people have very strong and varied views about what sex is and should mean. I think this is useful, especially for those about to go off to high school, where they will meet new friends, more diverse families and be exposed to much older teens with smart phones... it is much better they are prepared rather than being left to work it out by themselves.

*Sex can mean different things to different people. For some people they have very strong beliefs and values about sex. Some people think it is something that is rude to talk about. Other people find it funny. This is one of the reasons that many grown-ups find it difficult or embarrassing to talk about.*

*No one has the right to tell you how you should feel or believe and that includes your attitudes to sex. But sex should never be something you should be encouraged to feel guilty or ashamed about either. Sex is the reason we are all here, after all.*

*Sex is something that adults do. And it is something that is private as it involves our private parts.*

*A man and a woman may choose to have sex to make a baby; for this to work they will need to have what we call penetrative sex – when the penis fits inside the vagina. But this isn't the only reason that people may choose to have sex. And there is more to sex than merely putting a penis in a vagina.*

*In fact, two men or two women who are attracted to each other can have sex too…*

*Sex can involve lots of kissing, cuddling and touching each other all over, including touching each other's genitals. Some people may have sex to feel close to their partner or because it can feel good.*

*However, some people have sex for different reasons too that aren't so good… some people have sex to act grown up, to try and be cool (doing things to impress other people is never cool!) or because their partners pressure or bully them too. This is never ok.*

*Having sex is something you should choose to do – because you want to.*

None of these answers are set in stone – they are merely things I have found useful. You will have your own ways of explaining things, and your own stories to tell that are relevant to your family and your child. If you are stuck with a question that your child asks, I always think asking the same question back to them is a really good place to start. Reply, 'Oh, that's a great question, what do you think…?' This not only buys you some time to get the old cogs clicking – but also is an instant needs assessment for you. They will tell you what they have heard or understand, and you can either confirm what they think and say – 'Oh, that's right – I am so impressed' or 'So pleased you know that.' Or instead, you can correct what they have wrong, and then fill in the missing piece of the puzzle for them.

This is a really good way of making sure you are answering the question they asked to level that they understand. Plus, you may be surprised how much your child may have picked up by osmosis…

# References

Bennet, C. (2017). Parental approaches to teaching children about puberty, relationships and reproduction in the Netherlands. Available at: www.wcmt. org.uk/sites/default/files/report-documents/Bennett%20C%20Report%20 2017%20Final.pdf.

UNESCO. (2018). International technical guidance on sexuality education: An evidenced-informed approach.

# CHAPTER 5

# GET YOUR HANDS OUT OF YOUR PANTS, IT'S DIRTY...

There is one part of delivering parent meetings at primary schools that always makes me smile. And it happens every time. I deliver my presentation, usually explaining what RSE looks like at primary school, talking through what is covered and why – doing my best to cover the usual concerns as I go and to put everyone's mind at ease. As I am drawing the session to a close, I always ask, 'Does anyone have any questions?' Occasionally, there are the odd admin queries about when the school will be delivering the particular programme, or whatever – which are aimed more at the school than me... but generally, no one raises their hand – everyone just looks at each other and says nothing. I then thank everyone for coming and say I will hang around for a little while if anyone wants to come and have a chat before saying goodnight. And, without fail, half the parents form an orderly queue to ask questions.

Nine times out of ten, there is always at least one of those parents who comes to talk to me about the same issue every time. One occasion that stands out particularly was a dad who drifted around the school

DOI: 10.4324/9781003122296-11

hall, waiting for all the other mums to ask their questions, trying and failing to look inconspicuous. Once the last parent had finished and was making her way out of the hall he sidled over to me. He was a tiny Indian gentleman – now, I am only five foot six, and firmly classify myself as a Hobbit, so when I say tiny I do not mean to be disparaging, it is just my memory of him – he was so small and softly spoken and smiley. I warmed to him straight away.

He very quietly apologised for keeping me, before telling me about his six-year-old little boy. He explained that his son was a happy child, and at night they read stories together before he leaves his son to go to sleep. Dad had noticed that his son would always turn over to sleep on his front. However, more recently he had noticed that his son would often rub himself against the bed. At first, the dad had tried to ignore the behaviour, putting it down to his own imagination. However, eventually, dad – feeling concerned – had decided to bravely ask his son as they sat down to read their usual bedtime stories what was going on and why.

His son explained that he rubbed his privates against the sheets because it felt nice. And made him feel tingly and ready for sleep. He then asked his dad if this was OK.

At this point, I asked dad how he had responded.

He admitted that he hadn't the heart to tell him no, that it was wrong. He explained to me that when he was growing up he, was told this sort of behaviour was wrong and shameful. However, after speaking with his son and hearing his explanation, he couldn't see the harm… it seemed completely innocent the way his son had described it.

He then asked me if he had done the right thing. He was looking for reassurance that his son's behaviours were normal for a little boy.

It is understandable that as adults we are at a loss how to react when we catch our child fiddling with their genitals, especially when our child tells us that they enjoy touching their own body and that it feels nice. We are not very comfortable with enjoying the bodies we have been given in general. Most of us have grown up with notions of shame about our bodies and anything sexual in particular. This dad is certainly not the only parent to have sought reassurance that these behaviours are perfectly typical.

Indeed, I have the same conversation with countless parents, who confess their child's behaviours in hushed tones. We all like our privacy, but there are so many parents that all have the same worries and concerns. I am sure if we were able to share them, we would all feel much better and realise that the thing we are all so worried about is actually quite normal.

The same is true when I work with teachers. Again and again, teachers will say: 'I have a little boy in my class that sits with his hands down his pants or little girl who rubs against the chair…' It seems to be just as common amongst girls and boys – but the question is always: *'What do I do?'* How do we manage the situation, especially when the other children have started to notice too.

The traditional response to children who display these sorts of behaviours at school or home has always been: 'Get your hands out of your pants – it's dirty! Now, wash your hands!' Or perhaps, to make joking threats like 'It will drop off…' or 'It will make you go blind'. Whilst this may immediately stop the behaviour, it doesn't help us understand the problem or get to the root of the problem. The only thing shaming accomplishes is to create problems that need to be unpicked later and push children further away from coming to us with their worries.

If we return to the question I raised at the start of this book, what are we hoping for our children when it comes to sex and their future relationships? And what are we doing to get there? Think about it… if we make our children feel ashamed for enjoying how their body feels, and tell them it is wrong or naughty to make themselves feel nice, what message are we giving them for the future? Instead, it would be a much more positive move to talk about when and where it is appropriate, rather than if it is appropriate.

# Typical healthy sexual development

Often, as adults we assign adult feelings to children's behaviours. I understand how uncomfortable talking about children having a sexual development from birth can be. We do not like to put the words 'sex' and 'children' together for obvious reasons. However, there is a big difference between recognising that just as children go through a constant cognitive, emotional and physical development, so too they go through a sexual development.

Just as we can track a child's ages and stages of development in other capacities, we can also highlight milestones in children's healthy sexual development too. In Figure 5.1, you can see typical behaviours broken down to general age bracket as a guide. Just like milestones in physical or cognitive development, these are not set in stone and all children develop at their own rate. They are merely broad brushstrokes to give you an idea of a typical healthy sexual development.

## Understanding and managing self-soothing and self-stimulating behaviours

There are a number of reasons why a child may be having a fiddle, squeezing their legs together or rubbing against the furniture. Self-soothing or self-stimulation is perfectly common amongst small children and is a typical part of healthy sexual development. However, this is not to be confused with masturbation in the proper sense of the term. It is not until children reach puberty, when their hormones kick in and they become more consciously aware of their genitals, that children may start to masturbate in earnest.

Self-stimulation, self-soothing and masturbation are all different behaviours with a variety of different motivations behind their presentation. Many children, even in early infancy, will touch themselves because it feels *nice* – they may fall asleep with their hands in their pyjamas, as a comfort, like the boy in the example above; self soothe when anxious or enjoy touching themselves experimentally in the bath. Children at this age will say that it feels nice but there is rarely any conscious sexual undertone to this behaviour.

If a child is anxious and is touching themselves to self-soothe as a coping mechanism – similar to biting their nails or biting the skin around their fingers – shaming them is not going to make their anxiety better. Instead, it is better to concentrate on what is causing the anxiety, rather than the behaviour itself. Once you have discovered the source of the worry, we can then try to put in alternative means of managing the feelings, helping the child to build emotional resilience.

Whilst it can be embarrassing that your little girl squeezes her legs together and holds her breath and pants, when she does it on the bus, instead of

## Healthy sexual development and behaviours of children aged 0–4 years

Even at this stage, sexual behaviour is beginning to emerge through actions like:

- exploratory behaviours, touch, taste, looking, lots of hugs and kisses
- showing interest in body parts and how they work
- talking about private body parts and using words like poo, willy and bum
- playing games such as 'house/mummiesanddaddies' or "doctorsandnurses" withother children
- curiosity about the difference between girls and boys
- enjoying nakedness
- touching, rubbing or showing off their genitals
- Touching of genitals can give a pleasant sensation – including physical sexual responses.
- often, little girls are socialised out of this behaviour early, while there is more tolerance shown to boys
- self stimulation among children from around 3 months is common, involving friction, rhythmic rocking, pressing thighs together or rubbing genitals against objects. This can be self soothing and may be accompanied by facial flushing, grunting or moaning.

## Healthy sexual development and behaviours of children aged 5–9 years

As children get a little older they become more aware of the need for privacy while also:

- more exploratory behaviours with peers kissing and hugging
- curiosity about other children's genitals
- curiosity about sex, relationships, differences between boys and girls, where babies come from, how sex happens and same-sex relationships.
- showing curiosity about private body parts but respecting privacy, no longer wanting to bath with younger siblings.
- talking about private body parts and sometimes showing them off
- more questions and comparing of bodies to try to answer questions
- using swear and sex words they've heard other people say (even if children do not understand the meaning of the words they know it provokes a reaction from adults). Trying to shock by using words like poo, willy and bum
- playing 'house' or 'doctors and nurses' type games with other children
- touching, rubbing or showing others their private parts.

Figure 5.1    Healthy sexual development 0–17

## Healthy sexual development and behaviours of children aged 9–13 years

Children are getting more curious about sex and sexual behaviour through:

- kissing, hugging, holding hands and 'dating' other children
- changes that happen in puberty, hormones – become *conscious* of their sexual responses – and may experience *'feeling turned-on'*
- cognitively more able to understand and process information
- curiosity and asking about relationships and sexual behaviours
- actively looking for information about sex, this might lead to finding online porn. Interest in popular culture: fashion, music, online games and social media
- masturbating in private
- need for privacy
- relationship behaviours beginning talking of *boyfriends* and *girlfriends* but this may be name only.
- aware of their development and sense of themselves: are they attractive, do they have the right look?

## Healthy sexual development and behaviours of children aged 13–17 years

Children are getting more curious about sex and sexual behaviour through:

- as puberty kicks in, sexual behaviour becomes more private
- kissing, hugging, dating and forming longer-lasting relationships
- using sexual language and talking about sex with friends explicitly.
- looking for sexual pictures or online porn/ erotica
- masturbating in private and experimenting sexually with the same age group.
- now have knowledge and bodily desires – beginnings of adult bodies.
- consenting manual, oral, or penetrative sex, (including sexting) with others of similar age/maturity (alternatively choosing not to become sexually active)
- advanced relationship behaviours forming deep attachments
- emotional and romantic connections becoming important intensified by sexual desire and pleasure.

**Figure 5.1** Cont.

panicking about the stray eyes of judgemental strangers and chastising her in front of everyone, distraction can be a better tool.

Importantly, it is worth noting that abusers will often use shame as a means to control their victims. They will tell the child that they are dirty and no one will like them or believe them if they tell anyone what has been going on. As a safe adult we may well be merely attempting to manage an inappropriate behaviour but unbeknownst to us, we may well be reinforcing the words of the abuser and pushing the child further away from disclosing.

The important conversation to have with children is one about public and private behaviours. This is the same point I made to the dad in my story. Whilst it may feel nice, tingly or help make you feel calm when you have big feelings, there is a time and a place for these behaviours. Acknowledge that it can feel nice, just like picking your nose, and getting that crusty bit right from the back… but generally it is not considered polite to do it in public.

# Could it be something else?

In infant school especially, there are lots of reasons why children may be fiddling because they feel sore or uncomfortable. Not all children wipe or can keep themselves clean properly. Some children may have itched or have sensitive skin. Other's families may not have the means to wash or change clothes regularly enough. It is essential that we make space for children to come to us and ask for help.

Consider a child who has been playing with their friends or has been engaged in their lesson but needs the loo. In their haste to get back to the classroom and whatever they were doing, they didn't wipe properly. Inevitably, they are now sat in damp underwear – they haven't wet themselves, it is just a dribble – but nevertheless, it can be uncomfortable to sit during carpet time and listen to a story when your pants are wet. So they fidget, pull their pants away from their skin, trying to ease the discomfort. If, as the safe adult in the room, you tell them off and call them out in front of their classmates for being 'dirty' they are hardly going to come to you afterwards and say, 'Miss, I feel sore – can you help me?'

Equally, what if they have thrush? Or if someone has hurt them… shaming them will not encourage them to tell us what is wrong, nor is it fair.

A much better method of managing the situation is distraction; especially distraction that involves children moving around or using their hands. Ask them to stand up and fetch something, to give the books out or collect something from the office. Then, in a quiet moment, simply ask the child: 'Are you ok? You didn't look very comfortable before… is there anything I can do?' We need to give children permission and opportunity to ask safe adults for help.

Instead, when I work with teachers I advise them when they tackle this as a topic in class it is much better to focus on the private behaviours in private places message – *Now lots of people like to tickle or stroke themselves as it might feel nice. They might play with their hair, stroke their skin or they may even touch their private parts. This is really very normal; however, it is not polite to do it when other people are about. It is something we should only do when we are alone, perhaps in the bath or shower or in bed, a bit like picking your nose. It is certainly not polite to do in class when everyone is watching.*

This is not a script designed to encourage masturbation (that is not the right word) or even raise the topic with small children. It is a 30-second script designed to help teachers manage inappropriate touching in their classroom environment – in a way that doesn't shame children.

I have been asked a number of times why I would encourage teachers to bring this up in front of the whole class – surely it would be better to just talk to the children 'with issues' and not 'expose' other children to this behaviour. From my own experience, and the majority of people who have had the experience of working in a classroom will attest, this is a regular occurrence in an infant school classroom, and therefore an important topic to address in the classroom in a safe way.

Other children will often notice if a classmate is rubbing or making noises and can become upset or draw attention to the event, making the situation worse. They need an explanation that will make sense but will not shame the child in question. In addition, at school children will get changed for PE, perhaps go swimming and have to get undressed, will go to the toilet and will need to understand the difference between public and private spaces and behaviours. As part of teaching safe and appropriate touching, it makes sense that we should also talk to children about when and how it is appropriate to touch themselves.

Again, to be very clear: we are not teaching small children about masturbation. Masturbation is a sexual behaviour driven by sexual needs and generally starts at puberty. In the earlier years, we are talking about self-stimulation, self-soothing and exploration – these are rarely sexually driven behaviours. They are coping strategies or repetitive behaviours – like biting your nails or eating your hair – not sexually motivated.

I always recommend adults try to keep track of when these behaviour manifest themselves most commonly. Is it before a certain activity? At a certain time of day? Is it when they are in a particular mood? Often we only look for patterns when the behaviours are happening, but it is just as valuable to take note of what has changed or what is in place when the behaviours are absent too. There may be a particular protective factor that mitigates the behaviour. If you can find a pattern it may help to understand what is motivating the behaviour, and discerning the difference between stimulation or soothing or simply being uncomfortable.

As I advised the dad I spoke to in my story, agree at home where the private spaces are. In most houses usually these are the bathroom and bedroom. However, if your child shares the bath with a sibling, this is no longer a private space. Equally, if your child shares a room or they have a sleepover with a friend, their bedroom is no longer private either. Establish rules around shutting doors and knocking to preserve privacy and make sure everyone in the house respects each other's right to privacy. This can also help to set a precedent to save your own blushes too. Walking in on your parents having sex (or masturbating) is not a comfortable experience for anyone.

**Remember...**

There are no private spaces in school. Even the toilets and changing rooms at school are shared spaces, and therefore not private. This is equally true at the swimming pool or the public toilets in the shopping centre too.

The sooner you start to discuss notions of privacy at home, the better. You will notice as children get older, they will ask for more privacy when getting changed, going to the toilet or having a bath or shower. Children will often say they don't want to share a bath with a younger sibling or don't want you to come in when they are in the shower. Equally, as a parent, you too may want to reinstate your independence and reclaim the luxury of having a pee or a poo in private. There is a fine line between promoting a positive attitude to nudity and bodies, but also respecting everyone's right to privacy.

# Masturbation

With the onset of puberty, things change. Children will become far more aware of their genitals as they start to grow and behave as if they have a mind of their own. As stated above, putting boundaries in place before puberty starts can be helpful to create safe spaces for children to grow into their new bodies with a little privacy.

It is perfectly normal for children to start to explore their bodies during puberty and masturbate in the true sense of the word. You can pretend it isn't happening (and true, it may not be), but in all likelihood your child may want to have a good look and explore naked in a mirror, they may experiment with new ways of masturbating or start to look for material on TV, online or in books and magazines that gives them those little tingles in their undercarriage.

Be prepared to walk in on red faces, quickly changed channels, the closing of browsing windows or nonchalant looks as they pretend not to have noticed the passionate love scene on TV. Washing bedding and under-wear can lead to new surprises, as can emptying bedroom bins or tidying your child's bedroom. I say tidying, I do mean tidying and not snooping. You can embrace it or try to ignore it. There is a benefit to having your son or daughter taking responsibility for their own private space and doing chores – it can be a valuable trade for keeping their privacy. All families will have their own rules and boundaries, and I am certainly not here to tell you what they should be.

Equally, I am well aware some people have very strong beliefs about masturbation, whether they be cultural, religious values or simply how they were raised. Historically, masturbation has been seen as sinful, self-polluting and harmful to both the human mind and spirit. In Western cultures, the Church saw masturbation, along with any sensual pleasures as a danger that could undermine the family and devotion to work and order (Attwood, 2018). By the nineteenth century, notions of sin had been replaced by the medicalisation of sex with the introduction of sexology. Masturbation was no longer a sin but classified as a mental illness (Attwood, 2018). It had been firmly established by the medical practitioners of the time that a loss of semen was a serious danger to one's health (Lister, 2020). Men were warned not to waste their seed and by definition their strength through reckless masturbation and were instead encouraged to preserve it for the marriage bed.

These fairly toxic views of masturbation have led to the practice of both male and female circumcision (or Female Genital Mutilation (FGM)[1] as it is correctly called); various devices and punishments, including metal rings with teeth that were put on pubescent boys' penises to discourage erections; electric shock therapy; the use of carbolic acid to burn and desensitise the clitoris and most notoriously the invention of Kellogg's cornflakes, all in an attempt to stop *the harms* of masturbation.

This notion still persists today in online chatrooms amongst the *NoFap* community, who believe that ejaculating (fapping) will deplete their testosterone levels and their alpha male qualities. Just like in the nineteenth century this idea is based on some pretty poor science. There is absolutely no evidence to support the claim (Lehmiller, 2019). However, it does not seem to stop internet threads dedicated to the practice and the list of guys who buy into *No Nut November*. Yes, that is a thing where guys try not to ejaculate (at all) for the entire month to reset their testosterone and reclaim the power of their masculinity.

Whilst abstaining from masturbation is not actually a bad thing – everyone's hands need a rest now and then – unfortunately the *NoFap community* features heavily on *Incel* chatrooms along with *TheRedPill*. *Incel* is short for involuntary celibate. This group of predominately white men believe that the structures in society prevent them from finding a partner and have robbed them of their innate right to have sex with women. Conversations by *incels* often veer into woman-hating narratives that refer to *TheRedPill*, which is a motif taken from the film the Matrix,[2] where Morpheus offers Neo the choice between two pills. If Neo takes the blue pill he can return to a world of blissful ignorance; alternatively, he can take the red pill and see the real world beneath the facade. When referenced on chatrooms, the *real world* these men refer to is not the Matrix, it is one where masculinity has been robbed of its identity and power by feminist ideas aided by left-wing politics.

As Morpheus comments in the Matrix, if you take the red pill you can see how deep the rabbit hole goes. And it is one deep and dark rabbit hole on the internet of toxic views. Conversations that reference *TheRedPill* are characterised as highly misogynistic, homophobic and often racist and anti-Semitic to boot. It is a breeding group for extreme right-wing conspiracy theories, including the notion that the porn industry is run by the Jews to destroy society. As I say, this is a pretty dark area on the internet, and yet it is one click away from NoFap and *No nut November*. Anti-masturbation rhetoric has come a long way since the birth of the cornflakes but is still void of scientific evidence and still promotes toxic views and harmful practices.

Just in case you were in any doubt, there is absolutely no medical evidence masturbation is actually harmful. In fact, the opposite is true. Masturbation has been linked to an improved immune system (Haake et al., 2004) and a longer life (Smith et al., 1997). Masturbation can reduce stress (Ein-Dor and Hirschberger, 2012), relieve tension headaches, as well as improve sex with a partner as it can help you discover how your body works and what you like. Or, as Laura Bateman explains in her book *Girl Up*, 'actually it's pretty responsible (2016). We wouldn't go into any other major life experience without practising first, so what is so different about sex?' Indeed, you would never think of signing up for your driving test before you practised and took a few lessons. Well, masturbation is like the driving lessons but without the L plates.

All families will have their own rules and their own values. It is completely up to you to decide how you feel about masturbation and how you will manage situations at home. I am very aware people still hold very strong beliefs about masturbation and how they feel about things like pornography, which for obvious reasons kind of goes hand-in-hand (no pun intended). Indeed, we will discuss pornography and how to manage finding your child's search history later.

However, for me the important conversations are not about the rights and wrongs of masturbation – it is about setting boundaries about public and private behaviours. There are certain behaviours that should be done in private, not in front of grandma and certainly not at the dinner table. We all manage these conversation well enough when we are dealing with burping, farting and picking our noses… there is no reason why we need to deal with masturbation (self-soothing or self-stimulation) any differently.

Having conversations early about public and private spaces and personal boundaries can save a lot of blushes and embarrassment later. For everyone.

We know that the majority of human beings (and animals) masturbate at some point. Some a lot and some hardly ever – both are quite normal. People who do masturbate tend to fall into two categories: those who feel guilty and shameful about the behaviour and those who treat it as self-care.

As safe adults, how we respond to incidents where we catch our child with their hands down their pants, or walk in as they hastily pull a cushion over their laps, can have a lasting effect around which category they fall into. Ultimately, our brain is built on association. If our earliest experiences of feeling aroused are met with shame and being chastised, we associate arousal with guilt and shame.

For me, I am with the dad in my story earlier. I do not see the harm. I do not want my child to feel shame about her body or enjoying herself. I hope that she learns what she likes and frankly how to masturbate guilt and shame free…

But equally I always knock.

# Notes

1  FGM has been considered a form of child abuse in the UK since 1985. It was specifically highlighted in 2003 under the Female Genital Mutilation Act (England and Wales), which was later updated and amended in 2015 under the Serious Crime Act.
2  The Matrix (1999), Written and Directed by Lana Wachowski and Lilly Wachowski (as The Wachowski Brothers). Features Keanu Reeves and Laurence Fishburne.

# References

Attwood, F. (2018). *Sex Media*, Polity Press, Cambridge.
Bates, L. (2016). *Girl Up*, Simon & Schuster, London.
Ein-Der, T. and Hirschberg, G. (2012). Sexual healing: Daily evidence that sex relives stress for men and women in satisfying relationships, *Journal of Social and Personal Relationships*, 29, 126–39.
Haake, P., Krueger, T.H., Goebel, M.U., Herberling, K.M,. Hartmann, U. and Schedlowski, M. (2004). Effects of sexual arousal on lymphocyte subset circulation and cytokine production in man, *Neuroimmunomodulation*, 11, 293–8.

Lehmiller, J.J. (2019). Why you shouldn't buy into the whole 'No Nut November' thing. Blog post appeared on *Sex and Psychology* by Dr Justine Lehmiller of the Kinsey Institute. Available at: www.lehmiller.com/blog/2019/11/4/why-you-shouldnt-buy-into-no-nut-november.

Lister, L. (2020). *A Curious History of Sex*, Unbound, London.

Smith, G.D., Frankel, S. and Yarnell, J. (1997). Sex and death: Are they related? Findings from Caerphilly Cohort study, *BMJ*, 315, 1641–4.

# PART III
# SEX

# CHAPTER 6

# WHAT IS SEX?

**It doesn't matter whether I have a** room full of adults or young people, I always think these three words are a great place to open a session. The question 'what is sex?' is a fantastic starting point to help unpick people's attitudes and assumptions about sex and what it means – the who, the what, the where and the why of it all – and the bit we often skip – the how.

If we were in class, I would ask you to make suggestions and shout things out to make a big brainstorm on the board – but sadly we are not in class. However, don't let that stop you from having a go… grab a pen or a pencil and fill out as many answers as you can – what is sex, why do we do it, how do we do it, what it means, our motivations, other words for it – anything that springs to mind.

| What is sex? |
|---|
|  |

DOI: 10.4324/9781003122296-12

If you spend any amount of time on this exercise, you will quickly notice that there are an endless list of motivations when it comes to sex, beyond the obvious – to make a baby. Whilst it is important for young people to understand the mechanics of reproduction – the whole sperm meets egg, bakes for nine months of it all – that is not *sex*. That is reproduction. Sex is far more complicated, nuanced and messy – both figuratively and literally. Figure 6.1 shows an example of the typical answers that pop up regularly when I use this activity in my sessions.

Conversations about sex can feel dangerous and can take us into realms that are not always comfortable to navigate. The reason being, as a question, asking 'what is sex?' cuts to the heart of our fundamental beliefs and moral values. For a very long time sex has been framed in terms of sin, shame and society judgement – especially for women.

Sex can mean very different things to different people. There are so many different reasons why someone may choose to have sex; these are what Jennifer Hirsch and Shamus Khan refer to as 'sexual projects' in their study into sexual assault on College campus (2020). A person's sexual project is the goal they are aiming to achieve by engaging in sexual intercourse. This may be to 'do the college thing' (get drunk and hook-up), to seek intimacy, to lose their virginity or to gain social status for example (ibid.). Exploring the variety of motivations people have when it comes to sex is

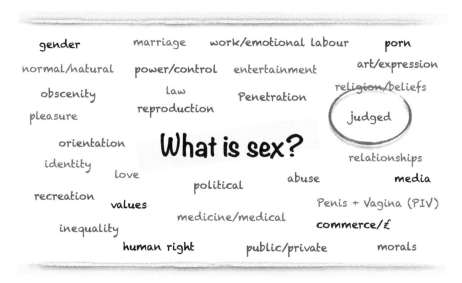

**Figure 6.1** What is sex? brainstorm

really interesting to unpick – especially when we think about which we see as valid and those we make judgements over.

For some people, sex is something that is special – it means: *I love you...* It carries connotations of marriage, mortgages, settling down, getting a dog, a goldfish or even a baby and living happily ever after. For others, sex is far more of a casual affair – a bit of fun, or something you might do on a night out. Despite what we like to pretend, neither of these views are *right* or *wrong* – safer or healthier than the other – you get to decide what sex means to you, regardless of what polite society would like to have us believe.

Often, we approach sex through a moral lens, especially when we talk to young people. The typical message young people were given was wait until marriage; now, the predominant message has moved to wait until you are in love. The message is still that sex should *mean* something special and be reserved for a committed relationship. Whilst this message may be well intentioned, it not only strips young people of their agency, but also can makes them vulnerable.

Two of the key topics I spend my days talking about are relationship abuse and sexual exploitation – both of which rely on someone falling in love with a person who treats them badly and actually uses their commitment and deep feelings of love to abuse them. We like to pretend that having sex as part of a committed relationship will magically make sex safe and more secure – however, this simply isn't so.

People in relationships often have sex because they feel like *they should* – even if they don't necessarily want to. There is certainly an expectation or a feeling of duty in a long-term relationship. This is true of both young people's relationships and adult relationships, as well. The majority of us have all had sex because it feels like it's expected – or because it feels like we *should*... the kids are staying at grandma's, you finally have a night without tantrums or teenagers – it's date night, it's your anniversary, or *their* birthday – an expected treat...?

But let's be honest, sometimes we would rather sit on the sofa in our slobs and watch Netflix (without the: *n' chill*). Unfortunately, due to our inadequacy or aversion of talking openly about sex, there is this, often unspoken, pressure to have sex, however bloated you feel from your cheeky takeaway. If you don't have sex now, there is no telling when we will next have a night off together without the kids... Sometimes it is easier to just have sex, get it out of the way, and then you can have the weekend to yourself, without your partner having a face on them! And they say romance is dead.

One-night-stands are often no better; they come with their own expectations. It is often assumed when on a date, or if you choose to go back to someone's house, that sex is a given. Implied consent by geography – you wouldn't be there if you weren't up for it (Hirsch and Khan, 2020). Indeed, a number of studies have reported that young women at university will often give a guy a blow-job at the end of the night as a tactic to escape when they don't want to have sex, simply because expectations are too high to leave without giving him something (Orenstein, 2016a; Hirsch and Khan, 2020). Equally, it can feel lonely being single, living alone or working remotely. Sometimes people chase a hook-up to try to fill a void of human connection, to make themselves feel better about themselves, to feel attractive, or wanted.

Regardless, of whether we are talking about sex within a committed relationship or as a one-night-stand, it can be disappointing and you can simply be going through the motions. You can't just turn it on if you are not in the mood. The most powerful sexual organ in the human body is the brain – not what is lurking in your underwear. If your head is busy with life, work or whatever, there isn't always room for sex – even when you are madly in love with someone. Indeed, just because you love someone will not prevent you occasionally feeling used, humiliated or disrespected and it will not automatically make sex safe.

Love is not a contraceptive. Love does not protect against STIs – chlamydia or HIV. Equally, love will not keep you emotionally safe either.

Having sex because you *want to* – because you *choose to* – is what makes sex safe. We should be honest: sex can be the most fun you ever have, but it can also be the worst thing that ever happens to you. Notice the difference in language between being engaged in the activity and being passive… if we are going to have conversations about sex, we need to talk about the darker side of unwanted sex too.

At this point it is worth emphasising that the majority of sexual assaults take place with people known to the victim – not strangers at the end of the night. The most likely person to perpetrate a rape is a partner, an ex-partner, a friend or family member – those people we love and trust (ONS, 2017). Whilst a lot of those incidents will be clearly recognised as rape or assault to all involved, we need to acknowledge, that some people will have assaulted others because they thought they were genuinely having sex (Hirsch and Khan, 2020). If we want to help young people to stay safe, we need to have broader conversations about what constitutes as consent, aside from duty, expectations and gendered social scripts. But most of all, we need to work on our ability to communicate about sex without shame.

# Issues of equality

This is where the importance of equality comes to the table. In our narratives of sex, we often reinforce prescriptive gender stereotypes. Sex is still something that men *do* to women. The social scripts and roles we assign to sex are far too narrow. Men are given the active role; it is up to them to initiate or push for sex. Women, on the other hand, are expected to take on the blocking role (Hirsch and Khan, 2020). Guys are supposed to work for it and girls are supposed to play hard to get – it is all in the chase. Nice girls don't chase sex or make overt displays of their sexuality and girls that do deserve what they get. Is there any wonder why these social scripts lead to misunderstanding about what consent truly looks like when 'no' merely translates as, try harder?

When I deliver the *'What is sex?'* starting point in a session with young people, I always add my answer at the end. I write the word 'judged', as highlighted by the ring around it in Figure 6.1. For me, sex is all about being judged… then I ask the group what they think I mean? Often people will raise the point that everyone wants to be good at sex, and people might judge you on your performance; others suggest that it might be more about being judged about your body and how you look.

These answers are definitely true – although we seem to judge ourselves much more harshly than our partners do. We are all a little insecure about others seeing us naked and vulnerable – literally with nowhere to hide! Regardless of how attractive our partner finds us, we all look in the mirror and wish we had a curvier bum, or a smaller bum… you get the idea. Nevertheless, it is often the bits of our bodies that our partner fall in love with – wobbly bits and all.

Whilst talking about our insecurities and body hang-ups is important, it is still not what I am getting at about being judged. Incidentally, it is usually one of the girls in the room who cottons on to my meaning and they often exclaim with venom – and rightly so – we don't judge men and women equally when it comes to sex.

We use sex to pass judgement on people. You are either having too much or not enough. You are either frigid or a slag and there doesn't seem to be anything in between. This is especially true for how we talk about women. If a guy has a reputation for sleeping around, he is a 'proper lad', emphasising the point that this is what lads are supposed to do. This is the role assigned to men. As a result, his social value increases. However, if a girl has a reputation for having multiple partners, somehow she becomes devalued. Labels such as *slag, slapper, slut, sket, hoe* and *whore* are branded around – and the rumours don't even have to be true. She has failed in her gendered role.

*Nice girls* don't sleep around. *Nice girls* aren't really into sex – they only have sex with their boyfriend – and only because it is expected of them. And this is the narrative that persists and sets the social scripts of sexual interactions. If you are given the passive role, how are you supposed to take control? How can you be expected to speak up and say what you want, what you enjoy or how far you are willing to go? And why would your partner listen, when it is an expectation of your role as a woman to resist and an expectation for him to convince you – it is all part of the same game.

# My issue with 'foreplay' and other words…

Social scripts are important, when it comes to setting the context of sexual encounters. These scripts not only dictate players' roles, but also how the scene plays out. And this is why I hate the word *foreplay*. When it comes to sex, language is important. The words we choose to use to describe and contextualise sex give it meaning – there is clearly a difference between 'making love' and 'I banged her'. For that reason, I loathe the term foreplay. You know those words that make you cringe – like 'moist' – well foreplay is that for me; it physically makes me shudder. In my humble opinion, I think the term foreplay is one of the most damaging words we use when it comes to discussing sex.

The implication of that word, foreplay, is that it is the warm-up – all the boring stuff you know you should do before you get to the game… like stretching. You only have to watch your local Sunday morning football club to see how seriously they take the warm-up to understand why using this sort of language could be a bit of an issue. The social scripts around sex are very unhelpful here. Not only are they very heteronormative, but also exclude those that get more out of oral, manual or anal sex. We use the word foreplay to belittle all the other fantastic things couples can do in bed together and this word emphasises the fact that under this narrative anything other than Penis in Vagina sex (PIV) isn't really proper sex.

For many people penetrative sex, i.e. PIV, can not only be problematic or painful – including those who suffer from Vaginismus,[1] but pleasure-wise may be a disappointment. It also helps to explain the well-known orgasm gap – the tendency for men to orgasm more than women – between heterosexual couples is cultural, not biological (Mintz, 2018). In contrast, there is little if no discrepancy between partners in same-sex couples when it comes to orgasm – simply because queer couples take a much broader view of what actually counts as sex.

**Did you know...**

Vaginismus is a condition which causes the involuntary contractions of the pelvic floor muscles – those that wrap around the vagina, making any sort of penetration either painful or impossible. If you think of a clenched fist, it will give you some sort of idea. Vaginismus causes a stinging or burning pain as the muscles go into spasm. Vaginismus is actually very common but little understood condition affecting around 27,000 people in the UK alone.

For a long time, many doctors assumed it was an issue with women being *unable to relax* and dismissed their distress – suggesting they drink a few glasses of wine before attempting sex as a solution! This is not an acceptable response and is merely another example of how women's genital issues are largely dismissed or ignored. Vaginismus is thought to have a number of causes – which include past trauma caused by medical examination, past painful consensual sexual experiences (where women have not told their partner that they are in pain and simply laid back and thought of England) or adverse sexual messaging that sex is shameful or will hurt. The body subconsciously reacts to expected pain in response.

So let's do a little activity.

Over the page you will find a copy of my sex act cards in Table 6.1. This is an activity I developed over ten years ago and have been using ever since.

**Table 6.1**

| | |
|---|---|
| Vaginal sex | Anal sex |
| Sexting | Dry humping (rubbing up against each other) |
| Stroking each other's bodies | Groping |
| Hand-job | Fingering |
| Sucking toes | Rimming (licking bums) |
| Going down on him | Going down on her |
| Kissing | Holding hands |
| Tickling | Hugging |

It is one of my favourites and is so versatile in opening up conversations around sex. Let me explain…

Very simply, you will find 16 separate cards each containing a different sexual act. Admittedly, some of them may not be explicitly sexual acts in themselves, like tickling for example; but I want you to consider them in a sexual context – between two people who are in a sexual relationship in some way.

If you want to go full Blue Peter with this activity, feel free to photocopy the page, print and cut out the cards. You can even laminate them if you are so inclined! Alternatively, you can grab some post-it notes or scraps of paper and copy each down in turn and do the activity that way.

Once you have a set of cards, simply all I would like you to do is sort them from the lowest level of sexual act you might do with your partner to the highest. You can put more than one sex act on the same line, if you think they are equal. There are no hard and fast rules for this – just order them from low to high.

I'll give you a minute…

I know it may feel daft, but it is a great activity to do for yourself – to help you get your own thoughts in order – but equally it is something you can do with your partner or teens. This activity can start some fantastic conversations… but more on that in a minute.

OK – have you got your line sorted?

# Debrief… sexual inequality?

My question to you is, how did you order them? I don't mean what order did you sort the cards into, for now I am more interested in *how* you ordered them – i.e. what was the criteria you used in your head?

- Was it risk?
  Have a look at your line: is it more risky as you move through the acts? What sort of risk are we thinking about? Is it physical risk, from unwanted pregnancy or STIs or is it emotional risk?
- Alternatively, was intimacy part of your decision making?

As you move down your line, do the acts become more intimate? Do intimacy and risk go hand in hand, do things become more risky as we get more intimate – on an emotional note… probably.

- Or did you separate them by chronological order – almost in bases, like first base, second base, that kind of thing?

  This seems to be the way most young people order their cards when I use this in class. Although when you unpick this further, it is most likely a combination of the three. Or, as one young person I worked with recently, ordered them – by how naked you would have to be to do them – risk increases by how much flesh you have on show, or how quickly you could get dressed again – in case you get caught.

A couple of points that are worth considering before we move on. The card that reads 'groping' often comes up in discussion during this activity as it makes people uncomfortable. Groping, the act of grabbing a handful of boob or bum and giving it a squeeze – is more often associated with unwanted touching. Or to be more specific, sexual assault; let's just call it what it is. Whilst, for those perpetrating the act, it may well be meant as only a laugh or a clumsy attempt at flirting, in reality it's a total disregard for another's personal boundaries. It is sad to think that the majority of the girls in the room, even as teenagers, can give personal accounts of being groped in public spaces, at gigs, festivals, on public transport or for the older ones, in clubs or bars. Unfortunately, I have often had young girls tell me they can't dress how they would like to, in skirts or shorts, at gigs because it attracts too much unwanted attention, and instead they have to sweat through jeans in the crowd as they dance or will only ever go if they have groups of male friends to stand around them. This card often brings out discussions of the inequalities felt in public spaces and the entitlement that men extort over women's bodies.

Another example of inequality in practice is evident from where young people (especially), but also adults, place the oral sex cards. Whilst it is not uncommon for the cards to be put together, it is equally common for the 'going down on him' card to come before the 'going down on her card', often way before. Blow-jobs are often a precursor to a couple having penetrative sex for the first time. A blow-job is an accepted holding point for those couples who aren't ready to go *all the way*. What I mean, is that girls will often offer blow-jobs as a consolation to their male partner who is pushing for penetrative sex, when she is not ready yet or into it. There is often an expectation that he needs to be given something to keep the peace – again, expectation and entitlement is still a huge part of male sexual social scripts.

In stark contrast, oral sex for her often comes after penetrative sex. There is definitely not an equal expectation that oral sex should be reciprocated. What is interesting about this, is that the young men I speak to are not opposed to the idea of going down on their female partners or uninterested, but in fact, it has more to do with young women's insecurities about their genitals. As we talked about earlier, girls are often raised to view their vulvas as both sacred and icky – not a conducive combination to allow your partner to put their head between your legs. The thought puts a lot of girls off the idea.

There is an added practical element to this disparity between oral sex. If you are giving a guy a blow-job, he doesn't need to be naked – he can just unbutton his jeans or pull down the top of his joggers – but essential to whip it out, he can still be fully clothed. To perform oral sex on a girl, you need to get between her legs – this generally involves pulling her trousers or shorts all the way down, or her wearing a skirt without tights. Unlikely, if you are trying to have a quick fumble in the bushes, at the back of the disco, or if your folks are home. In this way, social spaces – or the spaces which teenagers have to explore their sexuality – can severely limit their sexual experiences.

As I said, the language we choose to use to describe sex matters. Words can ascribe an act with added intimacy, or can casually remove it… for example, *stroking each other's bodies* – it just sounds sensual… whereas *hand-job*, by stark contrast, sounds tacky, rather than intimate. It sounds more like something Dave was boasting to his mates that Tracy did to him round the back of the bike shed.

In reality, manual sex – using your hands to stimulate your partner's genitals – can be both intimate and sensual. Hands are malleable, and able to switch between the lightest touch, barely making contact as they stroke and slide across your partner's body, featherlike, to a much firmer touch as your fingers massage, rub, probe and squeeze.

Again, the term *fingering* – as young people refer to the practice – is equally misleading as an indication of how the act should be performed. Most young people have the notion that fingering involves ramming as many digits as you can inside your partner's body like a handful of tiny penises, because that is what the term implies. However, a vulva is not a hand puppet.

Manual sex can be highly pleasurable for those with vulvas, simply because, as discussed in the chapter on anatomy, all the sensitive parts of the genitals are on the outside. The vulva is packed full of nerve endings, unlike the inside of the vagina – but it is rare that anyone tells young people about these facts. Or, more importantly, the basic rule of good sex: ask your partner what they like and how they like it.

# Are we having sex yet?

So far our little activity has led to conversations about risk and intimacy, the importance of the language we use when describing sex and the inequality of sexual social scripts. But we are not done yet.

I have two additional cards for you in Table 6.2.

Without rearranging the line of cards you have already sorted, I would like you to slot in these two extra cards: one reads *Sex* and the other *Virgin*. Where do they fit in your line. What act do you have to do in order to be classed as having lost your virginity and what act constitutes as having sex? So, wherever you slot your card in the line, all the actions that come before it are not sex, and everything after is what you would class as sex.

What do you think? And do the cards go together?

Would it make a difference who was having the sex? For example, would a young woman who only sleeps with other women define sex or virginity the same as a young man who only sleeps with other guys? Or were we all assuming we were talking about a heterosexual couple?

For most people, when I deliver this activity, they automatically assume we are talking about a heterosexual couple – we are all trained in heterosexualism. Equally, without too much thought people instinctively put both cards just before vaginal sex. That is how most people have been taught to think about sex – penis + vagina = 'proper sex' – the rest is just foreplay, except sucking toes, *which is clearly just plain weird.*[2] Equally, if I was to ask you what you need to do to lose your virginity before we did this activity, you would have most likely replied with: 'by having sex – obviously!' However, let's go back to our example of the young woman who only sleeps with other women.

Let's imagine she is 18 years old and is gay. She has never had penetrative sex before – but she has had a number of sexual partners. She enjoys oral and manual sex and all the other activities in our list – and she has had a pretty good time whilst exploring these acts with her sexual partners.

**Table 6.2**

| Sex | Virgin |
|---|---|
| | |

Would we still say she has never had sex? Or perhaps we would concede that yes, she has had sex, but would we still maintain she is a virgin? Would she really need to have penetrative sex to lose that label?

What about the gay young man in our other example? What would he have to do in order to lose his virginity or have sex? Most people (outside the LGBTQ+ community) would assume he would need to have bum sex – *because that is what gay men do, isn't it?* Well, no actually. Whilst some gay men do enjoy anal sex, as either a top or a bottom or both, there are plenty of gay men (and bisexual/pansexual men) who do not engage in anal sex at all, just as there are heterosexual couples who both do and don't engage in bum sex.

It is a fallacy that gay men have anal sex, heterosexual have normal – proper sex and lesbian… well…*who knows what lesbians do but I have heard it has something to do with strap-ons, and scissors…?!*

Regardless of your sexual orientation, human beings can have sex in four general ways:

1. we can use our hands to stimulate our partner's genitals;
2. we can use our mouths to kiss, lick or suck their genitals;
3. we can rub or grind our genitals together or against their body; or
4. we can penetrate our partner's genitals with a penis or a phallus[3] shaped object.

Or, even better, a combination of two at the same time. In fact, all of the cards (and it is not an exclusive list) are all part of sex – it is a very heteronormative view that sex can be reduced to sticking the proverbial plug in a socket.

# Losing it…

Culturally, we have put so much emphasis on PIV sex to the exclusion of other sexual activities that not only carry less risk, but also are often more pleasurable for all involved. It is rare for any sex education in school to include any mention of any form of sex other than penetrative sex (usually with the emphasis on reproduction, even if the aim is to highlight ways to avoid pregnancy).

This is not only a huge loss for young people who identify as LGBTQ+, like the young people in our examples above, but also serves the purpose of raising the stakes when it comes to virginity.

A few years ago I was delivering a whole year assembly to year nine pupils. There were around 150–200 young people in the hall. I was talking away – actually about the stuff we are exploring here, and I noticed this lad with his hand up. Whilst I try to make my sessions – even big assemblies – interactive and pupil led, I have them shouting out and getting involved – it is still unusual for someone to put their hand up without any prompt or in response to a question I have asked the room at large, especially with year 9s. So I stopped, and asked him what he would like to say… and this lad asked me one of the best questions I have ever been asked – it was brilliant.

This question was met with scoffs and giggles by the rest of the room. But fair play to the lad; he spoke over their laughter and explained…

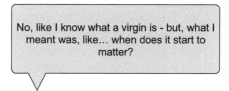

And he had a good point. When does it suddenly start to matter whether or not you've had sex yet? I would argue that it starts to matter as soon as walk through the gates at high school. Whilst sex may be a long way off when you first arrive in year 7 and 8, you will have definitely heard whispers and rumours circulating, along with the latest gossip about who's had sex or who hasn't.

But why are we so hung up on virginity and why does it matter so much? Well, let's admit it, virginity only really matters for women – not men. No one is carrying out traumatic virginity testing to join the Egyptian armed forces, or to confirm marriage rites in India. The rapper T.I is not accompanying his son to his annual doctor's appointment to confirm he is still *intact*...[4]

Historically, in the days before the contraceptive pill, becoming pregnant out of wedlock had a significantly larger impact on the mother than the absent father. It would be her family burdened by costs, which might go some way to explain why it is women's behaviours that were closely guarded rather than young men's. Furthermore, whilst it is always obvious who the mother of the child is, the father could theoretically be anyone – ascertaining paternity was not as simple as going on the Jeremy Kyle Show to have a DNA test to establish who the father was. In the majority of patriarchal societies inheritance of lands and titles flow down the male line, it was essential to ensure all your worldly goods went to your legitimate child and not to the good-looking stable boy's offspring.

The importance of virginity is mixed up with purity myths and money. Virginity is all about protecting ownership of men's possessions. We should not overlook the fact that under Christian marriage rights a woman is also seen as a possession of first her father and then her husband. Traditionally, her virginity is a gift to her new husband and is a prize to bargain with for her father.

Women throughout history have been ostracised or murdered due to rumours over their virgin status. Most famous are probably the Roman Vestal Virgins, who if they were accused of forsaking their sacred vows of chastity the punishment was to be entombed alive and starved to death. Despite the fact we like to believe we have turned our back on such nonsense, society is still firmly hung up on the importance of virginity. Indeed, even in the UK today women are murdered by their families in so-called honour killings.

Consider even the language we use to describe the notion – a choice between losing or saving your virginity. However, we know that there is no accurate way to discern a woman's sexual history – there is no such thing as an accurate virginity test, despite what T.I may believe. Indeed, in 2017 a systematic review was published by researchers at the University of Minnesota who found 1,269 separate studies exploring the reliability of virginity testing. They concluded, not only that any test is inconclusive and 'not a useful clinical tool' but also often 'physically, psychologically and socially devastating to the examinee' (Olson and García-Moreno, 2017). Furthermore, their research led them to label the practice as a clear violation of human rights and an example of gender-based discrimination. The following year the practice was further discredited when in response to the World Health Organization (WHO, 2018), the United Nations Human rights and United Nations of Women issued a statement calling for the end of virginity testing (WHO, 2018).

By still emphasising the importance of virginity and perpetuating the popping cherries narrative we serve only to further remove young women's control over their bodies and their sexual citizenship. Furthermore, we reinforce the notion of PIV as the only acceptable form of 'proper sex'. It is interesting to note, as Peggy Orenstein asks in her TEDWomen talk, 'why do we consider this one act, more often associated with pain and discomfort by young women, as the line in the sand of sexual adulthood?' (Orenstein, 2016b). Think about it… look back at your line of sex acts you have made – imagine a young person: Alex.

Alex is desperate to lose their virginity. All their friends have been talking about it and all the cool kids have already done it. They are feeling the pressure. They go to a party and have been drinking. They think: what the hell – may as well get it over with – so they keep drinking and eventually agree to go upstairs with someone. The sex is over quite quickly – literally a bit of kissing and straight to PIV. It isn't particularly comfortable. Wasn't pleasurable – and they feel confused and used afterwards… But hey – they are no longer a virgin…

Now consider: Bobby. Bobby has been sexually active for a while – but they haven't 'done it' yet. They have a partner – it doesn't matter particularly if they are a serious partner – if they are in love or merely friends with benefits – but they talk about their personal boundaries, what they are ready to try and what they are not ready for, but most importantly they also talk about what they enjoy. Together they are working through the various activities on our sex act cards and they have both had a lot of fun doing so…

Out of our two hypothetical young people, Alex and Bobby, who is really the most sexually mature or the most sexually experienced? To all intents and purposes, if we take virginity as the marker of sexual adulthood, we would have to say Alex, as Bobby is clearly still a virgin as they have not yet had PIV sex whereas Alex has already reached this milestone. However, I would argue Bobby's approach to sex is not only far more mature, but also much healthier too.

If you agree, then why as adults, as parents, as sex educators, do we spend so much time focusing on PIV sex and as a society on the importance of the notion of virginity? A concept that is not only impossible to prove but equally difficult to define… so why bother?

Personally, I have moved to using the term sexual debut in my classes rather than virginity, as I feel it is more inclusive and doesn't carry the same negative connotations. I am firmly of the belief that if we shift our conversation from focusing merely on PIV sex, to wider definitions of sex – as we have with our sex act cards – we can not only be more inclusive to those who enjoy other forms of sex, but also to remove the pressure for young people to rush to lose their virginity like Alex in our scenarios, at the expense of having sex that is actually enjoyable for all concerned. We do our young people a massive disservice by excluding pleasure from our conversations around sex. After all, surely we want our young people to only be engaging in sexual activities that they enjoy… is that not what we mean by making sex safe?

# Notes

1  There is help available for those who suffer with Vaginismus – I would suggest starting with: The Vaginismus Network www.vaginismusnetwork.com; @TheVagNetwork, a community for people who suffer with Vaginismus – who can help connect you with other people in the same situation and help you access proper medical advice and diagnosis.
2  **(Apologies)**, sucking toes is not weird. It is interesting though, how many people struggle with this card in practice.
   To be clear, the only reason the card with sucking toes is in the pack is to have

this conversation – we are back at my earlier point about how we judge people when it comes to sex. We are not very open with those around us about what we like and what turns us on – there will always be a number of people in the room when I deliver this activity, who really enjoy their feet being played with or someone sucking their toes (quite possibly, there may be a number of people reading this sentence right now). Sucking someone's toes is naughty and requires a level of intimacy in order to ask or be asked – and yet we often publicly shame these acts that other people enjoy and yet harm no one. Often we are quick to judge something we do not like – or something we do not speak about openly as weird or dirty. That is the reason the sucking toes card is included, to remind people that we should be mindful how we talk about sex – what we say may unwittingly shame others or may reinforce those inequalities that surround sex.

3 For those of you not in the know: a phallus is an academic penis!

4 In an interview with Nazanin Mandi and Nadia Moham in the podcast 'Ladies Like Us', the rapper revealed he has yearly trips to the gynaecologist to check her hymen – for which he was called out online as a breach of her privacy and for perpetuating the virginity myth.

# References

Hirsch, J. and Khan, S. (2020). *Sexual Citizenship: A landmark study of sex, power, and assault on campus*, Norton and Company, London.

Mintz, L. (2018). *Becoming Cliterate: Why orgasm equality matters – and how to get it*, HarperOne, London.

Office of National Statistics (2017). Sexual offences in England and Wales: Year ending March 2017: Analyses on sexual offences from the year ending March 2017 Crime Survey for England and Wales and crimes recorded by police. Available at: www.ons.gov.uk/peoplepopulationandcommunity/crimeand justice/articles/sexualoffencesinenglandandwales/yearendingmarch2017/ previous/v1#how-are-victims-and-perpetrators-related.

Olson, R.M. and García-Moreno, C. (2017). Virginity testing: A systematic review, *Reprod Health*, 18 May, 14(1), 61.

Orenstein, P. (2016a). *Girls and Sex: Navigating the complicated new landscape*, Oneworld Publications, New York.

Orenstein, P. (2016b). What young women believe about their own sexual pleasure, TEDWomen, October.

World Health Organization (2018). Interagency statement calls for the elimination of 'virginity-testing'. Available at: www.who.int/reproductivehealth/ publications/eliminating-virginity-testing-interagency-statement/en/.

# Quiz: sexual health

1. Why is the term: 'morning after pill' misleading?
2. How old do you need to be to access sexual health services?
3. What is the most common STI in the UK and why?
4. Are there any STIs you can pass on even if you are using barrier methods (condom/femidom/dental-dam)?
5. What are the four main ways a clinic may determine if you have an STI?
   
   i.                ii.                iii.                iv.
6. Up to how many weeks of pregnancy can you legally have an abortion in the UK?
7. Does shaving your pubic hair make you more or less likely to contract an STI?
8. What are the *Fraser Guidelines* and *Gillik Competencies*?
9. In what year were rubber condoms first introduced?
10. When is World Aids day?
11. What is Stealthing?
12. What is a merkin, and what does it have to do with sexual health?

# CHAPTER 7

# MAKING SEX SAFE

**W**hen we think about *safe sex,* **the** first thing that springs to mind is contraception. This raises the question: why not simply call this chapter 'Contraception' and be done with it? This is the conversation I often have with schools when they call up to make bookings, or a point I frequently address during training. As a topic, contraception is always on the list of lessons teachers and youth workers want to deliver – but assuming that safe sex is all down to using contraception is an oversight.

Whilst contraception is important – and is certainly something we need to cover – there is far more to making sex safe than merely contraception. By making contraception the sole focus, we not only make assumptions about the type of sex people are having, i.e. PIV (as we discussed in the previous chapter), again simply adding more importance to this particular act – but also, we make an assumption about who is having the sex… essentially, con(tra)ception is designed to prevent conception. By definition we are talking about heterosexual PIV. However, same-sex couples have sex too and equally need information to make that sex safe.

Imagine we have a typical class of 30 students. Statistically speaking, we can assume there is at least one young person who may not identify themselves as heterosexual. Equally, there will be other young people who are engaging in other types of sexual activity not PIV – they need information too. If I am the 15-year-old gay lad in the class and the teacher writes the word *'Contraception'* on the board in big letters as the title, I could be forgiven for thinking, *'what has it got to do with me?'*

DOI: 10.4324/9781003122296-13

However, if we take a step back and broaden the context of the discussion and instead write, 'What makes sex safe?' suddenly we have completely changed the context of the lesson. Not only have we made it inclusive to everyone in the room, regardless of the types of sex they may or may not be engaging in; their sexuality or their gender identity, but equally we have opened up the conversation to focus on much more than merely preventing an unwanted pregnancy. Suddenly we can discuss the wider risks of having sex, for example: What about STIs; questions of consent, coercion or feeling pressured; the emotional risks; trust, respect and other qualities of a healthy relationships; feeling used afterwards; or the practicalities of having somewhere private and safe to have sex in the first place? All of these (and more) are part of what makes sex safe.

Condoms are wonderful things. They will stop you catching Chlamydia and help prevent an unwanted pregnancy – but what they can't do is protect you from the emotional risks of sexual intimacy… they won't protect your feelings; they won't stop you feeling judged; or your photos being shared. They won't make you fall in love, guarantee you an orgasm, or prevent people talking behind your back.

Making sex safe is more than merely a conversation about contraception.

This raises the question: as the safe adults in our children's lives, what are the messages of safety we are providing for our youngsters? What words of advice or warnings do parents typically offer to their children?

However, even our parental conversations around contraception are often limited. If we are honest, the extent of the conversation will usually only be restricted to, 'and don't you come home pregnant, you're smarter than to go wasting your prospects on the word of some lad!' when addressing our daughters, or alternatively the equivalent for our sons, 'don't you go getting some girl pregnant – I am too young to be a grandparent!' unfortunately.

In the parenting handbook lexicon of safe sex, other helpful classics include advice on consent for teenage girls: 'you are not going out dressed like that!' and the all-encompassing safe sex advice of 'Not while you live under my roof - not in my house.' the magic words that when instantly spoken by a parent, immediately put a stop to all sexual curiosity and practices by our teens. Problem solved. As parents, you are well within your rights to lay down the law and assert boundaries for your teens; but it would be naive to believe the 'not under my roof' rule, will stop your teenagers from having sex. In reality, all it does is deny their right to sexual citizenship (Hirsch and Khan, 2020) and firmly shut the door on them coming to you for support.

Consider the real message behind these tired, misguided attempts to protect our children from the dangers of sex. Sleeping together in the same bed as your partner, at home, transforms sex into an act of intimacy, care and commitment. If we recognise the 'not under my roof' rule is unlikely to stop teenagers from becoming sexually active, but instead, only serves to send the message: sex is something to hide; to keep secret; and separate from family life (Schalet, 2011). Stern warnings not to 'come home pregnant' fails to offer any sort of solutions of how to negotiate the safe sex; again only serving the purpose to distance a teen who gets things wrong from the support network around them.

Becoming sexually active is a critical life skill (Hirsch and Khan, 2020). Unfortunately, many young people reach that milestone underprepared to do so safely. If we compare the amount of input most parents put into their child learning to drive safely. Driving, like sex, is a critical life skill; a sign of maturity, and a claim to personal freedom. Yet, we don't simply throw them the keys and expect them to figure it out by themselves. Why should sex be any different?

Indeed, one of the most important protective factors for young people engaging in a sexual relationship is having someone they can talk to. Someone who can share in their adventures and will listen without judgement. Whilst it is important to have someone they can talk to about their worries and concerns, to check if how they feel is OK and to point out the red flags, it is equally just as important to have someone to share in the daft and silly stuff too. Someone you can laugh with about the time you got cramp in the middle and had to stop and ask them to rub your toes in a very unsexy way… or the time you fell off the bed as you were a little too enthusiastic in your passion… or the time you banged heads, or the embarrassment of accidentally farting! The silly stuff is just as important.

Whilst there are not many parents that want that level of detail about their teenager's sex life – and I am not necessarily suggesting that is what you should be aiming for –wouldn't it be better if your child could talk to you about their partner and their relationship without fear of being shamed or ever hearing the words 'I told you so'. Some of these anecdotes are certainly better off as conversations between friends – after all, that is what friends are for – but teenagers should never be left alone to manage the worries and trials of a sexual relationship by themselves. There should be a safe adult around who can add age and wisdom (hopefully… and not merely cynicism and prejudice) to the conversation. Remember, building a safe space to engage in these conversations is not only about supporting your child with their problems but many teens also carry the burden of their friends' problems too. It may be your son or daughter who is supporting their best friend through a pregnancy scare or an abusive relationship and doesn't know what to do or say to help.

### Worried about a friend

A few years ago I helped to run a campaign in a college to encourage young people to talk to the advisers on campus. We ran the campaign under the title, '*worried about a friend*' as we found young people were more likely to approach the advisers about anonymous 'friends', real or imaginary, to seek advice – it is a great way for young people to test the waters and a chance for safe adults to prove their worth.

This is also a great distancing technique to use in lessons or workshops to help young people consider what advice they would give to a friend… what we are actually doing is helping them find solutions or support if they were ever in trouble themselves.

Being there to discuss with your child how they can support a friend is a great way to not only remove the burden from their shoulders alone, but also to talk to them indirectly and give them information about how to manage their own relationships too. It adds a little distance to the conversation, which can be good for both of you. But remember, why would they talk to you about their friends if you haven't first built that relationship? Why would they come to you, if every time they tell you about their friends you panic and tell them to stay away from them because any friend who is already sexually active must be a bad influence? It doesn't exactly encourage open conversation – but neither does indifference…

I know it is hard to keep up, and there are more twists and turns than the latest soap opera, but this is where you earn your stripes. Sometimes, young people will tell us as parents or safe adults about a friend's situation as a litmus test to see how we would react if it was them instead – if you can't cope with hearing about their friends, how can you be expected to cope when it is them…

If you want to be the one they call when things go wrong – if you want to be able to support them in their relationships – they need to know they can talk to you about this stuff. Whilst you don't have to talk about all the intimate details of your teen's sex life, it is important to build those lines of communication so they know they can talk to you if they need to.

A few years ago, I was working with a young person's project board on a project. Basically, they were a group of young people I trained in RSE and we would talk to them about various projects and get their input and advice. Essentially, stealing all their brilliant ideas and putting them into practice. Anyway, one day we were talking about mobile phones and how they helped or hindered their personal relationships. One of the girls in the group, Jess, talked about how she had used her phone to have a difficult conversation with her mum. Jess explained that back when she was 14/15 she had wanted to go on the pill, but knew if she'd approached her mum and said 'hey mum I want to go on the pill', her mum's immediate response would have been to explode and flip into panic mode: 'Oh my god! You are too young to be having sex what are you thinking…!' Or words to that effect.

Instead, Jess explained she decided to text her. At the time her mum was pottering around upstairs – changing the beds or something, and Jess was downstairs in the kitchen. She took out her phone and composed a text…

> Mum, I want to go on the pill… don't worry I am not sexually active or thinking about it but my periods are really getting me down. Will you come with me…?

Heart pounding, Jess said she heard the message ping upstairs on her mum's phone. *Ding*. And then she heard her mum sit on the bed and then nothing. She waited for what felt like an age for her mum to come back downstairs. Jess's mum simply walked into the kitchen and gave her a big cuddle.

By using her phone and sending a text message, it gave her mum time to read the message – reread it, catch her breath and process the conversation, before she reacted and ruined everything. That moment made all the difference. In the end they booked in to see the nurse at their nearest sexual health clinic and went together. This one incident changed their relationship. Now they talk much more openly about everything. I worked with Jess when she was 16/17, and was sexually active, but she said that she was able to talk to her mum about her relationship and about how things were with her partner as a result of this incident and she found it a real sense of support – even if she didn't always tell her everything, the knowledge that she knew she could made all the difference.

Over the next few pages we are going to discuss some of the things that help to make sex safe, besides having someone to talk to. First, we will deal with contraception, then STIs before we explore sexual citizenship and consent.

However, before we get stuck into exploring contraception and STIs, it is worth thinking about some of the more practical things first. Below is a *doing it* checklist. I pulled this together in response to being asked repeatedly, 'how do you know when you are ready for sex?' Obviously it's not an exhaustive list, but simply gives young people a number of things they might want to consider before they enter into a sexual relationship with someone. I have included it here as the items on this checklist are all centred around making sex a positive experience. As they say, knowledge is power after all.

Hopefully this list will prove equally helpful to you as a list of helpful topics you may wish to cover in your conversations with the young people in your life.

# Doing it checklist

**Practicalities**

✓  I have several in-date condoms and both I and my partner know how to use them
✓  I have latex-safe, water-based lubricant

✓ I know where my local sexual health services are and what they offer
✓ I have a location where I feel safe and comfortable in where I am able to relax to have sex

**Physical**
✓ I understand the basics of my own and my partner's anatomy and the basic mechanics of how to have sex
✓ I can tell when I am turned on and when I am not; I know what I need to be aroused or when I am simply not in the mood
✓ I can relax during sexual practices – including masturbation – without fear, anxiety or shame

**Relationship**
✓ I am able to create limits – to say no when I want to and can trust my partner to respect my decisions at all times
✓ I can assess what I want for myself and can separate it from what my partner, friends or family want. I feel able to trust my partner and am trustworthy myself
✓ I feel able to tell my partner easily what I want sexually and emotionally and when I do not like or want to do something
✓ I can talk to my partner about sex comfortably and honestly and they feel able to do the same with me
✓ I care about my partner's health, feelings and wellbeing

**Emotional items**
✓ I have someone I can talk to about sex that I trust and friends I can go to for emotional support or even just a giggle
✓ I am choosing to have sex because I want to for my own benefit and pleasure, and not to merely please my partner.
✓ I can separate sex from love and do not seek to have sex to use it to manipulate myself, my partner or anyone else
✓ I understand that having sex could change my relationship for better or worse and feel able to handle whatever may happen
✓ I don't have any strong religious, cultural or family beliefs or convictions that sex for me, right now, is wrong. I can take full responsibility for my own emotions, expectations and actions and can manage them
✓ I can handle being disappointed, confused or upset
✓ I have nothing to prove to myself, my partner or my peers

# References

Hirsch, J.S. and Khan, S. (2020). *Sexual Citizens: A landmark study of sex, power, and assault on campus*, W.W. Norton, New York.

Schalet, A. (2011). *Not Under My Roof: Parent, teens, and the culture of sex*, University of Chicago Press, Chicago.

# CHAPTER 8

# MAKING SEX SAFE: CONTRACEPTION

*'Don't you come home pregnant!' is a* lovely catchphrase but offers very little in terms of practical help or advice; not to mention being a less than warm invitation to an inclusive chat. It is the equivalent of shouting *'don't you crash the car!'* in place of driving lessons.

If, as parents or safe adults, we are hoping to add a little extra to our advice, it is important to make sure we have the right information first. This is especially true when it comes to contraception. I remember talking to a parent a few years ago about the implant; she was worried as her daughter had made an appointment to have an implant fitted as her chosen form of contraception. The mother was completely set against it, as she'd had an awful experience when she'd had one fitted years before. The mother was at her wits' end as she didn't want her daughter to have the same experience. What the mother didn't realise was the implant she'd had such issues with (Norplant™) was no longer on the market. It had been replaced in 1999 by a new licences contraception Implanon™, that had none of the issues she had experienced (Guillebaud, 2004). But why would she know?

For most adults, unless they happen to work in the field, their knowledge of contraception is likely to come from their own experience. Like the mother in our story, this might mean that some of the key information they need to help support their teenagers to make positive decisions

DOI: 10.4324/9781003122296-14

about their own contraceptive choice might be missing. In this chapter, we are going to readdress the balance. Below, I will give an overview of the various different methods of contraception available, with a brief explanation of how they work, highlighting some of the pros and cons of each method. This is not designed as medical advice and is merely an overview of the various options available.

As I am always at pains to explain to young people, if you want to find the right contraceptive method that works for you, you will need to talk to your GP or make an appointment at your nearest sexual health service (personally, I always prefer to recommend visiting a specialist contraceptive service – whilst GPs are excellent, not all GPs are experts in contraception or are up to date on all the options available). They will be able to talk you through your options, and make sure what you choose is right for you and your medical history. One of the great advantages of contraception is we have such a variety of options available nowadays; however, this is also our greatest drawback – one size does not fit all. Sometimes it can take a little while to find the right fit for you.

# The basics

As we mentioned in the previous chapter, contraception refers to the methods of preventing an unwanted pregnancy. But it is worth noting, no method is 100% effective. Often in literature you will see contraception efficacy rates – and they will give you two sets of figures: one for perfect use and one for typical use – and these can be quite different. Perfect use refers to clinical supervised trials. These are not real life – especially when you add in all the factors and stresses of everyday life, coupled with the heated emotions of sex. This is where typical use comes in. It is the reality of using that particular form of contraception by us mere mortals; horny and in a sexual relationship that is not perfect with jobs, shopping, family-life, dinners to cook and bins to put out.

It is worth remembering that sex is never 100% safe but contraception can greatly reduce your chances of having an unwanted pregnancy.

Unfortunately, as pregnancy is something that requires a womb, the majority of contraception is aimed at those who can conceive. Whilst there have been attempts at designing both an implant and a contractive pill for those with a penis, there is currently no such products licensed and

**A tip for those working with young people**

A question I use a lot with young men when discussing contraception and pregnancy choices – both often are seen as 'women's issues' and therefore not for them to worry about is this:

*Is it fair that a lad doesn't get any say whether his partner choses to carry on or end her pregnancy?*

on the market. For penis owners there is only one option – the condom. Despite their reputation and drawbacks, condoms are the champion of contraception as they are the only method that will prevent against both pregnancy and the transmission of sexually transmitted infections as well. But more of that later…

Regardless, contraception is something that is the responsibility of both partners. Men do not get to abdicate responsibility. In fact, as men get no say over what happens when there is an unwanted pregnancy, I would argue they should take their responsibility seriously. Once you have chosen to ejaculate and have deposited your genetic material inside your partner, there ends your decision-making capacity – officially. Legally speaking, men have no say whether their female partner decides to end or carry on with any resulting pregnancy (and rightly so. Is it fair? No – but it is the only ethical solution – women alone should make decisions over their own bodies). This is a point I often raise with disinterested young men during workshops – it certainly helps to grab their attention and often leads to interesting discussions around reproductive rights.

Contraception is certainly not a new concept. There are records throughout history, dating back as far as the Egyptians, of old wives' tales and recommended practices to avoid unwanted pregnancy. It is rumoured the Ancient Egyptians used crocodile dung and a concoction of honey and acacia leaves to block the entrance to the womb (Lister, 2020). Virginal douches have been used since the sixteenth century to try to wash away unwanted sperm (but are neither safe nor recommended); and the first reliable record of the condom goes back to Gabriele Falloppio (1523–62), an Italian physician who designed a fabric sheath to be used to stop the spread of syphilis (ibid.).

The contraceptive pill, heralded as one of the greatest scientific developments of the twentieth century, was developed in the 1950s, but was not introduced to the UK until 1961 and was originally only available to married women.

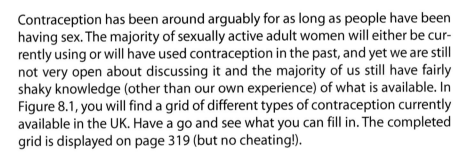

| Hormonal | Barrier | Other |
|---|---|---|
| | | |
| Emergency | Permanent | LARC |
| | | |

**Figure 8.1**  Contraception grid

Note: See Contraception grid with answers in the Answers section on page 319.

Contraception has been around arguably for as long as people have been having sex. The majority of sexually active adult women will either be currently using or will have used contraception in the past, and yet we are still not very open about discussing it and the majority of us still have fairly shaky knowledge (other than our own experience) of what is available. In Figure 8.1, you will find a grid of different types of contraception currently available in the UK. Have a go and see what you can fill in. The completed grid is displayed on page 319 (but no cheating!).

It is worth bearing in mind, not all women who use contraception, especially hormonal contraceptives, will be using it solely for contraceptive purposes. Many women choose to use contraceptives too help manage their periods, either to keep them regular, or to reduce painful or heavy periods. If you remember, this was the reason Jess, our project board member (from the previous chapter) had wanted to go on the pill. So, as a parent, if you happen to spot a pack of pills in your daughter's bag, bathroom or bedroom, don't panic and automatically assume they are already sexually active – it may not be the case (to be fair, even if they are sexually active, be proud of the fact you have raised a child who is resourceful and is empowered enough to take responsibility for their sexual health!). Indeed, there is even a particular brand of combined hormonal contraceptive pill Dianette™ which is prescribed to treat severe acne (Guillebaud, 2004).

The majority of contraception is hormonal based – this means generally it is designed to disrupt the menstrual cycle. However, as we discussed when we looked at puberty in Chapter 3, hormones can affect our bodies in different ways – both physically and emotionally – this includes our moods and our appetite; they can cause us to lose or gain weight; or can disrupt our skin and cause spots. This is true of hormonal contraceptives too. They can cause side effects, and these vary from person to person. But remember, contraception is designed to improve your life, not to make it more difficult.

If your teen complains about or is struggling with any side effects, don't brush them off as normal and something to put up with; instead advise them to go back to their health care provider and talk to them. As I said, there are lots of options available – sometimes it takes a little while to find what works best for them. However, it is worth noting, doctors will often advise to stick with a particular option for 3–6 months, as it may take a little time for their body to settle down and get used to the change in hormones. That said, if something isn't working and is causing side effects that are getting them down, it is important for young people to feel empowered enough to not take no for an answer, they need to feel able to tell their doctor or nurse it isn't right for them.

Final point, before we have a proper look at the various options available. It may be worth reminding your teenager, or any young people you are working with, that just because their best friends gets on really well with a particular brand of pill, doesn't mean it will work for them too. Whilst it is great they are talking amongst themselves and are aware of the options their friends have chosen, contraception is not a fashion statement, where you have to have the brand that matches your peers.

# Hormonal contraception

As stated above, hormonal contraceptives covers a range of different methods – the most common being the combined pill, more often simply referred to as 'the pill'. The combined pill contains both synthetically produced hormones oestrogen and progestogen, whereas the mini-pill is progestogen only. In general, hormonal contraception works by manipulating the menstrual cycle, and replacing it with a new cycle. This is done in three key ways:

1. Preventing ovulation – if there is no mature egg released there can be no pregnancy.
2. Reducing the thickness of the endometrium, making the womb inhospitable for implantation; even if ovulation did occur, the lining of the womb would not be thick enough for implantation of the fertilised egg.
3. Suppressing the production of excess cervical mucus, that act as sticky rope ladders for invading sperm cells, instead plugging the cervix with thick mucus, thus making it more difficult for sperm to get into the womb in the first place.

**The combined pill (CHC)** usually comes as either a pack of 21 pills or a pack of 28 pills (21 actual pills and 7 sugar pills). Traditionally, the pills are taken daily, for 21 days, and then you take a break for 7 days – or if you have a pack with 28 pills, you take the 7 sugar pills. In this time, most women experience what we call a withdrawal bleed. This is not strictly a period – but is a side effect from the sudden drop in hormones. This is usually lighter and less painful than a typical period. Then, after the seven-day break, she will start a new pack of pills and continue.

**The patch** is similar to the combined pill and contains the same hormones. However, you wear the patch, which is similar to a nicotine patch, directly on your skin. You wear a patch for 7 days, before replacing it with a new one. You do this 3 times, covering 21 days and then have a break for a week. Again, most women will experience a withdrawal bleed in this time.

**The vaginal ring** is a soft plastic ring that you insert yourself so it sits inside the vagina, resting against the back of the vaginal canal and the front wall of the vagina. It contains the same combination of hormones as the patch and the combined pill and is worn for 21 days before being thrown away. You replace the vaginal ring with a new one after taking a 7-day break.

*Updated guidance*: In January 2019 new guidance was released – finally acknowledging what had been known for a long time – there being no medical evidence of any health benefit to support encouraging women to take the seven-day break. Indeed, evidence suggests most women experience less symptoms by not taking the break (Guillebaud, 2004). This new guidance applies to the combined pill, the patch and the vaginal ring – but may take some getting used to for women who have been using the pill for some time and have been religiously taking a break and putting up with a withdrawal bleed every month – although some women like the reassurance of a bleed to reassure they themselves they aren't pregnant.

**The mini-pill**: the progestogen-only pill comes in packets of 28 pills. Simply you take a single pill every day (the window period is often shorter with the mini-pill, compared with the combined pill that has a 12-hour window to take, meaning it should be taken within 3 hours of the same time every day for it to be effective). One of the key benefits of the mini-pill is it is effective for those women who for whatever reason are particularly sensitive to oestrogen – including women who are breast feeding. However, some women experience irregular periods – although many women stop their periods altogether – which most women see as a plus rather than as a negative.

Obviously one of the key issues with the pill is it only works if you remember to take it. If you forget, it doesn't work. The key, is like brushing your teeth, making it part of your daily routine. However, as it is swallowed, digested and absorbed, it will not work if you are sick or have a dodgy belly. Equally, some antibiotics can affect the pill's efficiency – so it is always worth reminding your GP if they plan to give you any other medication.

For those with heads like sieves, there are other options available that do not rely on your organisational prowess and your memory…

**The implant** has changed since its first inception. It has been greatly improved in recent years, after initial problems with the original design. Now it is a single small rod approximately 4cm long, inserted under the skin, usually inside the upper arm. The implant slowly releases progestogen directly into the bloodstream. It is licensed in the UK to be left in place for three years – so it is classed as a one of four LARCs (Long Acting Reversible Contraceptives). The implant is put in place with the use of a dedicated preloaded applicator, with a cleverly shaped wide-bore needle – similar to those used for blood transfusions, that injects the implant just below the skin. This can be quite sore and is not unusual to leave some bruising behind or to feel tender for a few days. But on the plus side, that is your contraception sorted for the next three years – no memory needed. You can't forget it if you stay at your partner's place unplanned, or if you go on holiday. If you're sick or have a dodgy belly it still works. You can see why it is a popular choice, especially amongst young women.

**Injection** is another form of hormonal contraception and contains the synthetic hormone progestogen. The most commonly used injection is Depo-Provera (or DMPA). Depo-Provera and Noristerat must be administered by a doctor or nurse. However, there is now an injection called Sayana Press which you can be taught to inject yourself at home, meaning you may only have to visit a clinic once a year. Depending on which type of injection you are given, will depend whether you need to have an injection every 8, 12 or 13 weeks. As a result, the injection is classed as one of our four LARCs. Use of the injection has been linked with thinning of bone density, but this usually returns to normal once the injections have stopped. The most common side effect is a disruption of normal periods. They may become heavier, longer or may stop altogether. Once injections have stopped it is not unusual for it to take some time for your periods to return to normal. Women who are particularly sensitive to hormones may experience other side effects, such as weight gain, headaches, mood swings, breast tenderness, as well as irregular bleeding. Unfortunately, because the injection can't be removed from your body (like an IUD, IUS or implant – nor can you simply stop taking it like the pill), if you do have any side effects they are likely to last as long as the injection and for some time afterwards.

**IUS**: Intrauterine System is another form of hormonal contraception. It is a small plastic T-shaped device that is inserted, so it sits inside of the womb. This has to be done by a trained doctor (not all GPs are able to insert an IUS). The IUS contains progestogen in the collar around its neck similar to the implant. This releases hormones directly into the womb, meaning it can have a much lower dosage of hormones and therefore is less likely to have any negative side effects. However, having an IUS fitted can be uncomfortable, as a speculum is used, before the IUS is implanted inside of the womb with a special applicator. This can make the cervix go into spasm, which can be quite uncomfortable. That said, an IUS is another one of our methods classed as a LARC, as depending on which type is fitted, can be left in place either three or five years. Most women with an IUS have lighter and less painful periods; indeed, an IUS is often prescribed to women who suffer with heavy and extremely painful periods as they are known to help. Some women do not experience any bleeding as their periods stop altogether. The IUS is one of the most effective forms of birth control available to women.

As we have already mentioned, some people are particularly sensitive to fluctuations in hormones. These can have both physical and emotional impacts and cause unwanted side effects. It is not unheard of for some women to suffer with depression, weight gain, skin outbreaks or irregular bleeding. None of which are desirable. If you do find that you or young people in your life are experiencing any side effect, please go back to the doctor or nurse and talk to them. Contraception is supposed to be something to help you take control of your life, not make it more difficult. For those that do struggle with hormonal contraceptives, there are other options available to you.

# Non-hormonal contraception

**IUD** is short for the intrauterine device – but is more commonly known as the coil. The predecessor to the IUS, it is a small T-shaped device, that has copper coiled around its neck. Unlike the IUS the IUD is hormone free. Instead the copper coil acts as a spermicide, as copper ions are harmful to sperm. Again, it is inserted so it sits inside of the uterus; this has to be done by a trained doctor (not all GPs are able to insert an IUD). This is another one of our LARCs as it can be left in place between 5 and 10 years, depending on the type fitted. However, having an IUD fitted, again can be uncomfortable, as a speculum is used before the IUD is implanted inside of the womb with a special applicator. This can make the cervix go into spasm, which can be quite uncomfortable. But the plus side is that is your contraception sorted for over five years. This can be a very effective form of contraception – however, some women do experience painful cramps and heavy periods, making this form of birth control not compatible.

**Diaphragms and cervical caps** are dome-shaped devices (of either latex or silicone) that fit into the vagina and are designed to sit over the cervix, covering the entrance to the womb. Cervical caps are smaller and need to be put directly onto the cervix. Both are supposed to be used with spermicides which is a gel that is rubbed along the rim and the dome – spermicide gel contains chemicals that kill sperm, but have also been known to damage the balance of the bacterial flora in the vagina and may cause issues such as thrush and Bacterial vaginosis for those that are partially sensitive. Caps and Diaphragms are inserted inside the vagina before sex but can be left in place for a number of hours. As a result, they can be a little fiddly and may take a little getting used to before you're confident using them. After sex they must be left in pace for at least six hours (meaning you can fall asleep with them in and remove them in the morning) in order for the spermicide to work properly. Due to the fact they rely on being put in place correctly every time, neither are as effective as other methods of contraception.

**Fertility awareness/rhythm method**: involves monitoring your body temperature and cervical mucus in order to track the changes in your menstrual cycle and highlight your most fertile days. This can be done as a means to conceive or avoid pregnancy. If you are using this as a means to avoid becoming pregnant, then it means you must abstain from sex on your most fertile days. Whilst this is an option for those who cannot take hormone treatments for whatever reasons, it does take a lot of commitment and requires a few months of collecting data to get a true picture of your cycle. Things can be further complicated by having a naturally irregular cycle, from becoming ill or particularly stressed as these can cause fluctuations in your cycle. Another key drawback means you have to avoid sex on particular days – regardless of whether or not that is convenient or how aroused you may be – indeed, biologically you are designed to become more aroused when you are most fertile as a natural side effect of the hormones that control your cycle.

Finally, we have our barrier methods – the condom and femidom:

**The condom** is a sheath of extremely thin latex or often these days plastic, that fits over an erect penis before penetration. Equally a **femidom** (or female condom) works in a similar way but is inserted inside the vagina before penetrative sex. It is anchored in place with a plastic ring that sits inside the sheath. Both are different to all the other methods of contraception we have covered so far, as they put a physical barrier between both partner's bodies, restricting the transmission of sexual fluids from one partner to the other. This is not only effective in preventing pregnancy but also the transmission of infections too. Condoms are the recommended form of contraception to use with a new partner for this reason. The slight drawback to both, is that they have to be put on during sex – condoms especially require you to already have an erection before they can be used, making them a bit of a faff and a distraction. Although, as with anything, practice makes perfect and the more you use them the quicker and easier it becomes. Condoms and femidoms are both single use and should be disposed of hygienically after use.

There are also permanent forms of contraception known as **sterilisation**, although these are rarely an option for young people, unless there are underlying health conditions. A **vasectomy**, is available for those with testes, which involves having the tubes that carry sperm from the testicles back into the body cut and tied. Equally, for those with ovaries, can have their fallopian tubes cut, tied or blocked preventing the passing of a mature egg into the womb. These are both designed as permanent forms of contraception and are considered as irreversible. Although, on rare occasions tubes have been known to re-join – but those opting for these options are informed they are expected to be permanent.

Remember, none of the information in this chapter is designed to give you clinical advice, and instead is to merely give an overview to help you feel better informed of the options available. It is always recommended that anyone thinking of using contraceptives makes an appointment with a nurse or doctor before making any decision. Whilst it is amazing to have so many options available, it is worth bearing in mind, one size does not fit all. Sometimes it can take a little while to finds what works best for you or your teen. Our job as parents or safe adults is to be there to support in the meantime.

# References

Guillebaud, J. (2004). *Contraception: Your questions answered*, 4th edition, Churchill, Livingstone.
Lister, K. (2020). *A Curious History of Sex*, Unbound, London.

# CHAPTER 9

# MAKING SEX SAFE: SEXUALLY TRANSMITTED INFECTIONS

**W**hen I first started working in sexual health and RSE, the project I worked for used to deliver a workshop about STIs. Essentially, it consisted of a mix and match card sort activity, where students would have to match STIs with a description of their symptoms, treatment and an overly graphic picture of infected genitals. Many of us will have endured similar lessons, back in the day, where you were shown equally graphic medical photographs of infected body parts that displayed symptoms of infection. This serves absolutely no beneficial purpose, other than guaranteeing some poor lad faints (it always seems to be a lad!) in front of their classmates, whilst making the rest of the group feel nauseous or horrified.

This practice is the RSE equivalent of delivering a cooking course, where no food prep takes place, no knife skills, no actual cooking or eating and instead the entire session is focused on sorting horrific pictures of the effects of food poisoning. It is hardly practical and certainly not empowering for anyone involved – instead, like much of our RSE it is focused on messages of fear and shame. Most people leave these sessions thinking that people who catch STIs must be stupid, reckless and dirty. None of these opinions encourage open conversations about your STI status with prospective partners. Instead, conversations are tainted with accusations of the content of your character or personal hygiene.

DOI: 10.4324/9781003122296-15

# You do not get an STI because you sleep around or are dirty

Let's get a few myths out of the way. You do not catch a sexually transmitted infection because you are dirty, unclean or because you sleep around. You do not get an infection because you are particularly irresponsible or reckless. You catch them simply because you happened to have unprotected sex with someone who happens to have one.

An important point to remember is that many people who have an STI will not display any obvious symptoms, meaning people can be walking around oblivious to the fact they may be infectious. This is why it is so important to get yourself tested regularly, especially after any instance of unprotected sex – or when changing partner. This should be the key message and a much more helpful one than horror pictures of oozing genitals.

Generally, the definition of a sexually transmitted infection is kind of what it says on the tin – it is an infection, primarily passed on through the sexual fluids bodies make when getting ready for, or during sex – mainly semen, pre-ejaculatory fluid and vaginal fluid. Although some STIs are transmitted in other bodily fluids such as blood (e.g. Syphilis, Hepatitis and HIV) and can be passed on through other means. Equally, there are also a few that are passed on through close body to body contact through infected tissue such as genital warts and genital herpes or parasites such as scabies and pubic lice.

# What's the difference between an STI and an STD?

I know many of you will be thinking what happened to STDs? When I was at school, STIs were more commonly referred to as sexually transmitted diseases, and often the two terms are used interchangeably as synonyms – but this is not completely accurate. There is a difference between an STI and an STD. Technically, a disease has to cause some change in normal bodily function to be classed as a disease, whereas a person may have an infection (a foreign entity in their system) but not yet have any symptoms or changes in bodily functions. For example, chlamydia: the majority of people who contract chlamydia will not display any noticeable symptoms for some time – this is one of the reasons it is so prolific and the most common STI in the UK accounting for 49% of all new infections in 2019 (PHE). However, a Chlamydia infection can cause all sorts of problems if not treated, leading to Pelvic Inflammatory Disease (PID).

The term STI is not only the favoured term as it is more accurate a description in most cases, but also it was seen as having less stigma attached, compared with the term STD.

# How do you know if you have an STI?

The most common symptoms for having an STI include unusual discharge, from either the penis, vagina or anus. For those with a vagina, as we have discussed previously, vaginal discharge is perfectly normal and will change naturally throughout your monthly cycle, and everyone will be slightly different – some people produce more discharge than others – so the term unusual discharge can be a little vague and unhelpful. It means unusual for you. It may change consistency, colour, volume or odour. Healthy vaginal discharge doesn't smell bad – it smells like a vagina. This is why it is so important to get to know and pay attention to your normal discharge.

Other common symptoms can include a stinging sensation when peeing; pain during sex; tenderness in the lower abdomen; visible sores or blisters. However, it is common for STIs to be asymptomatic.

The only way to be 100% sure of your STI status is to get tested. You do not need to have had many partners to have an STI, you may only have slept with one person once and simply be unlucky.

# How are STIs treated?

Good news though: the majority of STIs are completely curable and all are treatable. The majority of infections are bacterial in nature, meaning you can take antibiotics and you are all clear. The most common two infections are chlamydia and gonorrhoea, both of which, whilst completely curable, can lead to PID and infertility if left untreated. It is worth mentioning that gonorrhoea is developing strains that are becoming resistant to the antibiotics we have available. This is why you will be asked to come back into clinic after treatment to be retested to make sure the antibiotics have worked properly.

Syphilis was almost irradicated in this country, however in recent years, like a boy-band from the noughties, has been making a bit of a come-back. Syphilis is a blood born, bacterial infection that ravaged Europe in the sixteenth century and only really became contained with the development of penicillin. At one time, Syphilis would lead to severe health conditions including blindness, paralysis, stroke, dementia and heart failure. However, it is very rare nowadays to reach tertiary stage of infection. On a positive note, the development of the condom as a means of protecting against STIs is largely down to attempts to slow the spread of Syphilis, as is the invention of the merkin – or pubic wig – as one of the symptoms of syphilis, and especially its previous treatment of prescribing mercury would cause sufferers' pubic hair to fall out. Sex workers would hide their sores, and their pubic hair loss from potential clients using a merkin – especially effective in dark alleyways.

There are still a few STIs that can't be 'cured' per-say. These are those infections that are virus based: HIV, Hepatitis, Herpes and Human Papillomavirus (HPV) but that doesn't mean they can't be treated.

Hepatitis A, B and C can all be passed on sexually, and causes an inflammation of the liver. For most people their bodies will naturally fight off the infection and they will be clear of the virus over time. However, some people can go on to develop chronic Hepatitis B and C. There are no specific treatments for Hepatitis, although antiviral medication may be prescribed to manage chronic conditions. There are vaccinations available for Hepatitis A and B which can be given to at-risk groups or people travelling to countries with high level of the disease.

Genital Herpes is caused by the Herpes Simplex Virus (HSV). There are two types, HSV 1 and HSV 2, and both can infect the genital and anal area and also the mouth and nose, causing what we commonly call cold sores. Some people will come into contact with the virus but will never have any symptoms, others will have repeated outbreaks. The virus is more likely to be spread through contact with open sores but can be passed on through sexual fluids in some cases even if the person is asymptomatic. Equally, if you have a cold sore you can pass on the virus through oral sex, and vice versa. There are topical treatments for visible sores, or alternatively you may be prescribed antiviral tablets, both of which can reduce the time an outbreak lasts for – although, they won't clear the virus from your body completely.

HPV is the virus that causes genital warts, although there are over 100 varieties of the virus – only two of which (type 6 and 11) are responsible for genital warts. Most people who are sexually active will have come into contact with a variation of HPV, but few people will ever develop visible warts. Most warts will disappear in time by themselves, however they can become uncomfortable and unsightly. They can be removed with either special topical creams or you can have them frozen at a clinic. These treatments can take time to be effective and warts may return as neither treatments remove the virus from the body. Some people will have a single outbreak, other will suffer with repeated episodes.

HPV has also been linked to cervical, throat and all cancers. In particular, strains 16 and 18 of HPV can cause cell changes that can lead to cervical cancer. However, in recent years young women in year 8 (aged 12+) were offered the HPV vaccination in school to help combat the prevalence of cervical cancer whilst also offering protection against developing genital warts.

Originally, there was some strong opposition to the jab as it prevents an illness caused by an STI and some people argued this was somehow sexualising young girls or would encourage them to become promiscuous. This is clearly nonsense. It is simply a vaccination to prevent one of the most common cancers in women.

In September 2019, the HPV jab was made available to boys too, after fights by campaigners. The immunisation programme has now been widened to include all young people, not just girls. There has been a fall in genital warts diagnosis because of the HPV vaccine and a fall in cervical cancer too.

HIV is an infection that first burst into the public consciousness in the early 1980s with the famous tombstone public health campaign which followed a national panic about this new disease, largely due to the lack of understanding about how it was transmitted, its connection with the gay scene of the day. Indeed, Russell T. Davis's heart-breaking TV series *It's a Sin*, which aired in February 2021, documents this moment in time as homophobia was rife and HIV was labelled as the Gay Disease. *It's a Sin* has been rightly been lauded with acclaim and credited with putting HIV back on the agenda, as HIV has slipped from public consciousness in recent years. Unfortunately, for most adults their only knowledge of the disease comes from the old plot line in EastEnders of Mark Fowler.

Fortunately, there have been huge strides in HIV treatment and prognosis in recent years, including U=U, PEP and most recently the uncapped roll-out of PrEP on the NHS. Indeed, in the UK HIV has been de-classified from a terminal illness, to a chronic illness – meaning that there is no reason why a patient who is HIV+ with medication can't live a full and active life. Nevertheless, most of these developments have gone largely unnoticed by the general public, without any national public health campaigns to champion these success stories. Instead, the public consciousness is still set to the original stigma and ignorance surrounding the illness. So, let's spend a little time bringing you up to speed.

### What everyone should know about HIV

HIV is short for Human Immunodeficiency Virus. Which all sounds very complicated but if we break it down it is actually pretty self-explanatory. HIV is a virus, which uses the cells of its host in order to replicate; in this case humans. The immunodeficiency bit, tells you what it does; HIV attacks the cells of the immune system, the very cells which help to fight off illnesses in our bodies. Eventually the immune system becomes so compromised that other illnesses we would usually be able to deal with become more serious and potentially deadly.

HIV infects vital cells in the human immune system such as T-helper cells – specifically those where CD4 protein is present, as it uses this protein to replicate. As a result, the infected person's immune system starts to fail. Once an individual with HIV develops a number of particular resulting illnesses, they are said to have AIDS: Acquired Immune Deficiency Syndrome.

Now this is where many of the misconceptions come in. You can't catch AIDS – it's not actually a thing, per-say. There is lack of understanding between the differences between HIV and AIDS as the terms are often mixed up and misused, especially within the media. To clarify, HIV is the illness you catch from another individual. When someone has HIV they are said to be HIV+. AIDS is simply a term we use to mean that a person is in the final stage of infection and their immune system is compromised. A person cannot catch or pass on AIDS.

**Did you know...**

Whilst we can now test for HIV using saliva swabs, bodily fluids such as urine, sweat or saliva do not contain enough of the virus to infect another person. You can't get HIV from spitting, coughing, sneezing, shaking hands, kissing, hugging, sharing cutlery or cups, sharing towels, toilet seats, or by using public swimming baths.

Whilst HIV is present in other bodily fluids, the most likely route of transmission is through unprotected sex. Both vaginal fluid (including cervical mucus) and semen can carry the HIV virus, so it is easily passed between heterosexual couples engaging in vaginal sex as well as through anal sex. There is still much discussion and argument about whether HIV can be passed through oral sex, however it is classed as a low-risk activity.

In order for infection to occur, the virus must be present in an individual, plus there must be a clear route of transmission from that individual to another. Simply coming into contact with an infected fluid is not enough, there must exist a route for the infection to be moved from one person's body into another. Inside the body HIV is very resilient, hard to contain or to destroy; however, outside of the body HIV is relatively fragile, surviving for next to no time in the open air. For this reason, there is nothing else you need to do, other than to follow usual health and safety guidelines for dealing with a person who is HIV+ when administrating first aid. There is no risk of transmission from spilt blood, vomit, urine or saliva – simply wear gloves and clean up in the normal way.

## PEP

Not many people are aware of PEP (post-exposure prophylaxis), which is an emergency treatment that can be given to someone who has become exposed to HIV as a last result, for example if a condom breaks. PEP will reduce the chances of them contracting the virus and becoming HIV+. PEP is not a cure and is not 100% effective, nor is it given to everyone. PEP is basically a four-week course of antiretroviral treatment (ART) which must be taken within 72 hours (at the latest) of exposure to the virus. You can be prescribed PEP from specialist sexual health and HIV services or from A&E.

In the UK, when giving blood transfusions all blood products are now screened for HIV and other illnesses, however this was not always the case; many haemophiliacs contracted both HIV and Hepatitis through infected blood product brought in from the USA due to shortages to be used for transfusions during the 1980s. It was thought over 5,000 people were infected with tainted blood products as a result, many of whom have since died. In July 2017, Theresa May finally announced after decades of refusing to accept responsibility for the scandal, and continued campaigning by victims and their families, there would be a public inquiry into contaminated blood. The Infected Blood Inquiry, chaired by Sir Brian Langstaff, is still ongoing.

Upon transmission most people experience flu-like symptoms, but this can be short-lived and most people will feel fine for some time after the initial infection. This poses a problem, as it is those who are undiagnosed that are a danger. Those who know their HIV status will be put on ART. HIV medication works by reducing the amount of the virus in the blood (viral load) to undetectable levels. This means the levels of HIV are so low that the virus can't be passed on – even through unprotected sex. We now have robust evidence to conclude that if one is on effective treatment there is *zero* chance of passing on the virus to a partner through unprotected sex – commonly known as Undetectable = Untransmittable or U=U.[1]

## PrEP: Pre-exposure prophylaxis

PrEP is a drug treatment for people who don't currently have HIV but who are at a high risk of contracting the virus. The roll-out of uncapped PrEP in England began on Thursday 1 October after clinical trials and another lengthy court case to force the NHS to provide the preventative measure as part of the NHS. As a result PrEP is now available for free on the NHS from some sexual health clinics but not all. PrEP is one of the new tools in reducing HIV transmission for those at high risk of contracting the virus.

Likewise, Testing has improved greatly over the last couple of years. It is possible to get an HIV test with accurate results from four weeks after potential infection. Results can be returned between 60 seconds or 2 weeks, depending on the test type. The test does not detect the virus itself but looks for the presence of antibodies your body has developed to fight the infection.

At one time, HIV was seen as a life sentence – now, with new treatments available, there is no reason why a person can't have partners, enjoy sex, have children and live a full, happy and healthy life. However, there are still huge disparages in life expectancy, treatment and health outcomes around the world. Poverty and government policy have played a huge part in inequality and the prevalence of this illness in parts of the world.

**Why you should always pee after sex**

There are a number of other infections that are not strictly classified as STIs but can be caused by sexual intercourse. Most common are things like urinary tract infections such as Cystitis, caused when bacteria from the anus or vagina makes its way into the urethra; or conditions such as thrush or bacterial vaginosis (BV), caused by imbalances in the bacteria flora. All of these conditions disproportionately affect women (BV only occurs for people with a vagina). This is partly due to the delicate balance of bacteria in the vagina, and also due to the anatomical design of the urethra being much shorter in women. There can be many cases of these conditions, however they can be caused through sex. Unfortunately, some women are particular prone to Thrush, Cystitis and BV.

**Top tip**

The safe-sex message we should be giving to all young people – especially girls is:

**ALWAYS PEE AFTER SEX.**

It is simple and easy to do but can greatly reduce your risks of infections such as cystitis. That does not mean you can't have a cuddle but it is a great habit to get into for all involved.

**Protecting against STIs**

A simple question: if we all know we should, why do people fail to use condoms? The majority of people are well aware that condoms (or a femidom – but not both together!) are the only methods of contraception to prevent against the transmission of the majority of sexually transmitted infections[2] – however, people still fail to use condoms regularly with new partners.

A 2017 YouGov survey of over 2,000 young people aged between 16 and 24 in the UK discovered that almost half (47%) of the young people surveyed failed to use a condom with a new partner (YouGov, 2017).

In 2019, there were 468,342 diagnoses of STIs made in England, a 5% increase since 2018 (PHE). Condoms are not new… so why are we still so bad at using them?

A quick point to make: don't think that it is just young people who are the issue when it comes to condom use. Adults are just as bad – in fact, I would wager worse. As we get older, sex and relationships do not become easier, or simpler. Adults make the same mistakes young people do – the only difference is, you don't have to explain to your mum when you get home. Just because you get to the age of 30 doesn't mean you suddenly have all the answers and magically become able to openly discuss your sexual health with a new partner – if anything, we accumulate more baggage as we get older. For example, between 2018 and 2019 there were increases in gonorrhoea, chlamydia and syphilis reported in *all age groups* of people aged 15 years and older – including the over-65s (YouGov, 2017).[3]

There are lots of reasons why (young) people would fail to use a condom. The obvious answer is inconvenience. As mentioned earlier when we discussed contraception, one of the key issues in using a condom is the fact you have to interrupt what you are doing in order to put it on. You are happily making out and enjoying yourselves but then you have to stop what you are doing, put the brakes on… as you open your bedside drawer, root around at the back to find one, check it's still in date, try to get the darn thing open, eventually resort to using your teeth to rip the thing open, faff around working out which way it unrolls, before trying to roll it on an increasingly diminishing erection, as your penis has become distracted by all the hassle and has decided it is no longer in the mood.

This is me being facetious – there is no reason why using a condom can't be incorporated into the sex you are having. With just a small bit of fore-thought, it is very easy to make condoms simply part of the action. But here is the issue – it takes planning. Sex is not always planned. People do not always carry condoms or expect sex to occur. It is easy to get caught up in the moment and in the fog of passion, common sense can get lost.

A few years ago, I was involved in a study designed to increase the uptake of young people's condom use (Newby et al.). I was employed to work with a project board of young people to explore some of the issues and reasons why young people fail to use condoms and to help design interventions that would tackle the problem. We have touched on two points that came out clearly in the voices of young people during the study, which need a little more explanation. Firstly, fear of losing your erection is a real issue for young men. Yes, I joked about it earlier to make a point about the inconvenience of pausing during a sexual encounter to put on a condom. However, this can be a huge barrier for some young men. If it has happened once, it can play on people's mind. As we talked about in the anatomy chapter of this book, you can't will an erection into being. It is controlled by the autonomic nervous system so is completely unconscious. It only takes a panicked experience as you struggle with a condom, worried your partner will be thinking you clearly do not know what you're doing and must be inexperienced, for the insecurities to set in and things begin to flop.

The mind works by association – suddenly, thereafter every time you reach for the condom packet, that shadow of doubt begins to pull at the recess of your confidence and things begin to flop.

Fear of losing one's erection is a real reason why some young men are wary to use a condom. But there is hope – practice makes perfect. A lot of the anxiety comes from fiddling around trying to put a condom on – like any skill, the more you do it the easier it gets.

One of the outcomes of the research study (Newby et al., 2017) was to employ young men as 'condom testers', the idea being, the more comfortable they became with experimenting with condoms by themself, the more confidence they would have when it came to using them with a partner; this is why, amongst private circles, the study became known as the *posh-wank study*.[4]

Another key point we have touched on is the issue of actually carrying condoms. If you have social scripts that are highly gendered that dictate your role in a sexual situation, this creates certain pressures that are difficult to overcome. The ridiculous thing is, young people often tell me that they were carrying condoms at the time, they just didn't want to pull it out because they were worried what their partner may think! The fear being confusion. Young men worry that their female partner will assume they were expecting sex if they are come to an encounter carrying condoms – their being prepared confused as expectation. Equally, young women explain they would be worried that their partner thought they must sleep around if they carry condoms…

This point was demonstrated nicely during a conversation at a post-16 training provider. I was working with a group of young women aged 16–18 who were all training to be hairdressers and beauticians. We were talking about carrying condoms and they all agreed that in this day and age, women should carry condoms and insist on their partners using them. They were clear carrying condoms was the responsible thing to do for both guys and girls.

During the session they talked openly about female empowerment and seemed to have very positive attitudes to sex. However, later in the session, I thought I would come back to the conversation. I gave them the scenario of being out in town on a night out – and they have walked into the toilets with their mate and as they are stood at the mirror a girl they don't know is touching up her lipstick in the mirror and her bag falls over on the counter and a couple of condoms fall out. I asked what they would say to their mate once the girl had walked out? Without pause, not even a heartbeat had passed before three or four of the group shouted out: 'Slag', 'Slapper', 'Hoe'…

When there is this amount of stigma attached to carrying condoms, daft decisions like carrying them but not using them, start to make sense.

### Look for the teachable moments…

So as parents, or as the safe adults in our children's lives what can we do to break the stigma? The answer is the same as I have already said – make them familiar. Encourage your teens to get used to having them around, touching them and carrying them. Similar to what we do with menstrual pads and tampons, give them something discreet to carry them in when they start going to parties. Encouraging teens to carry condoms is not the same as encouraging them to have sex. It is encouraging them to be prepared, to take responsibility for themselves, their partners. It is all about a change in attitude – and that can be led by example.

Unfortunately, condoms are rarely spoken about in films or drama. On the rare occasion they are mentioned, it is more often negatively, as if they take away from a sexual experience. The old adage of wearing a condom being like taking a bath with your socks on, or variations of the sentiment, is still repeated. Regardless, you can still use these as teachable moments to raise the subject of what they should be doing in that situation, or to question the narrative. There have been a few more positive TV dramas recently that have taken a more positive approach such as Netflix *Sex Education*, and BBCs *Normal People*, both of which are small rays of light in sex positive messaging. Condoms these days, especially those made of plastics, are getting thinner and thinner. The average condom is now thinner than a human hair! If you really believe that a condom, being the only thing between two people's writhing, sweaty bodies, as they touch and kiss, is really going to ruin the experience, you are doing it wrong.

Condoms should not detract from an experience, they should enhance it. Condoms should not be seen as an insinuation you think your partner is dirty, unclean or has slept around. It is a sign you care about their physical and emotional health. Carrying condoms is not presumptuous – it is responsible. Only by repeating these messages when we talk, whether seriously or in the off-hand comments we make on the storylines in the soaps and dramas we are watching, can we change the narrative.

> If you work with young people…
> Show them where their nearest clinic is, take them if you can or speak to the clinic and ask if they can come and talk to your young people. At least pop by and ask for some condoms to keep on site. Most services will help where they can.

I would firmly recommend if you have teenagers in the house visiting your GP or local sexual health service and getting some condoms for free to have in the house. You do not have to make a big deal about it but just put them somewhere they can be seen and accessed – leave them in the bathroom drawer or cupboard or, if there are younger siblings in the house you want to keep them secret from, put them in the teenager's bedside table. If you get them from sexual health services, they will usually come with a small leaflet with instructions of how to use them – it is a good idea to put this in the drawer with the condoms. Oh and don't comment when a few go missing – more than likely they were just trying them out by themselves. Or, as I mentioned earlier, you can get small discreet carry cases that can fit in your purse or bag as you would with menstrual products. Make them available and make sure they know you are happy for them to carry them.

I know for some parents this suggestion may not sit very comfortably; and I understand why. From my experience I have not seen any evidence that providing young people with condoms encourages them to have sex earlier. No more than making menstrual products available to daughters encourages them to start their periods any earlier. Instead, they merely translate the message that when they are ready, you understand and are there to support them. For me, it is all about opening doors and reinforcing the message – this is not something you need to feel ashamed about or something we can't talk about. It is that simple.

If you are really brave you could even sit down and show them how to put one on! To help, I have written out my step-by step instructions, how I would explain and perform a condom demon, should care to use them…

Whilst this is one thing that happens in most schools (and yes, we can all remember the giggles and embarrassment that filled the room), but it will be unlikely that your teenager took much from the session other than the collective feeling of being uncomfortable, or that they actually had the opportunity to do it themselves – it is more than likely they simply watched a very uncomfortable teacher demonstrate it on a plastic penis.[5] Having the opportunity to be shown in a less pressured or public environment can be extremely helpful, especially if they are then left with some to practise with. If you work with young people yourself, do what I do and use the excuse of needing to practise for work. Explain you have been on some training and need to be able to demonstrate and ask them to help you – again, this helps to provide a bit of distance and switches the dynamic from you lecturing them to them helping you. To be fair, I taught my daughter how to count to 12 when she was very little by helping me count condoms into paper bags ready for a distribution drop-in I used to run… although I am not sure she remembers that!

### How to put on a condom

There was a time when all I seemed to do at one point is perform condom demonstrations in classrooms… I do far fewer these days. I find most of my sessions are directed at exploring and unpicking people's attitudes to sex and creating a safe space for them to have conversations about sex they aren't able to elsewhere. It is often a better use of my time rather than talking about STIs and waving condoms around; however, it is something we should never assume everyone knows how to do so let's make sure we all know how to do it properly. In clinical trials condoms are 98% effective – in real life that drops because we mere mortals make mistakes (and don't live in labs with people in white coats).

1. **Check the expiry date.** Yes, condoms have dates on them. Most condoms have a five-year shelf life so this is something you can do before you put them away in your drawer or check periodically, rather than *in the moment!* Out-of-date condoms are more likely to break.[6]
2. **Look for the CE or British Standard Kite mark.** Like any product, condoms should meet certain requirements – those that do have safety standard marks. Unfortunately, you can purchase condoms that do not carry the mark – in small letters on the box they will say 'not to be used for contraceptive purposes'! What are you using them for… a puppet show?!

3. **Wash your hands.** Not only is it hygienic to makes sure your hands are clean before you start putting them on your partner's most intimate parts but oils from your hands can damage latex condoms. Massage oils, suntan cream, moisturiser, Vaseline – or even the grease from a bag of chips or pizza – can damage a condom.

4. **When opening the wrapper, look for the serrated edge.** It is much easier to rip open. It is best if you push the condom to one side first, away from where you are opening to make sure you don't damage the condom by mistake. If you really need to use your teeth (not advised as they are sharp!) again, push the condom to the side and out of the way first.

5. **Squeeze the condom out of the wrapper.** You don't want to be jabbing your sharp nails into the condom and creating a tear.

6. **Make sure it is the right way around.** Condoms will only roll on one way – if you get it wrong, it will end up looking like a little shower hat for your nob – and you will need to throw it away and start again (as any sexual fluids that are leaking naturally from the end of the penis will now be on the outside when you flip it round). The best way to check is think of a wizard's hat. A wizard's hat has a point and then a brim at the bottom. If you hold the teat of the condom between your thumb and forefinger, and then run a finger down the condom, if it gets caught in the rim, it is round the right way – if it pings off the side, you will need to flip it round… now you can roll it on your magic wand!

7. **Place the rolled-up condom on the tip of the penis.** Keeping the condom between your thumb and forefinger, place the condom on the head of the penis. With the other hand, gently roll it down the shaft – all the way to the bottom. Be careful not to curl your fingers under the condom – it isn't a swimming cap.

8. **Add lube (if you like).** Lubricant is a completely underrated tool – when it comes to sex, the wetter the better. This can help prevent the condom from slipping and can just feel great and add new sensations. Just make sure you use water-based lube with latex condoms, as oil-based lube can damage the condom.[7]

9. **Enjoy.**

10. **Withdraw.** Hold the base of the condom as you pull out to prevent it from slipping off – it is not unusual for penises to take a little nap after ejaculation and start to become flaccid. Take off the condom away from your partner's body and tie a knot in the end of it, making sure the fluid stays trapped inside. Dispose of the condom hygienically, in a bin. DO NOT FLUSH THEM DOWN THE TOILET.

# A few extra points to remember…

It is worth mentioning, you can pass on STIs through all types of sex, including using your hands during manual sex, using your mouth during oral sex, and through both vaginal and anal sex. If there is any transmission of sexual fluids you are at risk. You can get chlamydia and gonorrhoea in the throat. This is why they make flavoured condoms and dental dams – as protection during oral sex.

Dental dams are small rectangular pieces of very thin latex that can be laid across the vulva or anus during oral sex (flavoured condoms are designed for oral sex only for those who have a penis). Whilst these are available and often come flavoured, admittedly they still taste like kissing a rubber glove so are not widely used. When it comes to safe sex, we are constantly balancing what is safe and what is enjoyable – but it is worth pointing out that oral sex, whilst less risky, is not risk free of transmission.

Indeed, some people – who are particularly safety conscious or may be aware they are at high risk of contracting STIs as they have multiple partners – may choose to wear surgical gloves during sex too.

Condoms are designed for single use only. They are not designed to be used on multiple partners and if you are switching from anal to vaginal sex you need to swap condoms – otherwise you run the risk of transferring harmful bacteria.

Finally, it is essential as a parent or a safe adult working with young people, that you are aware of where your nearest sexual health service is and when it is open. When it comes to sexual health we are often very reactive. We wait until something has gone wrong and then panic before trying to find or visiting a service. It is the only part of our health we treat this way. Most people visit the dentist every six months for a quick check-up, regardless of whether their teeth hurt or not… there is no reason why our sexual health should be any different. At worst, you can stock up on free condoms.

# Notes

1  The landmark PARTNER 1 study (2014) looked at over 58,000 instances of sex without a condom, where one partner was HIV positive and one was HIV negative. There were zero cases of HIV transmission in couples where the HIV positive

partner was on effective treatment ('undetectable'). Due to the participants, the statistical certainty of the PARTNER 1 study was slightly lower for receptive anal sex with ejaculation than it was for vaginal sex. However, the PARTNER 2 study (2018), which looked at only instances of condomless anal sex, showed zero transmissions for both same-sex male couples and heterosexual couples. As a results of both these studies, scientists have robust evidence to conclude the chance of any HIV-positive person with an undetectable viral load transmitting the virus to a sexual partner is scientifically equivalent to zero. Recent combined studies PARTNER 1 and PARTNER 2, with 2017's Opposites Attract study, together make up approximately 126,000 episodes of condomless sex between partners, with no transmissions. We can now say with confidence, that people on effective HIV treatment can't pass on the virus.

2 Condoms protect against the transfer of sexual fluids keeping one partner's fluids on the inside and the others on the outside of the sheath. Although condoms don't protect against all possible infections; there are some that are passed on through close body to body contact – such as pubic lice, warts or herpes. Parasites can pass from one partner to the next regardless of condom use; equally, if there are warts or sores that are left uncovered by the condom.

3 The largest proportional increase in people aged 20 to 24 years for gonorrhoea (28%; from 13,623 to 17,443), people aged 35 to 44 years for chlamydia (17%; from 15,462 to 18,134) and people aged 65 years and older for syphilis (27%; from 115 to 146). Genital herpes diagnoses increased in people aged 20 to 24 years (2%; from 9,334 to 9,564), 25 to 34 years (4%; from 11,841 to 12,295), 35 to 44 years (5%; from 4,348 to 4,572) and 65 years and older (17%; from 344 to 402).

4 To be clear – this is NOT its official title and was only used by some of the professionals involved amongst themselves for amusement.

5 Having spoken to many adults of their past experiences of sex education I have heard of all manner of objects being used for condom demos. Very popular at one time were bananas and cucumbers; I have also heard of broom handles, the legs of stools and one person told me about their school that had specially designed metal rods…

However, there are properly designed demonstrators available to educations that are more appropriate. It is worth mentioning if you are demonstrating with a young person on the autistic spectrum, it is recommended you use a life-like demonstrator – as using fruit or something abstract can be confusing. As you will know, you will equally need to be very clear and explicit in how you explain and give your instructions.

6 I am a truly awful person. As I said, back in the day when I first started off in sexual health, I used to work for a youth work project, we used to deliver sessions, mainly in secondary schools, all across the city where I worked. We would regularly perform condom demos as part of these sessions. As part of the demo, I used to show the difference between a condom that was in date and one that had expired. The condom in date you could stretch like a resistance band, as you pulled your arms wide, quite happily (they will stretch to fit

on your head or you can wear them like a sock (not that we did that in class!) so anyone who says they don't fit is lying!)

Anyway, I would also carry out-of-date condoms and then show, when you tried to stretch them, they would snap – quite dramatically – with very little effort. This one time, as I stretched the out-of-date condom, it snapped as usual but this time it slipped out of my hand and floated with embarrassing precision to land in this poor girl's hair – and as luck would have it she had big frizzy hair too! I felt awful – this poor girl just went bright red and looked horrified… I, of course, apologised and did my best to make amends.

I learned my lesson, and afterwards stood well back from unsuspecting students during demos. As time went by and I continued to deliver session across the city; occasionally when the condom snapped part would again fly off and land like sexual shrapnel on the desk or floor and I would occasionally comment off-hand as (what I thought at the time) an amusing comment that it had once landed in a girl's hair…

One day (maybe two years later) I mentioned the story in the class I was teaching; suddenly the room erupted and everyone pointed at this poor girl! I hadn't recognised her but there she was in the room! I had managed to humiliate her not once but now twice doing the same demo! This girl must hate me – and rightly so. I deserve it. If you are reading this, I apologise sincerely for all the embarrassment I have caused. I am truly sorry.

7   If you are going to use lube – try to find one that is natural. It is ridiculous that KY Jelly is used as standard by many health care professionals, even though it contains glycerine and parabens, which are known to cause irritation in some women leading to conditions such as thrush and BV. Equally, many of the products on the supermarket shelves and well-known brands are not properly balanced and contain the same irritants. However, there are better products on the market. I always recommend Yes products: www.yesyesyes.org/blog/the-science-of-lubricants/

# References

Newby, K., Brown, K., Bayley, J., Kehal, I., Caley, M., Danahay, A., Hunt, J. and Critchley, G. (2017). Development of an intervention to increase sexual health service uptake by young people. *Health Promotion Practice*, 18.

Public Health England (PHE) (2020). Sexually transmitted infections and screening for chlamydia in England, 2019: The annual official statistics data release (data to end of December 2019). Published 17 June, updated 14 October. Available at: www.gov.uk/government/statistics/sexually-transmitted-infections-stis-annual-data-tables.

YouGov (2017). Campaign to protect young people from STIs by using condoms. Available at: www.gov.uk/government/news/campaign-to-protect-young-people-from-stis-by-using-condoms.

# CHAPTER 10

# MAKING SEX SAFE: CONSENT AND SEXUAL CITIZENSHIP

**A**ccording to section 74 of the 2003 Sexual offences act, in order to give consent a person legally needs three things: choice, capacity and freedom (Figure 10.1).[1] These tenets are interconnected and do not work in isolation – you can't have one without the other two.

**Capacity** refers to a whether under the circumstances a person has the cognitive ability to make the decision for themselves. There are number of things that could affect a person's capacity: their age, for example. In the UK the age of consent is set at 16, meaning a person under 16 years of age is deemed not to have the capacity to be able to consent to sex as they are thought to be not mature enough and unable to make that decision. If someone has Special Educational Needs or Disabilities (SENDs) they may not be considered to have capacity due to lack of understanding. As with driving a motor vehicle, if someone is drunk, or has taken drugs (whether legal or prescription), this may impede their capacity to make sound decisions. You would think it would go without saying but someone doesn't have capacity if they are unconscious or if they are asleep; unfortunately, there have been a number of cases where people have fallen asleep and woken to find their partner having sex with them. This would clearly not be considered as consensual.

DOI: 10.4324/9781003122296-16

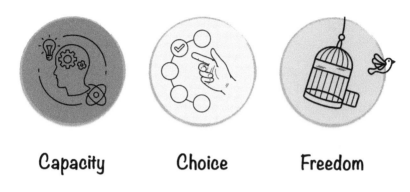

**Figure 10.1** Consent

**Freedom** refers to the emotional, financial and physical freedom to make up one's mind for themselves without consequence. If someone is being groomed, coerced, threatened, either physically, emotionally or financially – it would no longer be considered a free choice.

If a person is deemed not to have capacity or does not have the full freedom to make a choice for themselves, they can't be considered to have consented to sexual intimacy. There is more to consent than a simple yes or no. We also need to take into consideration structural power imbalances and gendered social scripts that lead to inequalities – as consent can only be seen to be given if there is a balance of power.

There is an activity I do, from time to time, when I am delivering year group assemblies to help explore consent. I usually use it with pupils from years 6–8, meaning the students will be between 10 and 13 years old, although I often talk through the activity as an example with older students too as I am going to do now. It provides a practical example of the issues surrounding consent and how we evaluate if it has been given.

Imagine an assembly, usually taking place in the school hall or theatre – basically a big room full of chairs, with all the students sat in rows. I explain to the room I need a couple of volunteers to help me with a brief demonstration – I promise it won't be difficult and I am not going to make them do anything too scary. Now, when you are working with young people of this age, there are still plenty of young people who will stick their hand up without too much persuasion – a little bit like Hermione (however, once you get to year 9, you have no chance – they are all too jaded and cool to volunteer… to be honest, after Pancake day in year 8 you can be pushing it!).

Looking through the sea of hands I try and pick two volunteers; although I purposely ignore all the young people with their hands up. The key is to pick young people who aren't staring at their feet petrified, just those that not quite making eye contact. I have got pretty good at judging who can cope and who won't be able to manage with the activity. You may be thinking, what is the point of asking for volunteers if you are going to ignore those that have their hands up? This is exactly the point of the exercise. I pick my two 'volunteers', point at them and ask them to head to the front of the room and join me – where, often to make matters worse, I will be on a stage.

Now every time, without fail,[2] the pupils trudge up to the front of the room like they are going to face a firing squad. I always feel bad as I watch them stare at their feet, refusing to make eye contact with anyone, as they shuffle up to the stage. Once on the stage they look out at their peers, which is a scary sight even for the most confident of young people so I make an effort to keep it quick. I get the volunteers to introduce themselves before asking them if they wanted to come to the front? And they always answer 'NO!', which is hardly surprising giving the manner they walked to the front.

Quickly, I thank them and send them – somewhat bewildered by what has just taken place (*was that it?*) – back to their seats, as I ask the rest of the room to give them a round of applause. Now comes the important part: the debrief. This is the bit that really matters.

Once everyone has settled down, I ask the room at large if they think the 'volunteers' consented to what had happened? I go further and explain that I didn't force them up to the front; it wasn't like I grabbed them by the ear and dragged them to the stage. Each one of them stood up by themselves and made their way to the front under their own steam. If they didn't want to come to the front, why then, did they? No one pulled or pushed them into moving.

The issue is, there is a huge imbalance of power in the room which makes true consent impossible in this situation. I am an adult but, more than that, I am a teacher (of sorts) stood on the stage at the front in charge of the class. Children are told from the day they can understand, they should always do as they are told and respect their elders. This is made worse by the fact I am a guest, and school children are always told to be respectful to guests. Further still, the stakes are raised even further by the handful of teachers positioned around the edge of the room, waiting to jump on anyone who misbehaves. This together creates a powerful imbalance, where it is nigh impossible for a young person to be honest and say the simple phrase, 'No, I don't want to', for fear of being thought of as rude or disrespectful.

However, there is even more added pressure as the room is also full of their peers. They are not only worried of being told off by the staff, but also ridiculed by their peers. If they say no, there is the fear of being called a *'pussy'*.

This is why they cannot and did not consent to the activity. When we get to this point I always apologise – as I have just given an example of how we often remove people's right to consent (which kind of undermines my point and is definitely a failing of the activity). To be honest, whilst it is effective – I have never been completely comfortable with putting young people through the experience of standing up in front of their peers and making them uncomfortable for the sake of the exercise. For this reason, these days, I do what I am doing now and simply talk everyone through the activity, rather than making people stand up and participate.[3]

The point of the activity is to demonstrate there is more to consent than merely waiting for someone to say no. There are deeper social conventions and power dynamics at work, not to mention relationships at stake, culminating in making it sometimes difficult, if not impossible, to say no.

Think about it; even as adults, we have all been in a situation when a friend or colleague has asked us out for a drink after work – but it's been a long day. You really don't feel up to it and just want to go home… and yet, how often do we feel able to simply say, 'No, thank you, I don't want to.' Often we feel the need to go anyway, not wanting to let anyone down or for anyone to think badly of us… or if we are quick thinking enough, we will more than likely follow social convention and make an excuse: 'I am sorry

I can't tonight, I have to visit my mother is in hospital…' Essentially lying in an effort not cause any offence.

Alternatively, when meeting someone new, even offering your hand to someone – there is little choice involved. You can't look at someone's offered hand and turn your nose up without it feeling like a deliberate slight.

There are countless examples where we ignore the notion of other people's consent and personal boundaries in the name of social convention or to be considered polite. This is especially true in how we treat children. We all remember what it was like when we were told to kiss a certain aged relative and how uncomfortable that felt. What message are we sending to children when we force them to kiss someone goodbye, despite their clear discomfort when they refuse? 'Don't be rude – grandma loves you. You will hurt her feelings… and she bought you all those nice things.' Are we really trying to teach our children that if someone tells you they love you and buys you gifts you owe them affection and physical affection in return, regardless of whether you want to or not?

Children learn from the behaviours they see and experience for themselves. What we want is for safe adults to model those positive behaviours we want children to display. And yet, how often do we sacrifice children's comfort in order to please and not offend the adults in the room? Personally, I don't really care if I upset Grandma – she is an adult and should be mature enough to manage her feelings. Although, to be clear, no one is saying that we can't show affection to our kids, or grandkids. No one is saying you can't kiss a child goodbye. Instead, they are merely highlighting one of our teachable moments – this is the perfect opportunity to reinforce a positive message rather than to undermine it. This gives children choice and autonomy.

# Missed opportunities for teachable moments

Lessons of consent should start young. As adults, we spend so much of our time teaching kids how to move their bodies through the world safely (Hirsch and Khan, 2020). There are so many opportunities for us as adults to reinforce positive messages; whether it is asking children if we can help them dress or undress, reminding them when they are playing games not to snatch, or encouragement to use their words to ask for what they want. These simple exchanges can make all the difference to build a mountain of practical experiences of negotiation and communication.

In essence, this is what consent is about. Unfortunately, whilst some of the hard work is already being done, often we miss the opportunity to connect these underlying messages of consent in these everyday interactions.

It is not unusual, for many of the teenagers I speak to in high school, for my session to be the first formal conversation any adult has had with them, explicitly exploring issues of consent. If things had been done correctly, they should have had experience of previous conversations about consent in primary school. Simple messages around safe and appropriate touching: 'No one should touch you without your permission, or in a way you don't like;' they should have heard mantras like: 'My body belongs to me,' and 'Stop and No are important words'. These should have been taught through exploring practical age-appropriate experiences they could relate to in terms of the games children play, of tickling and play fighting. Instead, suddenly they are in a workshop with me talking about sexual consent – this is the maths equivalent of starting off with quadratic equations rather than counting your fingers and toes.

With any luck, this will be changing with the introduction of statutory Relationship Education at primary level.[4] It would be lovely to walk into a room of year 9 pupils who sigh and complain, 'not consent again – we've done this to death!' but we are a long way off that yet.

When young people are lucky enough to receive formal lessons on consent, often conversations are focused around teaching the law (Bragg et al., 2020; Whittington, 2019). It is understandable why teachers, especially those who have not received specialist training, might choose to approach consent through a legal lens (Bragg et al., 2020). The law is solid; it has black and white rules that are set in stone: *the age of consent is 16. It is an offence for anyone to have any sexual activity with a person under the age of 16.* Young people are told the law and that they are not old enough to have sex, as if that is the end of the discussion. Whilst it is important for young people to understand the age of consent, this is not the barrier adults seem to assume it is; young people are well aware some of their peers didn't wait to be 'legal'. Equally, it is a very difficult law to enforce. You do not have the sex police hiding under your bed waiting to jump out and get you when you're 15 if you get a little too fruity with your partner.

Often adults like to state the age of consent as a means to deny young people's sexual citizenship; but the age of consent in practice is not like the legal age to vote – where young people do not get a say until they turn eighteen and their voting card turns up. Sixteen is not a magical age. No one goes to bed the night before their sixteenth birthday, thinking *'Night Mum, night Dad, I'm not ready for sex,'* and then suddenly they wake up the next day, blow the candles out on their cake and boom – they're ready for sex! That's not how it works. Some people are ready before and some people are ready much later.

The age of consent was never intended to prevent teenagers from having sex with each other – the Home Office guidance[5] is clear there is no intention to prosecute teenagers under the age of 16 where both mutually agree and where they are of a similar age. Instead, the age of consent was intended to protect children from adults who might groom and take advantage of them.

Another common message young people receive about consent from the adult brave enough to broach the topic of sex with their teens is, 'If they say no, then no means *no* and you have to stop.' Often the message of 'no means no' comes from well-meaning parents, who don't want their sons to get in trouble. I say sons as this is a message rarely delivered to the young women in our lives, it is reserved for the boys. To a large extent, consent is seen as a gendered issue, as sex is still seen as something men *do* to women, as it is governed by gendered social scripts. As Hirsch and Khan (2020) note in their study into sexual assault on campus at Columbia University in America, none of the women they interviewed had ever considered gaining consent from their male partners in their encounters – they had not even thought about it, as the assumption was guys are always up for sex.

Furthermore, this message adds credence to the notion it is the responsibility of the uncomfortable party to say *'No'* and make their protestations heard, rather than the perpetrating partner to seek permission; i.e. it reinforces the assumption someone has given consent until it is removed. This reduces consent to nothing more than a verbal transaction, and yet, as we have already noted, saying 'no' is far from simple to do.

Indeed, it is rare for discussions in formal lessons to cover the practicalities of how one might seek consent in real-life situations. There is little opportunity given to young people to practice the negotiation and communication skills essential to be able to talk about what you want and what you are not ready to do with a partner. Think about kissing: how many of you have ever asked – or have been asked – for a kiss? Does this mean that the majority of the kisses we have shared were non-consensual?

This is one of my favourite discussions to have with young people, asking them to talk me through how someone might go about kissing someone they fancy at a party. It is hilarious, as they talk you through the strange courtship rituals of body language, giving someone the eye, and their tips for a good bit of *flanter*.[6] *If they look you in your eyes, and then at your lips, and back to your eyes – it means you have something in your teeth… If they start playing with their hair – they might have nits…* The point is, no one ever (or rarely) walks up and asks for a kiss openly – instead we would rather lean in and go for it (hoping they don't pull away or slap you!) than ask. If we struggle to find the words to negotiate a kiss, how are they supposed to have the words to negotiate a sexual encounter.

Consent is rarely sought openly, more often it is interpreted through the implications of other behaviours, rather than spoken out loud. For example, there exists a notion of consent by physical presence – 'why would you invite me up to your room if you didn't want to have sex?' Which seems like a rational response, until you consider an interaction between two Freshers living in halls. A typical student bedroom at university consists of a bed, a desk, a chair and a wardrobe. Wanting to be alone with someone you like and sitting on the bed together (as you would on a sofa) suddenly escalated to a sexual situation due to the simple geography of the setting (Hirsch and Khan, 2020). It is easy to see why it could be confusing when we find it so hard to talk openly about sex. One student may have only invited the other with the intention of making out, but to the other there is an assumption that being 'invited back to their room' implies consent.

If you think back to our Sex Act Cards from Chapter 6, if we added an extra card labelled 'Consent' to the activity, where would it fit in our line? And would one card be enough?

Our student couple are sat on their student bed, making out – how does that interaction move to having sex. At what point should they stop and ask 'would you like to take this further and have sex?' (whatever that may look like). Often consent is taken as an open invitation – consent to a passionate kiss is assumed to be consent to everything thereafter. In practice, they will simply start moving through the various activities on our Sex Act cards, until they are naked and having sex, or someone moves the hand from up their top or says, 'stop' or 'no'. The expectation is for our partner to tell us if they feel uncomfortable, rather than for us to check-in and be sure. However, whilst they might be enjoying making out and a sneaky hand up their top or down their pants, it doesn't mean they want to have full sex. But here is the issue; if they say no or stop, just like our 'volunteers' in the assembly, they may be worried of the reaction they face. Whilst we would hope our partner would understand, we may also be concerned they may feel rejected or offended – and the sexy-stuff we were enjoying stops. Instead, a positive situation that was fun and exciting, has become awkward and left everyone feeling insecure. Is it any wonder why sometimes it may feel easier to just let things carry on even if we don't really want to?

There are many ambiguous realities when it comes to sex; many sexual assaults begin as sexual interactions that were consensual, until they weren't (Hirsch and Khan, 2020). If we do not teach young people to ask 'Is this OK?' or 'Would you like to try this?' as a matter of course as they switch from one activity to the other, there is the real chance that a consensual interaction can swiftly change into one that now feels like an assault. It is about learning to recognise those pivotal moments when things change. Unfortunately, the majority of young people come of age without the language to talk about their sexual desires or the knowledge of what they want.

## Sexual citizenship

Abstinence-only programmes of sex education, that are still consistently endorsed in America, have been shown to be ineffective in delaying the age of sexual debut or in reducing the frequency of sex or the number of sexual partners young people have (Kirby, 2007; Underhill et al., 2007; Fonner et al., 2014; UNESCO, 2018). Furthermore, young people who have been through abstinence-only programmes are less likely to use protection when they do have sex. The simple reason being: you cannot plan for something you do not acknowledge is going to happen. The same can be said for sexual assault. You can't effectively prevent sexual assaults, if you don't first acknowledge young people have a right to sex and prepare for it safely.

If we recognise sex as a critical life skill that helps to foster relationships, build intimacy, provides personal connection and a sense of self, we need to ask ourselves, what are we doing as the safe adults in our children's lives to help them prepare? Unfortunately, social conditions persist where attitudes to teenage sex are seen as problematic and the majority of parents and safe adults who work with them refuse to acknowledge young people's right to sexual citizenship (Hirsch and Khan, 2020). It is understandable why we as adults may struggle to recognise our teenager as an autonomous individual and to admit they are growing up. However, as parents there comes a time when we need to concede that our children's passage into adulthood inevitably will involve them making choices for themselves and their bodies we may find uncomfortable – whether that is getting a piercing, a tattoo or engaging in sex. But even if we have strong religious or moral values when it comes to sex, this is more reason why we should be engaging in conversations around their sexual citizenship – not less.

Consider the amount of time and energy we as parents and safe adults put into helping our children plan for their future careers and life projects. We don't wait for them to leave school to start the conversation; we start to put things in place early doors – perhaps by trying to get them into the right school, helping them with their homework and installing the values and work ethic we want to see. You may have a family trade, and young children are taken into the workshop or help out in the garden. You try and help spark their interest by taking them on days out or by encouraging hobbies outside of school. How many conversations do we have about what job they might want to do or 'what do they want to be when they grow up'. How old are they before we take an interest in what subjects they might choose; the college courses they might take or perhaps an apprenticeship would be better suited. How many University open days are we prepared to attend around the country to help them make their choice? The time we spend helping with homework, filling out job applications, or UCAS forms over the years. You teach them how to manage their money, to cook, clean, iron and generally take care of themselves.

We know as parents, the work or career our children choose will have a huge impact on the type of life they will be able to build. How much money they will have, how comfortable they will be, the opportunities they can provide for their family and their future happiness and well-being. As professionals who work with young people, again this is our focus too… But we also should recognise the equally important impact their future relationships will have on their future wellbeing. How many conversations are we having with our teens about this important aspect of their lives?

As safe adults, we are so good at giving our children messages of how to behave or how they should treat others when they are young and intervening when play goes too far. As parents, before we drop them at a friend's house, we tell them to be good, to be kind, to remember their pleases and thank yous, to be respectful, not to jump on the furniture and to have fun. But then it all stops. Why are we not still giving those same messages to our teenagers when it comes to sex? After all, the rules are the same – except for don't jump on the furniture – that is kind of the point!

We need to provide opportunities for young people to clarify their own sexual projects – what they want from sex and what it means to them, but also to critically reflect on how they can enact those projects in a way that recognises others have their own aims and their own sexual citizenship. Essentially, how will they connect with the most important people in their lives – and how they should treat others with respect and human dignity (Hirsch and Khan, 2020).

If we are going to do this, we need to move the conversation of consent to include broader discourse of pleasure. One of the most common questions young people ask me is how to be good at sex? The answer is the same as what makes someone good at consent: there is no magic move or button you can press that will guarantee everyone you sleep with has an orgasm – because everybody is different, and *every body* is different. The only way you can know what someone enjoys, is to ask: *Do you like this? Am I doing it right? Would you like me to go faster or slower? Is this OK? Tell me what you like?* Pleasure isn't static. What you enjoyed yesterday, is not what you want today – moods change and our desires change – what we enjoy is fluid. And this can be instantaneous; a particular type of touch can feel heavenly one moment, but suddenly become uncomfortable or frustrating the next. Consent is the same. We all have the ability to change our minds and the right to decide, actually, I am not into this anymore. Consent has to be constantly renewed and checked as the situation progresses – just like pleasure.

However, it takes real confidence to be blunt and open about what you want. And you need to be equally self-assured to ask your partner what they want in return. Confidence takes time to build. As parents we start to put the pieces in place with regards to our children's future life projects from the day they can walk and talk. There is no reason why we can't equally prepare them to fulfil their sexual projects safely too.

# Teachable moments – early messages of consent

The most powerful lessons we can give to our children are for safe adults to model those positive behaviours we want them themselves to display. As I mentioned earlier, children learn from the behaviours they see and experience for themselves. We spend so much of our time as parents or carers teaching children to manage their bodies and respect others' boundaries. This gives us countless opportunities to model messages of consent and to build their identity as an autonomous individual with a right to their own wants and feelings and to have control over their body. What's more, it doesn't have to be complicated.

For example, when getting dressed give them choices of what they would like to wear, even if it is framed as a choice between the two T-shirts you have already picked out: 'Would you like to wear the unicorns or the dinosaurs?' Simple interactions like this help to build a sense of choice and a confidence that what they want matters.

We can take this interaction further, rather than whipping off their pyjamas for them and pulling their chosen top on for them, instead ask: 'Would you like me to help or can you do it yourself?' Again, we are reinforcing the message that we should always ask permission before we touch others, even if we are trying to help, whilst also fostering a sense of independence.

In their interactions with other children, encourage your child to use their words to say how they feel and what they would like to do but also remind them that other children have the right to disagree and make up their own mind too. We don't snatch, we ask first – these are general messages of respect and how we should treat others, but can form the foundations for building strong notions of consent.

The key is to look for those teachable moments.

If we think back to the scenario of saying goodbye to grandma, mentioned earlier in the chapter: often situations like this have the potential to undermine the positive messages we have been drip-feeding to our child, if we then make them do something they are clearly uncomfortable with. Instead, all it takes is for us as the safe adult to take the lead and reframe the interaction to a much more positive exchange, where the child can feel like they have an element of control over the situation. All it takes is for us to say, 'Right, it's time to say goodbye and thank you to grandma… how would you like to say goodbye? Do you want to give kisses? A cuddle? Blow a kiss? A high five, a wave or a fist bump?'

**Simple messages to help build a strong foundation for consent**

- Your body belongs to you and you get to decide how and if people touch you.
- No one should touch you without your permission, or in a way you don't like.
- Equally, we must always seek permission before we touch someone else.
- Not everyone likes to be touched or shows their affection in the same way.
- Just because I like something doesn't mean everyone agrees.
- Giving permission once doesn't mean someone has given permission all the time.
- People have different personal boundaries and these need to be respected all the time.
- If someone says no, or stop, these are really important words and should be listened to at all times.
- If someone doesn't listen when we say no or stop, we can tell one of our safe adults.

But my personal favourite is:

- Is my fun, fun for everyone?

# Are cuddles always nice?

One of the starting points I use a lot with children in primary school, to unpick some of the subtle nuances of everyday interactions, is the question: 'Are cuddles always nice?' This is an age-appropriate way to introduce some of the complex issues and imbalances that underpin questions of consent. Children are perfectly capable of engaging with challenging issues that do not always have a straightforward answer, as long as they draw on their lived experience.

The answer? Well, it depends on the situation, as no two cuddles are alike. Children are perfectly capable of picking out the variants that will determine how a child may feel about any particular cuddle. They under-stand it will depend on who is doing the cuddling and how we feel about them? What are the circumstances? Who else is watching? And what mood we are in at the time. Simply, when you are seven years old, a cuddle from mum when you are upset or at the end of a long day can be great… but not at the school gates in front of all your mates! Consent depends on context.

# You reap what you sow

I have a duty to point out there is a downside to raising a fully autono-mous, free-thinking confident child who knows their own mind and is able to voice what they do and don't want. We as parents are rewarded with having to live with them. A compliant child is far easier to manage.

I have had countless discussions with parents over the years who worry about how you manage a child who is playing up and uses your messages against you as they yell *'You can't touch me – or make me, you're not allowed to touch me if I don't say so!'* when you ask them to do something they really don't want to do.

Yep, I can relate. I have certainly been there. We happen to have a very assertive and independent young woman in our house, who knows her own mind and who, in polite parlance, could be referred to as a stubborn and bloody-minded pain in the arse. Unfortunately, this is the price you pay – but take solace in the fact this is a result of all your hard work paying off!

In fact, would you believe me if I told you this is another of our teach-able moments? There are simple ways to manage this situation that do not undermine your message, but also help to defuse the situation. The key (as with all parenting) is to stay calm, manage your emotions – I am well aware it is frustrating and tiring – explain calmly that they are absolutely right: 'No one can touch you in a way you don't like but equally as your adult/parent/carer, I have a responsibility to make sure you are safe/keep clean/look after yourself/eat healthy etc… so you have a choice – you can do it this way or do it that way.'

For example, imagine you are out and about with your child. They are angry with you because you have told them they couldn't have sweets when you popped into the shops, or whatever. As you make your way back home, you come to the main road and as always you stop and ask your child to hold your hand. Immediately they respond, still in a huff and say 'NO, and you can't make me,' Trying desperately not to roll your eyes as you sigh, and ask again. Stubbornly, your child responds,

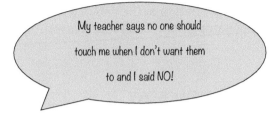

My teacher says no one should touch me when I don't want them to and I said NO!

Take a deep breath, and now tell them well done!

Well done – I am really pleased you remembered. You are right – no one has the right to touch you in a way you don't like… But as your parent, it is my job to make sure you are safe. We are by a busy road and we need to cross safely. I know you are feeling angry and annoyed right now and that's OK. But while we cross the road I need you to hold my hand. When we get to the other side you can carry on being mad at me... you can stick your tongue out and pull faces... but we need to cross the road safely – so can you hold my hand please...? Or how about, instead you hold onto the buggy, or my pocket... what do you think?

In this case, we are not undermining the key message, and instead we are giving them choices whilst explaining why sometimes we need to do things we don't like to stay safe or keep healthy. Children need to learn, with rights come responsibilities too. The same is true for brushing our teeth, eating our vegetables or taking a bath…

It is no different when we visit the doctors or the dentist. Let's be honest, none of us want to go – but it is all about keeping clean, staying healthy and taking care of yourself. It is good practice for doctors and dentists to always explain what they are going to do and to ask children for their permission beforehand if they need to touch them or have them undress. Taking the time to explain to your child why you need them to do something is essential; whilst it is much easier to simply play the 'because I said so' card, it doesn't set a very good example and undermines all of your hard work.

> **But I don't want to...it's my body!"**

> *You're right – your body belongs to you – but that means its your* **responsibility** *to look after it... and that means keeping it clean...* *So, you need to have a bath or a shower. Which one are you going to pick? Prove to me that you can do it properly, and you can do it by yourself next time.... Give me a shout when you've washed your hair so I can check it's clean and all the shampoo has been washed out...*

# Teachable moments – managing the teenage years

Personally, this is where we are as a family. Our daughter has just turned 13… the age of slammed doors and mumbled Mutley-style replies of 'I hate you!' under their breath. Conflict is never nice, or easy – but in the same vein, conflict is a natural part of managing our relationships. We need to learn strategies for managing our emotions and our behaviours, especially when they are in position to the people around us.

Whilst it is important for young people to develop a sense of autonomy, and to be aware of their wants and need as an individual – they also need to acknowledge that others too have their own right to autonomy and have their own wants and needs too. Needless to say, there will be times when what they want will be in conflict with the people around them. It doesn't matter what type of interpersonal relationship we are focusing on – we all need to learn strategies for managing our conflicts. This is no more true than in our most intimate relationships. If we want young people to become fully-fledged sexual citizens, it is essential they learn to acknowledge their partner's right to sexual citizenship and to recognise they will have their own sexual projects in mind too.

As parents and safe adults, we have the privilege of helping them pre-pare – i.e. we are the guinea-pigs they will practise various strategies on. They may rage at us; scream they hate us; ignore us; shut us out and test our limits. It is our job to weather the storm and be the safe harbour, no matter what they do – they need to know they are still loved. That doesn't mean we should give in, and let them have their way, far from it. It is our job to ignore the thunder and instead meet the noise by continuing to model healthy strategies to manage the conflict.

The psychotherapist and agony aunt Philippa Perry in her book, *The Book You Wish Your Parents Had Read (and your children will be glad that you did)*, explains there will be times when our teenagers may want to assert some independence and do things that they were previously not allowed to. For example, they might want to stay out late, go into town to a club or stay over at their partner's house. It is easy to overreact and simply put your foot down and categorically say 'No', end of story. And when your teen protests, revert back to the old favourite, 'because I said so, you are too young and you are not going!' Unfortunately, by overreacting, it only makes it more likely the lines of communication will be shut down. And next time they want to do something they are unsure if you will be happy with, they will in all likelihood simply lie (Perry, 2019).

Instead, return to the strategies suggested for when they were younger. Explain why and be honest. As children become teenagers and start to push at boundaries, whilst we all acknowledge this is all part of growing up, we need to admit, whilst they might be ready, it doesn't mean that we are. So be honest. Reply,

> *I know you want to go into town and I understand why. I know you can look after yourself and are responsible. But I am not happy with you going into town because I am afraid. I remember what I got up to at your age, and I am not ready for that yet… I need you to be patient with me and let me think about it.*

By letting them know, your refusal isn't you trying to assert your authority or spoil their fun, but is about how you feel. This can help to shift and reframe the conflict – now the solution lies in what they can do to reassure you – rather than being about a battle of wills. Now you are on the same team and can find a solution.

Ultimately, teenagers are safer if they can be honest with us about what they are doing or what they may get up to. That doesn't mean we have to always approve, or can't throw in the occasional eye roll. It is secrets that are dangerous, the things we can't talk about. If we can keep lines of communication open, we can work together to put mechanisms and strategies in place should they get into trouble. Even if part of our role as parents is to provide suitable opposition for them to learn to manage conflict. At the end of the day we are on the same team.

Essentially, that is the essence of consent – realising that it is not about how much you can get away with before someone stops you – you are on the same team. When it comes to sex, it should never be about winners or losers. We need to change the language of sex from being competition based, with lad-points, (the Americanism) getting to second-base, losing your virginity, or even worse taking someone's virginity. Sex should never be about taking what you can with no thought for your partner's feeling or enjoyment. Instead, we should keep in mind the message, is my fun, fun for everyone? It is a great message, whether you are 5 or 15, regardless of whether we are talking about tickling, play fighting, sharing toys, partying or having sex. *Is my fun, fun for everyone?* works.

# Notes

1 Under Section 74 of The Sexual Offences Act 2003, London: Home Office Communications Directorate, 2004.
2 I tell a little lie – one time I had a girl in year 9 who called me out on this. She stood up, and asked, 'do I have to…?'
    'I'd like you to,' I replied.
    She pulled a face at me and said, 'But I don't want to…'
    I smiled and tried to lead her a little further by saying, 'So, if you don't want to do something, what should you do?'
    'Not do it…'
    'And say what?' 'No.' At this point, a little over-excited I pointed at her and said 'Yes! Exactly.' I explained she was the only student who has ever been brave and assertive enough to say 'No'. I asked her name and asked everyone to give her a round of applause. I then talked through what usually happens. When I returned home, I emailed the head of year at her school and told them how brilliant she was in calling me out in a room full of people. I asked the head of year to pass on my praise and to say how impressed I was with her and her contribution in the session. This is something I try to do on a regular basis and I thoroughly recommend you email schools when you have a positive experience with a pupil. In my experience, people only give feedback to head teachers or year heads when they have thought a young person has misbehaved or been disrespectful. Often the only time anyone contacts a school is to raise a

concern. It makes a real difference to young people when they are pulled aside by a senior figure in their school because they have been praised – especially for the sort of young people who tend to do well in my kind of lessons – those who are often a bit gobby and get into trouble in other lessons. It can make all the difference to them – but also to the teachers and school as a whole. Who doesn't like to receive some positive feedback about one of their pupils or their school?

3   Indeed, Justin Hancock and Meg-John Barker wrote a fantastic journal article (2018), 'The use of porn in sex and relationship education', which echoes the sentiments as to why I feel uncomfortable with this demonstration.

The article is actually written in response to the suggestion by some commentators, educator should show still of pornography in class to show how unrealistic it is and to help young people think critically about what they are watching. However, they make an excellent point: 'If we are endeavouring to teach young people to engage in consensual behaviour, then it is vital to model this by not making the experience of SRE itself coercive' (pages 97–8).

For this reason I no longer actually deliver this exercise, only talk through it. It still works just as effectively but doesn't cause anyone any anxiety. I am constantly learning and updating my practice too.

4   The Relationships Education, Relationships and Sex Education and Health Education (England) Regulations 2019, made under sections 34 and 35 of the Children and Social Work Act 2017, make Relationships Education compulsory for all pupils receiving primary education and RSE compulsory for all pupils receiving secondary education.

5   Home Office, Children and Families: Safer from Sexual Crime – The Sexual Offences Act 2003, London: Home Office Communications Directorate, 2004.

6   Flirty-banter = flanter (this is not a word I ever say out loud).

# References

Bragg, S., Ponsford, R., Meiksin, R., Emmerson, L. and Bonell, C. (2020). Dilemmas of school-based relationships and sexuality education for and about consent, *Sex Education*, 1–15.

Fonner, V.A., Armstrong, K.S., Kennedy, C.E., O'Reilly, K.R. and Sweat, M.D. (2014). School based sex education and HIV prevention in low- and middle-income countries: a systematic review and meta-analysis, *PLoS One*, 9(3).

Hancock, J. and Barker, M. (2018). The use of porn in sex and relationship education, *Porn Studies*, 5(1), 97–103.

Hirsch, J.S. and Khan, S (2020). Sexual Citizens: A landmark study of sex, power, and assault on campus, W.W. Norton. New York.

Home Office (2004). Children and Families: Safer from Sexual Crime – The Sexual Offences Act 2003, Home Office Communications Directorate, London.

Kirby, D. (2007). *Emerging Answers 2007: Research findings on programmes to reduce teen pregnancy and sexuality transmitted diseases*. National Campaign to Prevent Teen and Unplanned Pregnancy, Washington, DC. Available at: http://thenationalcampaign.org/sites/default/files/resource-primary-download/EA2007_full_0.pdf.

Perry, P. (2019). The Book You Wish Your Parents Had Read (and your children will be glad that you did), Penguin Books, Milton Keynes.

Underhill, K., Montgomery, P. and Operario, D. (2007). Sexual abstinence only programmes to prevent HIV infection in high income countries: Systemic review, *British Medical Journal*, 335(7613), 248.

UNESCO. (2018). International technical guidance on sexuality education: An evidenced-informed approach.

Whittington, E. (2019). Understanding sexual consent: A participatory approach with young people, Doctoral thesis (PhD), University of Sussex.

# CHAPTER 11

# WHAT TO DO WHEN THINGS GO WRONG

The previous chapters have explored what makes sex safe. Whilst writing, a meme popped up on my Twitter feed, one that has done the rounds a number of time across the internet but seemed apt considering what we have been talking about – admittedly in my line of work some very odd, and not always sanitary things appear in my feed – it is a hazard of the job…

**How to fuck like a porn star…**

- get tested regularly
- share your status with partners
- discuss boundaries before you start

As I will be exploring issues raised by pornography in the next section, it seemed to fit well with the topics we have already discussed and provide a nice link to where we are going. To be honest, it made me laugh; there is currently a real fear young people are taking their lessons of how to have sex from pornography. However, this meme turns those fears on their head. There is no denying pornography has its issues – and I certainly wouldn't be recommending porn as a reliable source of sex education, any more than I would recommend watching *The Fast and the Furious* franchise as a reliable means of learning how to drive – however, we could do worse than learning how to *fuck like a porn star* safely.

DOI: 10.4324/9781003122296-17

Indeed, regardless of how responsible our young folk might be or how much they have learnt about the things they can do to keep themselves safe – inevitably, they will make mistakes. After all, none of us are perfect… it doesn't matter how mature or how careful they usually are, sometimes things go wrong. Condoms split, people get drunk, forget to take their pill or hurt the people they care about. Unfortunately, when it comes to our sexual health, we all tend to be reactive rather than proactive.

For many of us, both young and old, the first time we will visit a sexual health service or actually find out what they provide is when things have gone wrong and we need them. This only adds to the stress and worry of what we should be doing to limit the damage and clean up whatever mess we might be in.

It is worth bearing in mind, as adults, we often make all these same mistakes regularly too. We are not infallible, so it is important to rein in our holier-than-thou attitude and remember the only difference between the teenagers in our lives and ourselves, is we don't have to come home and explain to our parents what we have done or worry about them finding out.

If I could make one recommendation, it would be to encourage the young people in your life to become regulars at their local sexual health service. You do not have to wait until things have gone awry to make a visit. Instead, I would like to recommend a more proactive approach; just as we visit our dentist every six months for a check-up, there is no reason why we can't do the same with our sexual health. It is good practice to have a full sexual health screening regularly, at least every time you change partners. This also creates the opportunity to talk through your contraceptive choices or to have any questions or worries you may have put to rest. Becoming familiar with what services are on offer, how they operate and even what the waiting room looks like can massively reduce the stress of going when you are in need.

Most of us as parents, or professionals who work with young people, will only have our own experiences to go on, so it is unlikely we will all have the necessary information at hand to help support our youngsters in their moment of crisis. To help, in this chapter I have tried to pull together a step-by-step guide of what someone might need to know and what you might need to do when things have gone wrong. This can be used as a practice guide for those scary moments for you to work through or as a proactive guide of information you can drip feed to your teens ready for the inevitable. Always be prepared and all that.

But remember, if a young person has turned to you for help, whether as a parent or as a safe adult, the last thing they need is a lecture, any 'I told you so', or 'how could you be so stupid?' What they need now is a calm head and a warm shoulder… and maybe a cup of tea to start with.

# So you've had unprotected sex…

Meet Alex.

Alex has had sex and for whatever reason Alex didn't use a condom. At this point, the details as to the hows and whys are not particularly important – we will come to that in time. Regardless of whether it was alcohol induced; or simply getting lost in the heat of the moment; down to a lack of planning, lack of confidence, or lack of judgement; or perhaps, Alex did actually take precautions and things simply went wrong… condoms do break after all!

This is not the moment; there is nothing to be gained by pointing fingers or raising voices – we all make mistakes. What Alex needs right now is our help and support. There will be a time to reflect on the lessons learned later, but for now, take a deep breath as we deal with the situation at hand.

If you have had unprotected sex there are three key things we need to think about (Figure 11.1).

Two of these are quite obvious issues: avoiding an unwanted pregnancy and testing for STIs – or you would hope so, considering the content of the previous few chapters… nevertheless, they are staples on even the most basic sex ed curriculum. These are the ones people tend to focus on – perhaps, it is a human thing; when it comes to problem solving, as human beings we tend to be better at the practical stuff rather than the navel gazing, introspection and reflection necessary to tackle the emotional side of the equation. Consequently, the emotional impact of unprotected sex is often ignored.

Nevertheless, the clock is ticking and there is a time limit to deal with some of these issues so let's get to it.

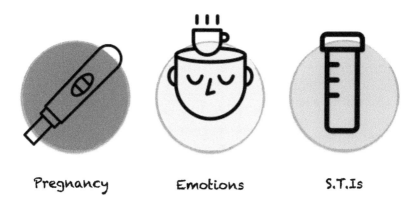

**Figure 11.1** Three key things to consider

# Avoiding an unwanted pregnancy

Assuming Alex's encounter was with a member of the opposite sex, avoiding an unwanted pregnancy should be high on the agenda and a good place to begin. It is no accident I haven't divulged Alex's sexual orientation and purposely chose a name that could be considered gender neutral as regardless of who you are or who you are having sex with, there are always risks associated with an unprotected encounter. Some of those risks may be higher or lower for some couples but there are still risks to manage. For example, if Alex was a CIS[1] young woman who only has sex with other women, obviously an unwanted pregnancy would not be an issue – lesbianism is a wonderful form of contraception when adhered to strictly. However, if Alex is a CIS, heterosexual, it would also depend on what type of sex Alex had with their partner. Pregnancy is only really a risk when having penis in vagina sex.

If the young person you are supporting had an encounter with a same-sex partner, you may want to skip ahead to part ii. But for the sake of argument, let's assume Alex is heterosexual for now (you can decide if they are male or female) simply so we can cover all the potentially necessary steps.

If you decided Alex was a young man, even though he can't get pregnant and he can't access emergency contraception himself – it doesn't mean he is exempt. He still has a responsibility and will most likely still be worried. Does he know if his partner is on some other form of contraception and is she taking it regularly (did he even bother to ask?). If not, it is at least considered polite to contact his partner and ask if he can do anything to help support her, maybe to access emergency contraception?

It is worth giving him a poke, and explaining that if his partner does take emergency contraception it can make them feel a bit rough for a few hours – similar to a hangover… it doesn't matter if the encounter was a one night stand, a friends with benefits type of situation or the love of his life – there is no reason why he couldn't drop her a text and check she is OK (as the bare minimum) and if there is anything he can do to support her. You got naked with this person – kindness costs nothing.

You do not need to be in love with someone to treat them with respect; there is absolutely no reason why we shouldn't *always* treat *all* of our part-ners with respect and empathy, even if it was just a one off or a booty-call.

# Why is the term 'morning after pill' misleading?

You may have noticed I keep using the term 'emergency contraception' rather than the *morning after pill* as it is more often referred to. There are a number of reasons why. Firstly, it can be a bit misleading. Often people assume that the morning after pill, is just that – something you have to take with your cornflakes, first thing or you have missed the boat. This isn't true. Depending on what options are available, emergency contraception can be used up to five days after unprotected sex.

When you did the quiz at the start of this section, and were asked how long after unprotected sex can you use emergency contraception, I am sure many of you will have written down 72 hours (3 days) after unpro-tected sex. You can have half a mark – as this is partially true. There are actually three options available to Alex (who for those of you who decide she was a girl and for the simple convenience of this next part we will now recognise as cis female) when it comes to emergency contraception, the most common of which is effective up to 72 hours.

1. Have an emergency IUD fitted
2. The emergency contraceptive pill Levonorgestrel (LNG)
3. The emergency contraceptive pill Ulipristal acetate (UPA) ellaOne

The most effective method is to have an **emergency coil fitted (IUD)** within five days (120 hours) of unprotected sex. As was covered in the contraceptive fact-files in Chapter 8, this would need to be fitted only by a trained doctor, and the process can be quite uncomfortable. However, once fitted, there is no need to have the coil removed, instead it could be used as a contraceptive going forward.

More often, however, women opt to choose to take an **emergency hormonal contraceptive (EHC) pill** instead. These can be accessed through a number of different services, including your GP and local sexual health services, but also can be obtained from most pharmacies (although there may be a cost involved).[2] When you visit a pharmacy, you will need to have a short chat with the pharmacist before you will be given EHC. They will ask you a few questions, such as when you had unprotected sex, where you are in your menstrual cycle and if you are taking any other medications. This is to ensure EHC is the most appropriate option, and you are given the medication that is most suitable for you.

**Levonorgestrel** (better known by its various brand names: Levonelle, Levonelle on step and Upostelle) contains the hormone progestogen and is most effective if taken within 72 hours of unprotected sex, although some services may offer it up to 96 hours (four days).

**Ulipristal acetate (UPA)**, better known as simply **ellaOne**, is most effective if taken within five days (120 hours) of unprotected sex.

Both forms of EHC can cause mild side effects such as headaches, feeling tired and worn out, breast tenderness, cramping and in some cases vomiting (if you are sick within three hours of taking EHC it is unlikely it will be effective – so seek further advice).

### Myth busting

Emergency contraception doesn't cause an abortion. The tablets used during an abortion end a pregnancy that has already happened, whereas emergency contraception prevents a pregnancy from happening.

EHC is not compatible with certain forms of medication taken to treat epilepsy, HIV and TB and can be affected by the herbal remedy St John's Wort. Neither is EHC designed as an ongoing form of contraception – it is just what it says, 'emergency' contraception, to be used when your normal form of contraception has failed.

If our friend Alex has had unprotected sex more than five days ago, she will not be able to use emergency contraception. Instead she will have to wait to take a pregnancy test… but more on that in a second.

# How old do you have to be to access EHC?

There are no age restrictions for accessing any form of contraception, including emergency contraception. There are no age restrictions on STI screening or testing. And a young woman can access abortion services at any age, even without her parents' permission.

It is understandable why some parents may feel shocked and horrified by this information, and why others may feel a little uncomfortable. However, these are really important rights for young people to have. No all young people can talk to their parents about sex and relationships; in fact, it is not safe for some young people to speak to their parents about being sexually active.

However, there are rules in place, which sit alongside safeguarding protocols and guidelines. These are referred to as the Fraser Guidelines or the Gillick Competency. Essentially, these guidelines allow young people under the age of sixteen confidential access to sexual health advice and treatment.[3] Whilst the age of consent in the UK is set at 16 – as we have already discussed in earlier chapters – this does not mean that all young people wait until they are 16 to have sex. For those that do choose to have sex before they are 16, and it is the minority we are talking about, the vast majority do wait until they are over 16 (BPAS, 2018; Council for Europe, 2020; Tanton et al., 2015; Lindberg and Maddow-Zimet, 2012), isn't it better they can do so safely?

Indeed, not only do the Fraser Guidelines allow young people to access contraceptive advice and treatment, they also provide a point of call and a safe space for young people to ask for help. This is an essential protective factor.

When I used to deliver condom distribution services, the final thing I would tell people before they left was for them to come back anytime and to let me know how they got on. Not because I had any interest in knowing the details but I wanted them to be able to come back and talk if they

## The Fraser Guidelines and Gillick Competency

Both the Fraser Guidelines and the Gallic Competency are designed to help professionals who work with children decide if they are mature enough to make decisions for themselves. Whilst the two terms are often used interchangeably, and both originate from the same legal case, there is a distinct difference between them.

In 1982 Victoria Gillick, a mother, took her local health authority and the Department of Health and Social Security to court in an attempt to prevent doctors from providing contraceptive advice or treatment to under-16s without their parents' consent, after discovering a pack of contraceptive pills in her daughter's bedroom.

The case went to the High Court in 1984 where Mrs Gillick's claim was dismissed. However, in 1984 the Court of Appeal overturned the decision, before the judgment went to the House of Lords and the Law Lords in 1985 where Lord Scarman, Lord Fraser and Lord Bridge ruled in favour of the original judgment.

As a result, Lord Fraser set out guidelines to help determine whether a particular child was deemed mature enough to give their own informed consent, and to set the conditions under which contraceptive advice or treatment could be given without informing their parents.

The Fraser Guidelines apply specifically to advice and treatment about contraception and sexual health, and may be used by a range of professionals working with under-16s. Following a further ruling in 2006, the Fraser Guidelines can also be applied to advice and treatment of sexually transmitted infections, and accessing abortion services.

The Gillick Competency is often applied to wider contexts to help assess whether a child has the maturity to make their own decisions and can understand the implication of those decisions.

Whilst the Gillick Competency mainly applies to medical advice and treatment, these days, it is also used for young people who want to access therapeutic support without their parents' or carers' knowledge; to access confidential services around substance misuse; or want to change their future living arrangements which may conflict with their parents' or carers' wishes.

The Fraser Guidelines state:

Practitioners using the Fraser guidelines should be satisfied of the following:

- the young person understands the health professional's advice;
- the health professional cannot persuade the young person to inform his or her parents or carers;

- unless he or she receives contraceptive advice or treatment, the young person's physical or mental health or both are likely to suffer;
- the young person is likely to continue having sex with or without contraceptive treatment;
- the young person's best interests require the health professional to give contraceptive advice, treatment or both without parental consent.

(Gillick v West Norfolk 1985)

wanted or needed to. And not necessarily because something had gone wrong. Sometimes when people first start having sex, they can feel a little confused about how they feel; sex isn't always how they imagined. It can take some help to get things into perspective.

However, imagine if Alex had been brave enough to go along to her nearest drop-in clinic to get some condoms for her and her partner. For argument's sake, let's say she is 15 years old in this scenario; and when the nurse asks her how old she is, their response is to tell her, 'It is against the law to have sex before you are 16 and you could get into real trouble'. And once they have told her she is too young, they send her on her way, empty handed.

Do we really believe it would stop her and her partner from having sex? Especially considering she has made up her mind and has already made the effort to attend my clinic? Surely this is something that should be commended rather than sneered at? Alex is showing real maturity and is clearly wanting to take responsibility for herself and her partner. But the real issue is, when things do go wrong, she isn't going to come back to the clinic and ask for help – because if she does, the staff get to tell her 'I told you so!' All they have succeeded in doing is shutting the door firmly in her face and removed a key safety factor from her support network.

It may make us feel uncomfortable as parents to think of our teens accessing these services behind our backs; but perhaps the question we should be asking ourselves instead is why do they feel the need to do it without talking to us first. Are we really doing everything we can to keep those doors open?

# Taking a pregnancy test

For whatever reason, poor Alex has missed her opportunity; it is already more than five days since she had unprotected sex. This means emergency contraception is no longer a viable option for her. Unfortunately, Alex now has an anxious wait on her hands – and this is when she will need real support and understanding. Although, it is worth noting, unprotected sex doesn't always lead to pregnancy – a lot of it comes down to luck. Nevertheless, this will not stop Alex from worrying. Whilst Alex could take a pregnancy test and be done with it, most likely it will be too early for that yet.

A pregnancy test usually involves peeing on a small plastic stick, with a special absorbent end. The test works by reacting to the presence of a hormone called human chorionic gonadotrophin (HCG), which is only present in the urine of someone who is pregnant. However, it can take a while for the hormone to build up in the body in significant volumes to be detected. This means there is little point taking a pregnancy test immediately after unprotected sex as you are likely to get a false negative.

In order to get a reliable result it is better to wait two weeks (14 days) after unprotected sex or immediately after a missed period, whichever is sooner. You can buy a pregnancy test from most supermarkets and pharmacies but they can be expensive, especially the branded one with fancy LED displays. Essentially, they all work the same – just because it has flashing lights and a ring tone doesn't make it any more accurate, just a little easier to read. Pregnancy tests are also available for free from your GP or at any sexual health service.

If the test is negative, then it is more than likely Alex will not be pregnant. However, if her next period is late, or lighter than usual, it is always worth taking a second test a week after the first, just to be sure. No matter the result, this will definitely be an important time for Alex to have someone safe and non-judgemental to talk to. Even if she is relieved and ultimately it is for the best, that doesn't mean she won't feel disappointed, upset or confused; our emotions don't always make sense. But please, if you are a parent or professional supporting a young person with a pregnancy test, remember this is not about how you feel. Do not start whooping and dancing around the kitchen with relief, or alternatively get upset you're not going to be a grandparent, or whatever – at this moment right now,

Alex will need her parents to hold and manage her feelings – now is not the time.

Alternatively, if the test is positive Alex now has more difficult choices on her hands. However you feel about this, as stated – now is not the time. Alex is going to need people she can trust and people who will listen, not tell her what to do.

# Pregnancy choices

Essentially, Alex has three options available for her to choose from:

1. Continue with the pregnancy and raising the child herself (hopefully with support from her family).
2. Continue with the pregnancy but relinquish the child for adoption.
3. Choose to end the pregnancy by having an abortion.

For Alex, it may be an easy decision. She may feel clearly she isn't ready to be pregnant, and is simply happy she lives in an age and a country where she has options available to her – as this isn't the case everywhere in the world. In fact, women's right to access safe and legal abortion is coming under attack around the globe.[4] Alternatively, Alex may find it really tough,

 **Top tip**

The best piece of advice I have ever heard regarding pregnancy choices, is to recommend to anyone trying to make the decision to keep a journal. Encourage them to write down how they feel, their current circumstances and ultimately why they come to whatever conclusion they decide in the end. Not only will it help them collect their thoughts but it will be useful in the future. Advise them to put it away at the back of the drawer somewhere and forget about it. In the years to come, they may need it. Sometimes when our futures don't turn out how we plan, or we are struggling with setbacks, we like to romanticise the past, and may start to think 'what if…' The thing is, you can't make decisions in hindsight. You can only make decisions on how you feel and the information you have now. That way you will always know you made the right decisions for you – at the time – which is all we can ever ask for.

as she ums-and-ahs over it and goes around in circles trying to decide what to do. The important thing though, it has to be her decision. After all, it will be she that has to live with the choice.

I have delivered pregnancy testing training to professionals, usually youth workers and school nurses, for years and this is something we spend a lot of time discussing in training. It doesn't matter what your views, values or beliefs are, you have to be able to keep them to yourself and sit on them. Even better, put them in a bag and bury them – and then sit on them. Your job is simply to be there and listen. However challenging that may be.

Some people are against abortion for moral or religious reasons, and they have the right to their beliefs. If you do not agree with abortion then, when it is your turn to choose, no one can force you to have one. However, it is not OK to take away other people's rights to health care or to make choices about their own body, based on your beliefs. Unfortunately, in countries where abortion is against the law, women resort to self-induced abortion or care provided by unregistered healthcare professionals – known as 'back-street abortion'. These are rarely clean or safe and, as a result, thousands of women die each year from unsafe abortions.

## Myth busting

People who are against abortion for moral reasons often publish false information to convince women they are acting in their best interest.
However, abortion does <u>NOT</u>:

- lead to future infertility
- increase the risk of miscarriage, ectopic pregnancy or a low placenta in future pregnancies
- increase the risk of developing breast cancer
- cause or lead to mental illness

(FSRH and RCOG, 2019)

Equally, current evidence does not suggest a foetus is able to feel pain under 24 weeks.[5]

Abortion is a really emotive topic, but there is a reason why young people have the right to access these services without parental consent or knowledge. If you want to be there to support Alex, make sure you do just that, and not allow your feelings to get in the way. What is right for you, may not be what is right for Alex. If, for whatever reason, you are unable to offer this kind of support, perhaps you might want to consider who else is in Alex's support network who can?

If Alex decided she wanted to end her pregnancy, under the Fraser Guidelines she could have an abortion without her parents' permission, even if she is under 16 years of age. Some people can talk to their parents openly about their situation and their decision to have an abortion and will be lucky to have their support throughout the experience. Others may choose not to tell their parents; they may be afraid of what they might say or may be concerned as to how they would react to the knowledge they have had sex. Although healthcare professionals would encourage Alex to talk to her parents, we must remember it may not be safe for her to do so. We do have so-called honour killings here in the UK. Should Alex decide not to talk to her parents or carers, health care professionals would ensure there are people around to support her.

Sometimes it is easier to speak to someone who is completely outside of your life, rather than having to deal with the added complications of family members. For this reason, Alex might choose to take advantage of the free impartial counselling offered as a key part of abortion care. All abortion services have specially trained counsellors who will offer an opportunity for Alex to talk about her decision. They will listen and help her come to a decision, but the decision will be hers; they will not pressure Alex in any way. However, it is important Alex is aware there are other organisations known as 'Pregnancy Crisis Centres' that pretend to offer 'impartial' and 'unbiased' advice. In reality, they use counselling to persuade people not to have abortions – they are run by pro-life organisations and use disinformation to emotionally blackmail women. For this reason, it would be much better for Alex to go straight to a specialist abortion service. In many parts of the country Alex could refer herself straight into abortion services without going to see her GP.[6]

When speaking to young people about accessing abortion care, I always recommend going straight to their nearest service provider, rather than visiting their GP. This is simply because it can remove an unnecessary barrier from proceedings. Under The Abortion Act 1967, there is a 'conscientious objection' clause, which permits healthcare professionals to refuse to participate in authorising abortion care if it conflicts with their religious or personal beliefs. However, doctors who have an objection to abortion *must* tell women of their right to see another doctor and refer them on to further care without delay. At the end of the day, GPs have the same right to their beliefs as anyone else – however, the healthcare professionals who work at an abortion care provider you can be sure do not have moral obligations that abortion is wrong.

# Having an abortion

When Alex attends the service, she will first be assessed by a doctor or nurse who will answer her questions and talk her through the procedure. After the assessment Alex would be given a separate appointment to return to the clinic at another time – you do not have the procedure on the same day as your assessment. However, this process, from start to finish, should take no longer than two weeks – as time is a key factor when it comes to abortion care.

Generally there are two ways of ending an unwanted pregnancy: a medical abortion which involves taking two separate medications also known as the 'abortion pill' or a surgical abortion which requires a small surgical procedure. The type of abortion you have will depend on a number of factors, including how far along the pregnancy is. Generally, the earlier you opt for an abortion, the more options available and the less invasive the procedure. However, you should always have a choice over your preferred method, as long as it is appropriate for your personal situation.

Before having an abortion it is likely Alex will be offered blood tests, screening for STIs and be given an ultrasound to confirm how far along the pregnancy is, so the doctors can assess the best procedure to use. Finally, Alex will be given a consent form to sign, to confirm she understand what is about to happen to her. However, Alex could still change her mind at any point, even after she has signed the form.

## The law

It may surprise you to know, abortion is 'technically' still not legal in England, Scotland and Wales. The 1967 Abortion Act renders lawful the conduct of doctors that would otherwise be unlawful under the 1861 and 1929 Acts. This means there are strict rules as to who may perform an abortion and under what circumstances. A woman can have an abortion up to 24 weeks of pregnancy, only if two doctors decide, 'in good faith', that one or more of the grounds specified in the Abortion Act are met.

These grounds are:

a.  the continuance of the pregnancy would involve risk to the life of the pregnant woman greater than if the pregnancy were terminated.
b.  the termination is necessary to prevent grave permanent injury to the physical or mental health of the pregnant woman.
c.  the pregnancy has not exceeded its 24th week and the continuance of the pregnancy would involve risk, greater than if the pregnancy were terminated, of injury to the physical or mental health of the pregnant woman.
d.  the pregnancy has not exceeded its 24th week and the continuance of the pregnancy would involve risk, greater than if the pregnancy were terminated, of injury to the physical or mental health of any existing child(ren) of the family of the pregnant woman.
e.  there is a substantial risk that if the child were born it would suffer from such physical or mental abnormalities as to be seriously handicapped.

The vast majority of abortions are carried out under ground C.

The Act also permits abortion to be performed in an emergency if one doctor is of the opinion formed 'in good faith' that an abortion is immediately necessary:

f.  to save the life of the pregnant woman.
g.  to prevent grave permanent injury to the physical or mental health of the pregnant woman.

Procuring an abortion in Northern Ireland was still a criminal offence until July 2019, when MPs voted to bring Northern Ireland in line with services in the rest of the UK. A new framework for lawful abortion services came into effect on 31 March 2020 allowing abortion up to 24 weeks.

In May 2018 Ireland chose to legalise abortion in a historic referendum. From January 2019, Ireland opened its new abortion services. The new law allows abortion on request to 12 weeks and beyond 12 weeks in a few, very limited circumstances.

The Abortion Act 1967 also does not apply in the Isle of Man, Jersey or Guernsey. Some women from these areas who wish to have an abortion travel to mainland Britain or another European country for the procedure.

The majority of abortions take place in just one day, with no need to stay overnight – this can be especially helpful for young people like Alex, who would have to find an excuse to explain where she has stayed overnight – should she wish to keep it a secret. Alex will need to take some menstrual pads and spare underwear with her, as it is common to experience bleeding similar to a heavy period and it's good to be prepared.

The vast majority of abortions performed in the UK take place early in pregnancy. For example, annual statistics for England and Wales produced from the Department of Health show that in 2017, 90% of abortions took place at under 13 weeks with 77% at under 10 weeks (FSRH and RCOG, 2019).

As with any medical procedure, it is normal to feel a bit wobbly and it is good to take some time to rest and recover. It is normal to experience some bleeding after an abortion, but it should stop after a week or so. Abortion is extremely safe and there are rarely any serious complications. Nevertheless, it is normal to feel a little sore or uncomfortable afterwards, which can be managed with normal painkillers like paracetamol.

The majority of people who have abortions say that the main emotion they feel afterwards is relief.

But there is no right way to feel. It is perfectly normal to feel upset, confused or guilty, even if you know you have made the right decision. If we return back to Alex, regardless of how she feels having a sympathetic and non-judgmental ear is always helpful. Whether it is from a trusted friend or a safe adult, she will manage better if she knows there are people around her who care for her, no matter what. Even if she doesn't want to disclose what has happened, or talk directly about her abortion, knowing people are there should she choose to is often enough.

If you are interested, in series one of the Netflix drama *Sex Education*, episode 3 is dedicated to exploring abortion as one of the central characters Maeve finds out she is pregnant. As with most things in the show, it is tackled with empathy and honesty without making moral judgments of any of the characters. It is lovely when Otis collects Maeve from the clinic (whilst mistakenly thinking he is going on a date); he doesn't pry or think worse of Maeve. He treats her with dignity and respect, and even clumsily offers her a shop-bought prawn sandwich and packet of crisps.

**Did you know...**

One in three women in the UK will have an abortion during her lifetime, although many people who have had an abortion choose not to talk about it through fear of stigma. This is a real shame when it is a part of so many women's life experiences. It is worth remembering, more than likely, a woman in your life has had an abortion, even if they haven't told you that they have.

Whilst I would always advise taking TV dramas with a pinch of salt, I would recommend watching the series as each episode tackles another key relationship issue or challenge relevant to a teenager developing their sense of sexual citizenship. As I said, it is sex positive in its outlook and sympathetic to the characters without ironing over their flaws – if you can convince your teens to let you watch it with them, it can be a great conversation starter. Although, if your house is anything like mine, TV viewing often happens in separate rooms and they have already watched it without you whilst being locked away in their room. Nevertheless, it may give you a different perspective and allow you to start a conversation.

We digress... Alex hasn't got time for watching Netflix, they have an appointment at the GUM clinic.

# Checking for sexually transmitted infections

Whether Alex happens to be in a same-sex relationship or a heterosexual relationship; whether they are male or female; regardless of what type of sex they have engaged in (most often encounters involve more than one type of sex) – potentially they may have contracted an STIs or may have passed one on to their partner. Remember, some people will not be aware they have an infection as there are not always obvious symptoms.

Whilst STIs are more likely to be passed on through penetrative sex, either vaginally or anally, STIs can also be passed on through oral sex and manual sex – chlamydia and gonorrhoea will quite happily live in the back of the throat – and can survive on the hands for a short amount of time, so if they are using their hands to stimulate themselves and their partner, there is the potential to pass sexual fluids between them. This is also true if partners have shared sex toys or rubbed their genitals against each other. Although, there always needs to be a clear route of transmission into the body from one partner to the other.

These days many local authorities now fund postal kits that can be sent direct to your door in a nice discreet package. However, not all local authorities pay to screen for all infection – usually just chlamydia and gonorrhoea. This means that even if you get a negative result, it doesn't guarantee you still haven't got an infection, it would just be one they haven't tested for. For this reason, we are going to send Alex for a full sexual health screening at their local Genito-Urinary Medicine (GUM) clinic.

Like most NHS services GUM clinics vary across the country. Most have walk-in clinics, however some are by appointment only. If you have symptoms, it is likely you will be seen much quicker than if you are just after a precautionary check-up. A good tip if it is a drop-in clinic is to check the opening hours and try to get there a few minutes before they open in the morning or after lunch. Yes, it might mean waiting outside a closed door for 10 minutes but it will save you much more time sitting around in the waiting room, trust me.

Many people find the thought of visiting a GUM clinic intimidating or, worse, embarrassing. There is still so much stigma around sex and STIs – there is a general fear that people will assume you are dirty, irresponsible or must sleep around. Clearly none of these things are true. There are hundreds of reasons why someone might be at a GUM clinic, especially now due to funding cuts, many separate services have been combined, so GUM and contraceptive services are all in one clinic. Visiting a GUM clinic is the responsible thing to do. You only have to look around the waiting room (where being British, no one makes eye contact) to notice there are all manner of people from all walks of life using the service. Making sexual health a normal part of general wellbeing would make a huge difference – so please normalise sexual health services with your teens!

On arrival, Alex will have to check in and fill out a form. It is worth reminding Alex that all sexual health services are completely confidential, even for young people under 16. The only time health professionals would need to share a young person's details is for safeguarding purposes if they believe they are at risk of harm.[7] As part of the form, Alex will be asked to provide their personal details, such as their name, date of birth, a contact number to receive the results, and if they have any noticeable symptoms.

It is common in most services to be triaged by a nurse who will ask Alex some questions, which under normal circumstances would feel a bit too intimate – such as when Alex last had sex; what type of sex they had; the gender of their partner; did they use any contraception; and also about previous partners. Whilst these questions may feel judgemental or down-right rude, there is no ill intention involved. They ask everyone the same questions – regardless of their age. This information is essential to not only ensure Alex is screened properly but also to follow up on subsequent partners should it turn out Alex has an infection. This is why it is imperative Alex tells the truth. If, for example, Alex had anal sex and failed to mention it because Alex was worried about what the nurse would think, something might be missed. It might be worth reassuring Alex that these doctors and nurses literally do this for a living. They have seen and heard it all before – there is nothing Alex can say that will shock them so there is no need to be embarrassed. They are there to help, not judge.

There are four main ways a clinic will screen for an STI:

1. **Urine sample**: the majority of infections can be detected with a urine sample these days. They are easy to perform; the nurse will give you a plastic cup and ask you to fill it. It is worth remembering not to pee the hour before you attend the clinic, otherwise you may be waiting around until you can fill the cup. If you are waiting and haven't been seen, but are desperate to go, ask at reception for a cup (although they often have spares in the toilet, just in case.

2. **Swab sample**: vaginal swabs are used to detect STIs after vaginal sex. Essentially they are a cotton bud but on a long stick, that comes in a plastic tube to keep it sterile. These days a nurse will give you a swab and ask you to take the kit to the toilet and perform the swab yourself, which is far less intrusive than the nurse performing the swab for you. The cotton bud is inserted into the vaginal canal, where you brush the walls of the vagina before replacing the swab back in the plastic tube. If you have had unprotected anal sex, a nurse will get you to lie on your side before taking an anal swab in the same way. Occasionally, they may also perform a penile swab, where a thin swab is inserted just inside the urethra; however, these tend only to be used if you have symptoms and they want to be sure what the infection is, as swabs can be returned often within 30 minutes with a result. To be clear, penile swabs are much smaller than vaginal swabs, and whilst it may feel a little odd, really do not hurt – they just feel very strange, as generally people tend not to insert anything down their penis.

3. **Blood test**: some STIs are most easily tested through a simple blood test. Infections such as HIV, Hepatitis, Syphilis are tested this way.
4. **Visual exam**: if you have any lumps, bumps, sores or unusual discharge, then it may be necessary to have a visual exam. But this is only done if you have symptoms.

Once Alex has been screened they are free to leave. Now, Alex will have a nervous wait for their results, which they will usually receive within two weeks. These days, results are most often sent via a text message to the mobile phone number provided when Alex filled out their form. However, how much time has passed since Alex had unprotected sex will determine whether they are invited back for a second test in a couple of weeks' time. Many STIs have a window period, in which the infection may not show up on the tests and will instead return a false negative result.

If Alex is clear of infections their test will simply read: 'the test you recently took has come back negative.' To help retain privacy, it will not mention it was an STI screening or that the test was from the GUM clinic. Your business is your business.

If, however, Alex has an infection, they will be sent a number to call to arrange an appointment to return to the clinic and receive treatment. Obviously, the treatment will depend on what infection Alex has but as we covered in Chapter 9, the majority of STI can be treated with a course of antibiotics, and even those we can't cure, we now have ways to manage them safely.

Alex finding out they have an STI will not be a nice experience, but it doesn't have to be the end of the world either. It doesn't make Alex a bad person, it doesn't mean they are irresponsible, or that their moral compass has gone a bit skewiff! It just means Alex had unprotected sex and was unlucky this time. However, there is something important Alex will need to do. It is Alex's responsibility to inform their past partners. In Alex's case, they have only had unprotected sex once, with their past partner – so this shouldn't be too much of an issue. Yes, calling your partner, an ex-, or someone you had a one-night-stand with, to inform them you have tested positive for an infection is never going to be fun – but hopefully, they will be grateful they know and can now make sure they are tested and treated too. If you are mature enough to be sexually active, you have to be mature enough to take responsibility for your actions – and you had sex together. There is no point in playing the blame game. You both failed to use protection, therefore you are both equally responsible (assuming the situation was consensual).

If, however, Alex made a habit of having unprotected casual sex, partner notification may get a little trickier. Alex couldn't be sure how long they had been carrying an infection, so would have to contact all their past partners since they were last screened or since the first time they had unprotected sex to let them know about their STI status. Here the clinic can help; GUM clinics are experts in track and trace[8] and have experience of contacting people out of the blue to invite them to be tested. Partner notification can be done anonymously, as people are merely informed that someone they have had sexual contact with in the past has tested positively. The professionals who perform this service are experts in being discreet, if you are not able to contact people yourself.

# Repairing the emotional damage

Now all the practical parts are crossed off our to-do list, Alex can turn their attention to assessing the emotional damage caused by the experience. As you will have noticed, as we have made our way through the various steps there is a huge amount of anxiety and waiting involved in getting the all clear. The quicker Alex responds to the problem and faces up to what needs to be done, the less stressful everything is. For example, it is far easier for Alex to take emergency contraception than it is to go through waiting for a pregnancy test, and perhaps an abortion. But Alex can only access emergency contraception if they understand how it works, where to access it, and that they have a right to access it if they are underage. As they say, knowledge is power. And that is the message of this chapter. The more information we as the safe adults around our children can provide, the easier it will be for them to manage their problems.

Sex can be stressful but so too can be managing relationships. Throughout this chapter we have talked about an imaginary teenager (who spontaneously changes gender, sexuality and age as is convenient), but somewhere is an equally imaginary partner, who we have not mentioned yet. They too will be working their way through these issues. It would be nice to think that they have been along for the ride every step of the way but that may not be the case.

It would be much better if, as a couple (regardless of whether their relationship is serious or not), they could support each other along the journey of managing the situation – there is no reason why they couldn't attend the clinic together and be tested together. Whilst I wouldn't exactly class it as a romantic second date, it certainly beats waiting on your own. Personally, in my eyes, what could be more romantic than attending a GUM clinic together. It shows you want to take responsibility for your partner and keep them safe. It also draws a line under both your pasts and shows that if you move on, you can do so together, without the fear of infections and you are making these choices together. What could be more romantic?

As parents and carers, we have a huge part to play in whether or not Alex's partner is there to offer support and work through all this together. If Alex feels safe to bring their partner home, because you accept their relationship and treat them both with respect and whatever relationship they have as valid and real, it will make all the difference. Why would Alex bring their partner home if they know you will not make them feel welcome or worse, will blame them for the pickle they are in. It is up to us as parents to make our children's partners part of our family, rather than place them in opposition to the family. No child should be made to choose between their friends or family.

This is an especially important point when addressing unhealthy or abusive relationships. It is easier to see from the outside when a partner treats our child with a lack of care or respect and this is awful as a parent to watch. It may be counterintuitive but this is even more reason to make them welcome in your home. Abusers work hard to drive a wedge between their victims and their support networks. If your child has to see their partner behind your back, due to fear you will not approve, this makes them more vulnerable and plays into the abusers hands. Keep them close, invite their partner for dinner, be kind – then it is impossible for them to use your behaviours as an excuse for them to talk you down or say you are trying to split them up and place the blame on you. You can't drive a wedge between a family that talk openly. It doesn't work.

Nevertheless, regardless of whether the partner is on the scene, there is still important emotional baggage for our Alex to address. As I keep going back to again and again, the best way of dealing with our feelings is to talk about them with the people we trust. Sharing your misadventures, whether you're laughing or crying over them, is an excellent way to make sense of everything and get things into perspective.

We brushed aside earlier the reasons why Alex had unprotected sex. This needs to be addressed, otherwise we risk making the same mistakes again and again. However, there are positives in all this; we know having a pregnancy or STI scare can actually provide a valuable opportunity for behavioural change (Newby et al., 2017). There is a small window of time where Alex is more susceptible to influence as they worry about the consequences of their action. This is an ideal time to put interventions in place to positively change behaviour in the future. This may be about carrying condoms more regularly, reflecting on how much they drink at parties or about learning to be more assertive in demanding the use of a condom. It may also be a time to reflect on how healthy their relationship actually is. You could help them to think of ways they might respond differently should the same situation present itself again.

Perhaps the reason Alex failed to use a condom was because their partner didn't want to or talked them out of it. Perhaps they didn't really want to have sex but felt obliged. Think back to all the arguments we unpicked surrounding consent. This could be an ideal time to help Alex work through some of those issues, whilst they are in that malleable space to reflect and change how they view their own rights to sexual citizenship.

Carrying condoms, and having the confidence to insist on using them, shows responsibility and maturity. It will help protect Alex from unwanted pregnancy and STIs. Condoms protect physical health. However, condoms do not protect your emotional health – yes, they can reduce the stress of sorting out all this mess we have been discussing; but they will not ensure Alex's relationship is safe or healthy. A condom will not ensure Alex enjoys the sex they have or that they feel good about themselves afterwards. Condoms are wonderful things but they don't do that.

Alex has that responsibility. Our responsibility is to help. To be there with a warm shoulder, a kind ear and a cup of tea.

# Notes

1   CIS – is a term for someone who recognises themselves as the gender ascribed at birth. It is a term used to avoid the word 'normal'. One thing history has taught us is trans and non-binary folk are perfectly normal and have existed throughout history in every civilisation (although have been marginalised and persecuted in many). Equally, it is accepted (by most) and well evidenced, biological sex is not binary; science points to the fact gender cannot be simplified to a just male/female category, whether we are looking at chromosomes, gonads or secondary sex characteristics.

It is worth mentioning, however, if Alex or their partner were trans, pregnancy may still be a risk – depending on the type of sex they had. Simply, if one partner has a penis and the other has a vagina and they engage in penetrative vaginal sex, pregnancy would still be a risk.

2  Most local authorities have programmes where they will fund local pharmacies to deliver EHC for free to young people in education, although the breadth and age limits of the scheme will vary depending on your local authority. Emergency contraception is also available to buy over the counter if you are over 16 and will cost around £25 for Levonorgestrel and £35 for ellaOne.

3  In Scotland, section 2 of the Age of Legal Capacity (Scotland) Act 1991 sets out the conditions of when a person under-16 can consent to medical treatment or procedures.

4  In October 2020, women in Poland marched through the streets of Warsaw in protest after the government tried to bring in a wholesale ban on abortion: www.bbc.co.uk/news/av/world-europe-55077166. Around the same time, in Hungary, their European neighbours co-sponsored an anti-abortion declaration dubbed the Geneva Consensus Declaration; the thrust of the document was a non-binding yet clear denial of the international right to abortion under the guise of promoting women's health. The Geneva Consensus Declaration was signed by 30 countries including President Trump's America, where abortion rights have always been controversial. Other signatories included Brazil, Egypt, Indonesia, Uganda, Saudi Arabia, Bahrain, the United Arab Emirates, Iraq, Sudan, South Sudan, Libya. www.theguardian.com/world/2020/oct/22/us-trump-administration-signs-anti-abortion-declaration

5  The clear conclusion presented by the Royal College of Gynaecologist (RCOG) after reviewing the neuroanatomical and physiological evidence in the foetus, it was apparent the connections from the periphery to the cortex, necessary to sense pain, are not intact before 24 weeks of gestation. The RCOG concluded that the foetus can't experience pain in any sense prior to this development. RCOG. Fetal Awareness, Review of Research and Recommendations for Practice. March 2010. www.rcog.org.uk/globalassets/documents/guidelines/rcogfetalawarenesswpr0610.pdf

6  To find your nearest service, visit either British Pregnancy Advisory Service (BPAS) www.bpas.org/ or Marie Stopes www.mariestopes.org.uk/ for further details.

7  It is worth noting that sexual health services were the organisations that gathered a huge amount of the intelligence on the Rochdale CSE gangs. The young women who were exploited had been accessing the services, and the health care professionals who worked there had raised their concerns with Police and Social Care a number of times before anything was done. The services not only gather intelligence and evidence, as the girls talked about their 'boyfriends', but also provided invaluable support to the young women giving them a safe place to visit.

8  Which begs the question why the government failed to use these experts during Covid? We literally have teams of people trained in partner notification tracking infections!

# References

bpas (2018). Social media, SRE, and sensible drinking: understanding the dramatic decline in teenage pregnancy. Available at: www.bpas.org/media/3037/bpas-teenage-pregnancy-report.pdf.

Council for Europe (2020). Commissioner for human rights. Comprehensive sexuality education protects children and helps build a safer, inclusive society, 21 July. Available at: www.coe.int/en/web/commissioner/-/comprehensive-sexuality-education-protects-children-and-helps-build-a-safer-inclusive-society 8-8-2020.

FSRH and RCOG (2019). Abortion and abortion care factsheet – to support relationship and sex education in secondary schools. Produced by the Faculty of Sexual and Reproductive Healthcare and Royal College of Obstetricians and Gynaecologists. Available at: https://pcwhf.co.uk/wp-content/uploads/2019/03/fsrh-rcog-abortion-care-factsheet-rse-lessons.pdf.

Gillick v West Norfolk and Wisbech Area Health Authority, UKHL 7 (17 October 1985) Available via (BAILII) in the law reports (appeal cases) [1986] AC 112.

Lindberg, L. and Maddow-Zimet, I. (2012). Consequences of sex education on teen and young adult sexual behaviors and outcomes, Journal of Adolescent Health, 51(4), 332–8.

Newby, K., Brown, K., Bayley, J., Kehal, I., Caley, M., Danahay, A., Hunt, J. and Critchley, G. (2017). Development of an intervention to increase sexual health service uptake by young people, Health Promotion Practice, 18.

RCOG (2010). Fetal awareness, review of research and recommendations for practice, March. Available at: www.rcog.org.uk/globalassets/documents/guidelines/rcogfetalawarenesswpr0610.pdf.

Tanton, C. et al. (2015). Patterns and trends in sources of information about sex among young people in Britain: Evidence from three National Surveys of Sexual Attitudes and Lifestyles, BMJ Open, 5, e007834.

# PART IV

# SEX MEDIA

# Quiz: sex media

1. How old do you have to be to watch porn?
2. How old do you have to be to buy a *top-shelf* magazine from a newsagents or petrol-station?
3. How old do you have to be to buy erotic fiction like *Fifty shades of Grey*?
4. What is the 'watershed' when it comes to TV viewing?
5. What does 'Rule 34' state?
6. Who was prosecuted in the biggest pornography obscenity trial in British legal history?
7. Goya's painting 'The Nude Maja' (1797) is the first European painting to show what feminine attribute?
8. What is Outcome 21?

You may have come across the following terms in the media – but what are they?

9. Deepfake
10. Upskirting
11. NoFap
12. Cyber-flashing

# CHAPTER 12

# PORNOGRAPHY AND SEX MEDIA

**M**any people assume pornography was invented in the late 70s along with the VHS, shortly followed by the 80s bush. However, pornography has a long history (Box 12.1). Whether we are talking about obscenity, morality or pushing the of boundaries of acceptability, pornography has always been a battleground.

The term pornography was first coined in the mid-nineteenth century and has become entwined with the creation of the Secret Museums in Naples and 'Cabinet of Obscene Objects' housed at the British Museum in London (Attwood, 2018). Curators sorting through the recently discovered artefacts from the archaeological sites of Pompeii and Herculaneum, were concerned of their suitability to be put on display to the general public due to their sexually explicit nature. It was decided they would remain locked in the Secret Museum, to ensure they did not fall into the wrong hands of the easily corrupted. The exhibition was reserved only for the Upper Class Gentry, as only they were considered to be of a suitable disposition to be able to cope with the sexually charged relics. Women and children needed to be protected, whilst the working classes were already considered equally deviant and dangerous, and there was real concern they might use the sexually explicit materials in the wrong way (Mulholland, 2013).

A few years later in 1857, this culminated in the introduction of *The Obscene Publications Act*, the first official laws in England to control the reproduction and distribution of pornography. For many people, this period marks the start of the battle over who controls the obscene and who needs to be protected.

DOI: 10.4324/9781003122296-18

## Box 12.1 The history of porn

Porn is not a new phenomenon. As soon as early humans could pick up a piece of chalk they began producing images that were sexual in nature. Whether they were early sculptures of fertility symbols, erotic works of art, or illicit writings, human beings have always been obsessed with the human form and exploring the erotic. History is littered with sexual images and representations; however, the term *pornography* is relatively new being coined in the mid-nineteenth century. Throughout history, pornography has been associated with those in power policing the illicit. The history of porn is a battleground of morals, values, obscenity, human rights, and new technologies. Indeed, Dr Kate Lister coined the phrase *Kink Blink* which she describes as the time it takes for new technology to be turned to facilitating sex in some way, be it the invention of the paint brush or VHS.

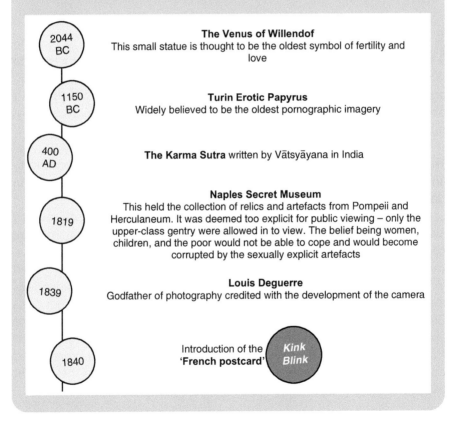

**2044 BC**

**The Venus of Willendof**
This small statue is thought to be the oldest symbol of fertility and love

**1150 BC**

**Turin Erotic Papyrus**
Widely believed to be the oldest pornographic imagery

**400 AD**

**The Karma Sutra** written by Vātsyāyana in India

**1819**

**Naples Secret Museum**
This held the collection of relics and artefacts from Pompeii and Herculaneum. It was deemed too explicit for public viewing – only the upper-class gentry were allowed in to view. The belief being women, children, and the poor would not be able to cope and would become corrupted by the sexually explicit artefacts

**1839**

**Louis Deguerre**
Godfather of photography credited with the development of the camera

**1840**

Introduction of the **'French postcard'**

*Kink Blink*

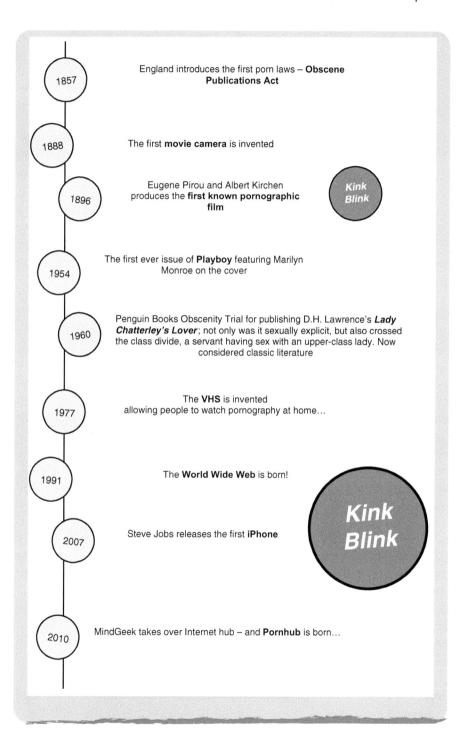

**1857** — England introduces the first porn laws – **Obscene Publications Act**

**1888** — The first **movie camera** is invented

**1896** — Eugene Pirou and Albert Kirchen produces the **first known pornographic film**

*Kink Blink*

**1954** — The first ever issue of **Playboy** featuring Marilyn Monroe on the cover

**1960** — Penguin Books Obscenity Trial for publishing D.H. Lawrence's **Lady Chatterley's Lover**; not only was it sexually explicit, but also crossed the class divide, a servant having sex with an upper-class lady. Now considered classic literature

**1977** — The **VHS** is invented allowing people to watch pornography at home…

**1991** — The **World Wide Web** is born!

**2007** — Steve Jobs releases the first **iPhone**

*Kink Blink*

**2010** — MindGeek takes over Internet hub – and **Pornhub** is born…

**Did you know...**

The term pornography first appeared in the Oxford English Dictionary in 1850 taken from the Greek:

*graphos* – writings, descriptions
*pornei* – prostitutes

meaning the writings of prostitution.

Over the intervening years, what has been classed as pornography has changed along with cultural values and sensibilities. In the 1950s, society was scandalised by Penguin Books' decision to publish the then-banned D.H. Lawrence novel, *Lady Chatterley's Lover*, leading to the most famous obscenity trial in British legal history. These days, the book is a staple of the majority of undergraduate literacy courses. This begs the question, what is porn and who gets to decide what is obscene and what is culturally acceptable?

With the introduction of any new technology, history has shown it doesn't take long before the ingenuity of humans manage to manipulate it to sexual ends. Historian Dr Kate Lister, author of the *Curious History of Sex*, named this phenomenon the *kink blink*, which feels apt in a chapter exploring pornography. The first thing we did when we invented the camera was to start taking naked pictures of each other; similarly with the video camera. Indeed, many attribute Sony's refusal to engage with the porn industry the deciding factor in the format war of the VCR home video system, between Betamax and VHS, despite their Betamax machine being superior in every way to VHS (Sulivan and Mckee, 2015). Nevertheless, VHS won the day; considering at the time, X-rated tapes made up over half of all sales in the late 1970, you can understand why (ibid.).

In days gone by, before the birth of the internet, pornography could only be sold in licensed adult video stores; these were discreetly placed in the less-nice end of the high street, situated as standard, between a betting shop and a dodgy-looking second-hand jewellery store. Innocent passers-by were protected from reading the titles of the DVD and videos on offer inside, by the blacked-out windows, and a sign 'for over 18s only' would police the door, along with the shame-inducing stares from the lady who ran the laundrette over the road.

For most of us growing up, our only brush with pornography would be through the occasional, discarded, slightly damp copy of the *Daily Sport* caught in a hedge by the park – or perhaps an older sibling discovering a mucky video tape or magazine hidden at the back of dad's wardrobe.

However, we are currently living through possibly the greatest *kink blink* of all, through the influence of the internet and the smart phone. It is easy to see why many adults are worried. Whereas at one time, adult material was easily locked away from prying eyes, suddenly porn is only a few clicks away for anyone to access.

The ease with which young people can now access online pornography, and the vast array of content available frightens many parents. It feels like Pandora's box has been opened and blacked-out windows are no longer enough to keep the content hidden.

# Problem policy

In response, UK government policy in recent years has focused on filtering and blocking pornography and other harmful content, in a similar fashion to a digital *secret library*. The flagship policy of The Digital Economy Bill (2017) was the disastrous attempt at trying to instigate Age Verification (AV) restrictions, better known as the *porn block* (which at time of writing has now been scrapped).[1]

Whilst government policy here in the UK has focused on attempting to block porn, elsewhere there have been more positive steps forward in address the issues of pornography with young people. For example, Dr Emily Rothman's Porn literacy programme, as explained in her *TEDtalk: How porn changes the way teens think about sex* (2018).[2] The programme is evidence informed and designed to help young people critically think and engage with pornography (although none is shown in class) in its broadest context. The idea is to help young people contextualise pornography in a similar way as we explore film or adverts in media studies. As Andy Phippen, Professor of Digital Responsibility points out, 'it is far easier for a politician to say "children are watching pornography, we must stop this" rather than the more complex "Children are looking at pornography and whilst we can't stop this we can provide tools that might mitigate exposure and put education in place…"' (Phippen, 2017, p. 140). The real public health crisis is not pornography, but the fact we are not providing comprehensive relationships and sex education for every adolescent to tackle the issues we are levelling at porn. Unfortunately, many young people are looking to porn for their sex education. This is a flaw of the RSE on offer, both at home and at school, not a flaw in pornography.

## The porn block

When taken at face value Age Verification (AV) seems like a sensible step to protect children online. This would require commercial sites to verify the age of their users before they can view sexual content in a bid to prevent children accessing pornography or other content deemed as harmful. If you have ever (accidentally of course) stumbled across an online porn website, you will know, as you arrive on the site, you will be met with a pop-up box that reads something like, 'this website contains adult material suitable only for those over the age of 18.' And then you get the really difficult security question: 'Are you 18? Yes or No?' And that is it. To be clear, no 15 year old has ever clicked onto a site, stopped and clicked 'no'! By clicking yes, you absolve the distributor – in this case the website – of any responsibility. The idea with AV was to require visitors to register their personal details, to confirm their age, such as driving licence, passport or credit card, which would be checked and verified. Whilst this sounds simple, privacy advocates raised substantial concerns around the safety of having a database of people's porn viewing habits, and their personal Id – which feels like a hackers dream come true, especially after what happened with the Ashley Madison[3] data breach in 2015.

Further concerns were raised when it emerged Mind Geek, had been given the government contract to design the software.

In practice, however, the proposal was not only impractical, but many online safety experts suggested it may lead to putting young people at further risk (Blake, 2019). As those desperate to access material may be forced into more dangerous areas of the internet to secure fake IDs, and cheap VPNs (Virtual Private Network) to sidestep the restrictions.

Interestingly, as AV policy was developing and unfolding, as part of my regular sessions with young people, I would ask if any of the young people in class had heard about the porn block – almost without fail, teenagers had not only heard about the policy, but had also read articles or watched videos on YouTube explaining how to sidestep the restrictions. Young people regularly brought up the solutions of VPNs, which allow a user to hide their IP address and the location they are searching from. Conversely, when I spoke to professionals during trainings and asked them the same questions, they were none the wiser (except for the ICT teachers). Unless, AV was designed to make it more challenging for middle-aged, non-tech savvy adults to watch porn, it seemed less than effective.

Indeed, much of this policy seems to be based on ideology rather than evidence of what will work to make young people safer. Whilst young people having access to pornography is an issue, blocking it is unlikely to help. Instead, a much better solution is to teach young people how to engage with porn and other forms of media safely. That does not mean encouraging them to watch it; but neither does it mean shaming them if they do.

Pornography, by its very nature, is an emotive topic and a battleground of people's values. There have always been those who find the idea of pornography offensive; the reasons vary from the objectification of women; concerns over sexual violence or are based on religious or culture values of sex, marriage and relationships. However, on the other side are those who enjoy pornography, see it as a valuable outlet of sexual expression and a means of sexual liberation, especially for marginalised communities such as LGBTQ+. Regardless of what side of the fence you sit, it doesn't really matter. One thing's clear: we can no longer keep children in a bubble safe from sexualised media. With the dawn of digital TV, even the watershed doesn't exist to shield children from adult viewing.

Before we go any further it is worth taking a moment to reflect on our own feelings about pornography as this will affect how we manage future discussions. Take a moment to think about the question below; feel free to write your answers down, as then you can look back at them later, as you read through the rest of this chapter.

# What are our problems with porn? (And are there any benefits?)

One of the key worries for adults is about what effect pornography may have on children and for parents, what to do if they discover their child has been searching for porn on the internet. Before we go any further, please do not assume this only relates to sons and not daughters. Teenage girls will often search for porn, watch porn and enjoy porn.

It is considered developmentally normal for young people (regardless of gender) to be curious about sex and to seek out information, especially around the age of 10/11/12 and the onset of puberty (Lehmiller and Rothman, 2020). It is essential not to punish kids for being curious about sex. Punishing the child will only increase their feelings of shame about sex, and confirm they can't come to you with their valid questions. In this case, it will only teach them to hide their behaviours better in future. Instead, I would advise you to take this as an opportunity and a valuable teachable moment.

# Teachable moment

**Younger children**: Discovering your child has seen something they shouldn't is always worrying. But you can mitigate the shock by how you deal with the situation. With younger children, it is more than likely they came across pornography by mistake whilst searching for something else. Research shows that if young children stumble across sexually explicit material online, seeing the material itself is less upsetting than their fear that you'll be angry at them for seeing it (Spišák, 2016). The most important lesson for younger children to learn about staying safe online is to ensure they know: *if they see anything that they think they shouldn't, anything that seems odd, or strange, or makes them feel a little uncomfortable, they should come and to talk to you.* You won't be mad (and this needs to be a promise you can keep), and you will help them manage and answer their questions. If you get mad, why would they ever tell you? Explain that there are things on the internet that are especially for grown-ups, just like there are shows on TV that are for grown-ups. Ask them what they were originally searching for and help them find the answer to what they were looking for in the first place. If they have any questions about what they have seen, try to answer them. Remember, you can always defer and say: 'That's a great question – let me have a think so I can give you a great answer too!'

This may also be a time to review the safe search feature on the home computer, laptop or tablet. Having separate profiles on devices can really help, especially if you have children of different ages and stages, or who all share the same devices. Most devices now have very simple to use child-friendly filters that can be turned on with only a few clicks. It is worth speaking to older children in the house too; remind them to clear their search history, and not leave tabs open for their siblings to find either.

**Older children**: When it comes to teens, it is more likely any material they have found, they have looked at intentionally. Older teens rarely come across porn by mistake and these days porn does not accidentally pop-up from nowhere. Although, it is possible they may have been sent something by friends and some of the material may have been meant as a joke, to disgust, or freak each other out rather as a sexual stimulus. However, with older teens we have more to unpick, and this will not be solved in a single conversation. How you react will depend on past discussions you have had around sex, your values and what messages they have been given previously. As with younger children, how we react now will greatly affect how easy our children will find it to approach us in the future – however uncomfortable, this can still be a valuable opportunity to open a dialogue.

# What is porn?

Before we can talk about porn properly we need to be clear what we are talking about. A good place to start is to define what we mean by porn. We have been talking this long as if we all know instinctively what porn means and all have the same specific picture in our heads. Does porn only cover what you find on the internet? What about top-shelf magazines? What about erotic fiction? Audio-erotica? Where is the line between porn and art? We take coach loads of kids to art galleries on school trips and allow them to wander around the exhibits often littered with images of nakedness.[4] It's not enough to merely echo the famous sentiments of US Supreme Court Justice Potter Stewart, who said: 'I know it when I see it… (*Jacobellis* v *Ohio*, 378 US 184 (1964)). We need something more concrete to work from.

Often the word porn is associated with disgust or excess: M&S food is referred to as *food-porn* as are Nigella Lawson's cooking shows. Documentaries have been accused of being voyeuristic poverty-porn or trauma-porn (Sullivan and McKee, 2015), relishing in seedy undertones. Unfortunately, there is no universal recognised definition of what porn is. Whilst we may not want children to be reading *Fifty Shades of Grey*, there are no age restrictions on buying books. Yes, particular shops may have their own policies on what they deem suitable to sell to particular patrons, but there are no legal requirements for them to do so. The same is true of top-shelf magazines. You know the ones with plastic covers hiding the front image; despite the fact they are often referred to as porno-mags, they are not technically classified as porn, not if they can be sold in a newsagents, or petrol stations, otherwise they would need to be sold from a licensed sex-shop. The reason they are on the top-shelf is there is an unofficial height restriction: you need to be this height to ride the ride, sort of way.

It is equally important to be clear about what is *not* pornography. However we may feel about porn, there is no arguing it is becoming seen as more legitimate and more mainstream. There is no such thing as *child porn*, a term often used by the tabloids. They do not make pornography for children or of children; and in the UK, successive acts of Parliament prohibit the production, possession and distribution of films or images of anyone under the age of 18.[5] Instead we should refer to this thing more accurately and call them what they are – *indecent images of children*, or *images of child sexual abuse*. Language matters.

Rape is not pornography. Neither is sexual assault, coercion or human trafficking, neither is revenge porn.[6] These are all clearly criminal offences in their own right and should not be confused with the legally produced adult entertainment. However, these issues are often used by abolitionists to muddy the waters when discussing the harms of pornography. In our discussion we will only be talking about pornography that is legally produced, commercially for distribution.

The definition I find most useful is the one put forward by Sullivan and Mckee (2015) – see Figure 12.1. This is the one I use with young people in class and in the training I deliver to professionals. I think it's helpful as it encapsulates the key components of the intention and function of pornography whilst helping to distinguish it from other forms of media.

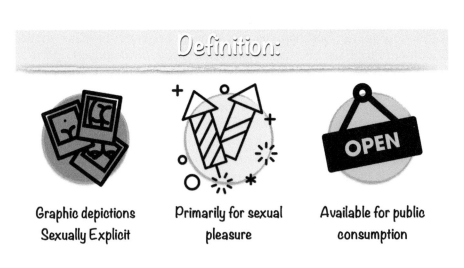

Definition:

Graphic depictions Sexually Explicit

Primarily for sexual pleasure

Available for public consumption

**Figure 12.1** Pornography definition

Fundamentally, pornography has three primary criteria.

1. **Sexually explicit**: offers highly graphic depiction of genitals and/or incorporates explicit sexual acts.
2. **Publicly mediated**: intended to be made available for public consumption but the act is physically separate from the audience.
3. **Sexual pleasure**: intended to incite sexual pleasure.

However, the sex on display is not 'real'. The very presence of a camera changes the context of what is on display to a performance. There is an audience, even if mediated through the lens of the camera; what we see is no longer authentic, even if the events involve a real couple having real sex. Like any performance, actors play to the audience.

This is an essential point to keep in mind when putting porn into context for young people. Like any performance, the act has been carefully choreographed to give the best show possible. Camera angles, lighting, make-up, sound and narrative have already been dealt with off screen. Just as in a Hollywood action movie, we may see the actor on screen pick up a broom and defeat four armed assassins but what we don't see is the hours of work, practice, choreography, training and out-takes it took to put the shot together. Why should porn be any different? Rather than thinking of them as porn stars, perhaps we should think of them as *sexual athletes* who are trained to perform sex acts and positions the average person simply couldn't manage, or perhaps *sexual stunt performers* would be a better and more apt description (Sullivan and Mckee, 2015).

Adult entertainment is not a euphemism. Pornography is designed for adults, to enjoy – not as an instruction manual or to replace sex education for teenagers (Rothman, 2018). I say again, *it is not real*. Copying what you see on screen is no guarantee that it would be pleasurable or enjoyable, more likely it was just convenient for the camera angle. The analogy I always describe to teenagers is, if you want to learn to drive, sitting up playing *Grand Theft Auto* on your PS4 and watching the boxed set of *Fast and Furious* – whilst it may be fun isn't all that helpful and won't give you the skills you need to past your driving test. Porn is no different. It is no more a true reflection of sex as *Fast and Furious* is of driving… but it can be exciting.

### Deepfake

Channel 4 recently released a video of the Queen's Christmas speech, in which she dances around the room. Clearly this was fake. They did it to draw attention to deepfake technology and videos online designed to spread fake news. Up until recently the programmes necessary to produce deepfake videos were expensive, and reserved for expensive Hollywood Movies (similar to how Peter Cushing managed to appear in the new Star Wars films, despite having been dead for years); however, it is now readily available. If you have enough pictures of someone (which isn't hard for celebrities) using Artificial Intelligence (AI), you can create films of them saying and doing whatever you want. There has been a craze of deepfake porn, where celebrities faces have been pasted onto porn performers bodies making it seem as they have filmed the scene. At one time, this would look clearly fake, however the technology now looks seamless. Deepfakes have now moved to the world of revenge porn, as people create and post films to humiliate or shame their victims online. This is a new form of image-based sexual abuse.

## Changing the conversation

When I am asked by schools to talk to young people about pornography, my starting point is never porn. Unfortunately, when adults talk to young people about porn, the topic is usually framed from the perspective of 'why porn is harmful'. I know if I open the session there, I will be met with resistance. Those in the room who do watch porn will immediately have their backs up and be worried they are being judged. Why would I talk to you about porn if you are going to talk about me like a sexual predator and make me feel ashamed in front of my peers?

Instead, I find asking the question:

#### *Where do we learn about sex from?*

enables me to sidestep these problems. Within a matter of minutes, young people will be talking about the gaps in teaching RSE at school; the issues of talking with their parents; the TV shows and films they are watching; the content they read on social media; and porn will always get a mention. But this time, the conversation was started on their terms. They brought up porn, not me – which means they have an opportunity to frame how we approach the topic. This makes all the difference in the classroom. We now have a forum, where we can critically evaluate which of these sources are reliable and why people may prefer to choose certain places to seek their answers.

Young people will speak at length of the benefit of the internet. Google doesn't judge or shame you if you ask questions about sex. It isn't embarrassing, you don't have to look anyone in the eye, or worry about it shouting at you. It is private. But equally, young people are quite savvy – they know not all information on the internet is true or reliable… or safe. Young people will talk about the negative influences porn has, and like the adults around them will blame porn for many of the negative attitudes and experiences they witness. Young people are quick to explain that porn is harmful to younger kids, or to other people who aren't as clued up as them – in what is known as the third person effect (Davidson, 1983).

One thing that becomes clear from this conversation with young people is, if we – the safe adults – are not providing opportunities for young people to ask questions about sex, and explore sex and sexuality in a posi-tive way, young people will simply find their answers elsewhere. The one place you can find out all the ins and outs (excuse the pun) of sex, is by watching porn. Young people watch porn to see how to have sex, to see what bodies and genitals look like, and to discover how to pleasure their partner. Unfortunately, the majority of porn was never designed for these ends. If you want to know how to truly pleasure your partner, what it takes is communication and finding out about them personally.

Young people also watch porn for the same reasons adults do – as a sexual stimulus. We use this phrase, 'watch porn' as a euphemism. People do not *watch* porn – people *wank* to porn. Apologies for being crude but no one sits down with a bowl of popcorn and a cup of tea like they do with a show on Netflix to watch a porn film. Generally, pornography viewing is some-thing that is done in private, by yourself, with your underwear around your knees or on the floor – which is another reason to put boundaries in place with your teens regarding privacy and knocking before entering private spaces. No one wants to see that.

# Is porn harmful?

And so we arrive at the million-dollar question: is porn harmful? In par-ticular, is it harmful for young people? The honest answer, unfortunately, is – it depends. I am sorry but it is true.

You could be forgiven if you assumed there would be a simple answer. Especially if you were to listen to the rhetoric of politicians on both sides of the Atlantic (more so in America, where a number of states have actually declared pornography a public health crisis), and the sensationalist tabloid articles declaring there is an epidemic of porn addiction or that online porn is the digital equivalent of crack-cocaine (Attwood, 2018). Indeed, porn addiction websites such as *Fight the New Drug* and *Your Brain on Porn* claim porn 'rewires' the brain, and the only way to combat the damage is a practice they describe as '*rebooting*' the brain to overcome the addiction.

Anti-porn activists have levelled claims that porn damages relationships or the way viewers relate to their partners as it promotes a lack of intimacy. Pornography causes violence against women and promotes misogynistic views of women as objects for men's satisfaction. Pornography is warping young people's notion of what *normal sex* should look like and pressures young people into trying niche practices. However, how much of this is actually true?

We know, for the vast majority of people, porn does not seem to be a problematic source in their lives (Lehmiller and Rothman, 2020; Grubbs, Perry, Wilt, et al. 2019; Marston, 2018). Indeed, there is little evidence to support the claims posed above. There is particularly little evidence of any harms of pornography consumption on young people (Marston, 2018). There is a tendency to blame porn for wider social problems, however porn does not exist in a vacuum. It is part of culture and society as a whole, which means it will always be difficult to determine if porn is the actual cause of harm.

## Is porn addictive?

On 16 May 2012 Gary Wilson, one of the co-founders of the website *Your Brain on Porn*, delivered a TEDx talk in Glasgow. His wife was friends with one of the organisers. His talk *The Great Porn Experiment* has now been seen 13,839,223 times on YouTube and his views have been used as some of the key evidence in the 'science' of porn addiction. The slight issue is: Gary Wilson is not a scientist. He has no scientific or academic qualification and has never published any peer-reviewed research anywhere in the world.

Ted have distanced themselves from the talk, and it does not appear on their website. However, as mentioned you can find his talk on YouTube, under which you will find the disclaimer:

NOTE FROM TED: This talk contains several assertions that are not supported by academically respected studies in medicine and psychology. While some viewers might find advice provided in this talk to be helpful, please do not look to this talk for medical advice.

And yet *Your Brain on Porn* is quoted in magazines and newspaper articles. Amongst the #Nofap and 'Reboot' followers he is a cult hero despite four separate peer reviewed studies having been published which unpick his ideas as pseudoscience.[7] But porn addiction is big business. In an interview with the Kinsey institute, Dr Nicola Prause sets the record straight:

> Pornography does not 'hijack' anything in the brain, it does not 'flood' the brain with dopamine, it is not a 'superstimulus,' and it absolutely is not 'more addictive than cocaine.' This common panic language shows a basic lack of education in neuroscience.
>
> (Dr Prause in Lehmiller, 2020)

## #Nofap

(N.B. to fap = ejaculate)

The notion of Rebooting to beat porn addiction, has led to the rise of an online community often associated with the #Nofap. These men believe by abstaining from masturbation, they can boost their testosterone and therefore their manhood. Their ideas are based on the 'science' of Gary Wilsons and his website Your Brain on Porn. There are strong links with the views promoted by the misogynistic group known as Incels (involuntary-celibate) who believe men are split into Alpha and Beta. Betas are emasculated by feminism and 'woke' ideas of equality and LGBTQ inclusion.

Rebooting will help them to become Alphas. Their chat groups often feature conspiracy theories of the New World Order, The Red Pill and antisemitic conspiracies that porn industry is orchestrated by Jews to bring down society. Yes it is bizarre. Members have been investigated for harassing scientists (especially female) who publish peer reviewed studies that disprove the addiction model for pornography or undermines the practice of 'Rebooting'.

NB: To be absolutely clear there is no scientific evidence to support #Nofap or their views are anyway beneficial to health.

Indeed, neither the Diagnostic and Statistical Manual of Mental Disorders, Fifth Edition (DSM-5) nor the International Classification of Diseases

(ICD-11) classify pornography use as a mental disorder or addiction.[8] However, the term porn addiction is banded around in public discourse and mainstream media as if it was an actual clinical diagnosis. As I have said repeatedly, language matters.

Nevertheless, there are certainly a number of people who struggle with their use of pornography and these people should not be discounted. What is particularly interesting to note about individuals who report 'feelings of addiction' is their feelings of distress have no correlation to their frequency of use of pornography. Instead, the only correlation, was those who felt their use of porn were most problematic had more conservative views and stronger beliefs pornography was morally wrong (Zimmer, Imhoff, 2020; Grubbs et al., 2019; Perry, 2019). This phenomenon was put down to moral incongruence in pornography use; which put simply is distress caused when someone's own behaviours clash with their intrinsically held beliefs (Grubbs et al., 2019).

It would seem that those who hold more conservative, religious or moral beliefs that sex is shameful, are more likely to report feelings of their porn use being problematic. This highlights again the importance of avoiding shame in how we respond to young people's sexual behaviours and identities.

## Not all porn is the same

When we talk about porn, we talk as if it is all the same. It isn't. These days there is far more variety in pornography available; with many different forms, styles, genres and artistic merit. With the introduction of the internet, pornography diversified as production and distribution cost plummeted. This meant it was easier for feminist and LGBTQ+ producers to move into the mainstream (Sullivan and Mckey, 2015). On one side of the spectrum you have ethical and feminist porn; there are real couples who post their intimate videos on sites like *Make Love Not Porn;* there is cartoon porn, dominated by the Manga style Hentai films; there is queer porn; fetish porn and BDSM porn. And then there is the standard – *I've come to fix your boiler – oh what big tools you have – let's have a threesome*, style porn which promotes unrealistic expectations for how British Gas works. On the other end of the spectrum, we have the darker side of actual abuse that is filmed and posted online, however that is *not* porn – it is illegal.

My point is, when people ask if porn is harmful, it is extremely difficult to say. There is such variety available, it depends on what you are watching. Will pornography warp young people's sexual attitudes, or their values? If you think back to the question I posed earlier, 'From where do young people learn about sex?' The answer to the question is from a myriad of sources, their friends, family, the TV shows they watch, the music they listen to (and, on a positive note, the safe adults and professionals who are brave enough to engage with them on the topic – here we have an opportunity for real change). Harmful ideas circulating amongst young people pertaining to sex and their personal relationships, will be affected by all these areas of society and not just from whatever porn they might be viewing (Marston, 2018).

To put it another way, if we think about fast food. Is fast food harmful? Again, the answer depends on what type of fast food; how often you eat it; what the rest of your diet is like – do you only consume fast-food or is it a once a week treat? Do you have any underlying health conditions? Are you fit and active or are you already obese with type ii diabetes? The same applies to porn (Lehmiller and Rothman, 2020). Any effects pornography will have will depend on the material consumed and the context of consumption (Marston, 2018).

It stands to reason, if your only source of information about sex and how sexual relationship are formed and maintained is pornography, you are going to be in far greater danger than someone surrounded by a variety of positive voices and experiences. This would be further exasperated if combined with being raised in a sexually conservative household, who believe pornography is immoral and sex is shameful.

## Is there a link between sexual violence and pornography?

Another common accusation levelled at pornography is that it is becoming increasing violent and in turn perpetuates male sexual violence against women. Again, we are back at the same issue of causation – does violent porn push people to become violent offenders or do violent offenders seek out violent porn?

There are those who have suggested that viewers are becoming desensitised by 'soft' porn and there is a demand to produce more violent and degrading porn. However, a recent study, aptly named, *'Harder and Harder'? Is Mainstream Pornography Becoming Increasingly Violent and Do Viewers Prefer Violent Content?* showed there is no evidence to support this claim (Shor and Seida, 2019). Indeed, the study examined 269 popular films uploaded to a free tube site over the past decade. They discovered not only was there no increase in aggression over time, but if anything the aggressive content had decreased. What was particularly interesting was videos that did display acts of aggression were both less likely to receive views and less likely to be ranked favourably. Incidentally, the videos which ranked highest were those which showed female sexual pleasure (even if it was performative pleasure) (ibid.).

When it comes to the effects of pornography, it seems one's pre-existing sexual attitudes are the deciding factor. If an individual has developed a positive sense of their own sexual citizenship and part of that realisation is their recognition of others equal right to their own sexual citizenship, pornography has little influence on their attitudes to sex. The concern that more frequent engagement with porn would desensitise the viewer's acknowledgement of others right to sexual citizenship does not bear out in practice. Those who watch porn more it seems, do not become more comfortable with depiction of nonconsensual situations through their viewing (Dawson et al., 2020).

Both of these results correlate with what we see in broader society and cultures around the world. We see sexual violence as most associated with societies that have extremely conservative attitudes to sex; that see women as second-class citizens; where patriarchal control of the family is still the norm, and notions of male entitlement still reign (McNair, 2014).

It would seem that cultures with a more progressive attitude to sex and pornography are actually less violent, and women tend to have more sexual freedom. This is not to assume that the availability of porn is the deciding factor. Again, there is a difference between correlation and causation. It is more likely the recognition of sexual citizenship as a basic human right.

# The influence of Pornhub

It might be a positive step forward that pornography has diversified with the help of the internet. However, it is all well and good having feminists and ethical porn available in the market, but by definition it only remains ethical if you pay for your porn. Young people do not pay for their porn.

The majority of young people access pornography through aggregate sites, such as *Pornhub, YouPorn, xHamster and Redtube*. If you are not familiar with these sites, it is essentially a version of YouTube but instead of being populated with cat videos, or make-up tutorials, it is populated solely with pornography. In the same way YouTube makes money through algorithms, search engine optimisation and targeted advertising, so do the aggregated porn sites.

Currently the company behind Pornhub – MindGeek – has the share of the market with an estimated 115 million visits daily. Their business model is based on users uploading their own content, much of which is pirated from other sources. Whilst the array of different bodies and categories of porn available on the site instantly destroys the myth that everyone in porn looks the same: that ethical, feminist porn movie that was 25 minutes long as it set the scene, as our lovers built the tension, and intimacy in the encounter – it finished not with the money-shot, but instead showed the aftercare of the encounter as the partners basked in the afterglow of their love-making – has now been cut to 6 minutes (guess which bits they clipped?) and is now two people banging away. Yes, it is artily filmed, but it loses its intimacy when it's been renamed 'teenage slut take a full load'.

The language of the titles are awful. There is no other way of saying it. Many of the titles are purposely chosen to push the film to fit in the current most popular trend or category. A real sex film, between a couple in an actual relationship is suddenly tagged as 'Step-sister seduces her Step-brother, let's hope their parents don't find out' when clearly that is not the case. There is a fear that the algorithms have become caught in their own feedback loop as the porn becomes cyclical. A particular tag is pushed to the top of the favourites, so producers make more content to fit the tag, which then makes it even more popular, even though in reality that may not be the case.

# Teachable moments – talking to young people about porn

There is a reason why, when I am asked to talk to teenagers about pornography, I never label my lessons 'pornography'. I either introduce my session as being about sex media, or simply exploring where we learn about sex from. The reason is, if you look back at the list of your answers to the original question…

## What are our problems with porn?
## (And are there any benefits?)

If we are honest, the majority of the answers can apply to all media in general. Porn is an intrinsic part of culture and society – it does not exist in isolation. Is porn realistic? No, but then neither are the sex scenes in Hollywood movies. Does porn give unrealistic expectation of sex and relationships? Certainly, but so do the majority of romantic comedies. How many TV shows can you think of that provide positive representations of consent? Issues about body image, the pressure to look or act a certain way… you only have to think about the #MeToo movement to know that misogyny, sexual violence and male entitlement is every much a part of mainstream culture. The same negative messages are everywhere. 'The problem isn't that the media is teaching young people to have sex… the problem is too much of the sex on offer isn't grounded in principles of respect, consent, diversity, equity, and open communication…' (Sulivan and Mckee, 2015, p. 125). So why are we so hung up just about the issues of porn?

Take a moment to think about a sex scene in a big-hit Hollywood movie… think of one of the classics you grew up with – how realistic is it? What expectations does it raise, and if you were watching it to learn how to have sex, how helpful are its instructions? Would Rose's first time in *Titanic* (1997) really have been worth dying for, in the back of a car in the frozen arctic – sounds cold and uncomfortable to me?

Porn is designed as adult entertainment. Comedy films are designed to make us laugh, releasing endorphins into our body and making us feel good. Horror films, like roller-coasters, are designed to scare us, to get adrenaline pumping through our veins and help us to feel alive. That makes perfect sense. However, we also pay to go to the cinema to watch films about someone's struggle with the death of a loved one, or being diagnosed with Parkinson's and leave the cinema in floods of tears? But watching a film with the aim to turn us on is considered strange…? Why do we see sex as any less valid a human experience?

If we were in class I would click to my slide of Disney princes and princesses to talk through the awful messages of relationship abuse, gaslighting and gender roles that appear in the films we show to small children without a care in the world… but I will save that for the next chapter.

My point is, talking about pornography is no different than any of the other topics we have covered in this book. They are all part of the same fabric of helping your child become a fully-fledged sexual citizen, able to recognise their own sexual rights and pleasures but never at the expense of others. If we can ensure pornography plays the role it was intended to play – that of entertainment (yes, of a sexual nature but entertainment nonetheless) rather than it taking on the role of sex education, we can reduce the potential for harm for young people. Pornography doesn't need to be a problem, or no more of a problem than the rest of mainstream media.

As parents and safe adults we are good at pointing out the injustices in the world children see about them, and teaching children how to combat them. We can help them understand what a healthy relationship looks like… that boys and girls do not have to conform to certain gender stereotypes, gender roles or social scripts. We can give them messages of body positivity: *our bodies are fantastic and each of ours is special and beautiful in their own way*. We can teach them about consent, asking permission and respecting other people's boundaries. We can teach them sex, their bodies and their feelings are nothing to feel ashamed about. We can talk to them about our attitudes and values when it comes to sex and help them form their own. We can teach them the importance of recognising their own right to sexual citizenship and the importance of acknowledging others too. We can teach them that not everything they see on TV or social media is true; we can teach them to critically evaluate what they see and unpick the messages they are given.

If we can do all this, and provide young people with the comprehensive RSE they deserve, what is left to teach them about porn?

# Notes

1 Age Verification was one of the flagship policies included in The Digital Economy Bill (2017), which was due to come into effect in October 2019, after already being delayed. However it was scrapped after immense opposition, and the realisation that the policy in its present form was unworkable. It has since been replaced with the proposed Online Harms Bill (2019), which sets out strict new guidelines that will requires platforms to abide by a new code of conduct that sets out their responsibilities towards children. The bill requires the most popular sites to set their own terms and conditions, or face fines if they fail to stick to them.

2 If you wish to watch Dr Rothman's Ted talk, the link is here: www.ted.com/talks/ emily_f_rothman_how_porn_changes_the_way_teens_think_about_sex>

3 Ashley Madison, an adultery dating site with the strap-line 'Life is short, have an affair' catered for well-off married individuals. In August 2015, Hackers dropped

information about users' details including names, and email addresses. Amongst the addresses were emails associated with US military, US government, including executives in high-level positions and email addresses linked to the White House, NASA, not to mention the Vatican and the United Nations. Others included senior professors at top universities, local and national government employees in the UK.

4  Have we ever considered the pressure for women to shave their pubic hair is not due to pornography, but instead due to depictions of the classical body in paintings and sculpture? Did you know Goya's painting 'The Nude Maja' (1797) is considered the first European paining to feature public hair… that is a long build-up of social pressure to trim the bush?!

5  The Protection of Children's Act 1978 (s. 1); The Criminal Justice Act 1988 (s. 160); The Sexual Offences Act 2003 (s. 45).

6  We will discuss the issues with the term 'revenge porn' in Chapter 15, which deals with sexting.

7  In 2013, Dr Nicola Prause psychophysiologist and neuroscientist, published a peer reviewed paper based on a study she was running into the porn addiction models (Prause, Ley and Finn, 2013). Her finding completely undermined the claims made on Your Brain On Porn website, which contradicted Gary Wilson's claims. Ever since she has been targeted and harassed by #Nofap and Reboot enthusiasts, to the point of receiving death threats for publishing her work.

8  In 2016 the American Association for Sexuality Educators, Counsellors and Therapists (AASECT) announced that it *didn't* find 'sufficient empirical evidence to support the classification of sex addiction or porn addiction as a mental health disorder', and did not find 'the sexual addiction training and treatment methods and educational pedagogies to be adequately informed by accurate human sexuality knowledge'.

# References

Attwood, F. (2018). *Sex Media*, Polity Press, Cambridge.

Blake, P. (2019). Age verification for online porn: More harm than good? *Porn Studies*, February.

Davidson, W. (1983). The third person effect in communication, *Public Opinion Quarterly*, 47(1), 1–15.

Dawson, K., Noone, C., Gabhainn, S.N. and MacNeela, P. (2020). Using vignette methodology to study comfort with consensual and nonconsensual depictions of pornography content, *Psychology and Sexuality*, 11(4), 293–314.

Grubbs, J.B., Perry, S.L., Wilt, J.A. et al. (2019). Pornography problems due to moral incongruence: An integrative model with a systematic review and meta-analysis, *Archives of Sexual Behavior*, 48, 397–415.

Hancock and Barker (2018). The use of porn in sex and relationship education, *Porn Studies*, 5(1), 97–103.

Lehmiller, J. (2020). A conversation with Dr Nicole Prause Kinsey Institute. Available at: https://blogs.iu.edu/kinseyinstitute/2020/07/16/the-kinsey-interview-series-a-conversation-with-nicole-prause/.

Lehmiller, J. and Rothman, E.F. (2020). The truth about porn, sex and psychology podcast, hosted by Dr Justin Lehmiller, Episode 15, 9 December. Available at: https://podcasts.apple.com/gb/podcast/sex-and-psychology-podcast/id15 05460817?i=1000501861477.

Marston, C. (2018). Pornography and young people's health: Evidence from the UK sixteen18 project, *Porn Studies*, 5(2), 200–3.

McNair, B. (2014) Rethinking the effects paradigm in porn studies, *Porn Studies*, 1(1–2), 161–71.

Mulholland, M. (2013). *Young People and Pornography: Negotiating pornification*, Palgrave Macmillan, New York.

Perry, S. (2019). *Addicted to Lust: Pornography in the lives of conservative protestants*, Oxford University Press, Oxford.

Phippen, A. (2017). Children's Online Behaviour and Safety – Policy and Rights Challenges: A case study of child *online safety in the UK 2010–2015*. Palgrave Macmillan, Basingstoke.

Prause, N., Ley, D. and Finn, P. (2013). The emperor has no clothes: A review of the 'pornography addiction' model. *Current Sexual Health Reports*, January.

Rothman, E.F. (2018). TED: How porn changes the way teens think about sex. Available at: www.ted.com/talks/emily_f_rothman_how_porn_changes_the_ way_teens_think_about_sex.

Shor, E. and Seida, K. (2019). 'Harder and harder'? Is mainstream pornography becoming increasingly violent and do viewers prefer violent content? *Journal of Sex Research*, 56(1), 16–28.

Spišák, S. (2016). 'Everywhere they say that it's harmful but they don't say how, so I'm asking here': Young people, pornography and negotiations with the notions of risk and harm, *Sex Education*, 16(2), 130–42.

Sullivan, R. and McKee, A. (2015). *Pornography: Key concepts in media and cultural studies*, Polity Press.

Webber, V. and Sullivan, R. (2018). Constructing a crisis: Porn panics and public health, *Porn Studies*, 5(2), 192–6.

Zimmer, F. and Imhoff, R. (2020). Abstinence from masturbation and hypersexuality, *Archives of Sexual Behavior*, 49, 1333–43.

## CHAPTER 13

# READING BETWEEN THE LINES OF MAINSTREAM MEDIA

**O**ne of my favourite sessions I deliver to both young people and adults is the one around media social scripts. I will quite often tack it on to the end of a session about porn or attitudes to sex – generally, I squeeze it in wherever I can as I think it is fun.

It makes sense following our discussions around pornography, to pick up some of the themes from the last chapter and show some of the ways you can use mainstream media to instigate discussions with your children. In the last chapter we explored some of the issues and concerns raised by pornography, and certainly some of our fears. Whilst it is important to engage children in conversations around what they see on the internet and the negative messages perpetuated within porn, it is not like you can sit down as a family and point them out.[1] However, you can with mainstream media – you can ask questions as you watch a film, you can ask what they would do if they were in the character's shoes, who they could talk to or ask for help. You can discuss which relationships are healthy and which might be considered abusive. The same goes for the books you are reading or the songs that play on the radio in the car.

DOI: 10.4324/9781003122296-19

# The stalkers' theme tune

It is amazing: you never pay as much attention to the lyrics of songs playing on the radio until your small child starts singing along from the backseat. Whilst there are arguments about the content and themes of contemporary music, such as overtly sexualised lyrics of Cardi B's song 'W.A.P.', which have recently caused such a stir. Arguments reign over whether the lyrics are a sign of female sexual empowerment or simply vulgar and a sign porn culture has gone too far?

However, challenging lyrics are not a new things. There is an old song from 1986 that I find particularly troubling in its lyrics and its content. And yet this song appears on every *Greatest Hits* album of the decade, and most ironically on those compilations of the *Greatest Love Songs* that come out around Christmas and Valentine's day. The lyrics are creepy, possessive and obsessive, and reflect a really unhealthy attitude to women and relationships in general, and yet it is considered one of the greatest love songs ever. I am of course talking about 'Every Breath you take' by The Police (1986). When you have a moment, read through the lyrics – *read it in a creepy whisper* and you will see what I mean. It is the stalkers' theme tune.

It is interesting what narratives of *love* we idolise…

Some of the first stories most of us fall in love with as children are fairy tales. On the surface fairy tales are simple stories filled with magical creatures, princes and princesses, heroes and villains; but beneath the surface they are dark and raw with often very twisted notions of morality comically brought to life by Roald Dahl in his own interpretation of some of the classic stories *Revolting Rhymes* (1982). Fairy tales were never meant to be nice, or suitable for children. They were scary stories designed to highlight moral behaviours – however, many have been sanitised over the years, cleaned up and retold over and over again to fit the sensibilities of the day.

These days, not all children are read fairy tales – but instinctively, somehow we all know the stories. For most children, the Disney versions will feel like the originals and will be their first experience of the tales.

# Once upon a time…

It is the rule: we have to start with 'Once upon a time[2]…' There was the story of *The Snow Queen*,[3] or there would have been if Disney actually named the story correctly. Have you noticed how the last few 'princess' movies have all been titled with adjectives rather than with the name of the central female protagonist: *Rapunzel* was called *Tangled* (Disney, 2010), *Merida* was *Brave* (Disney, 2012) (and *The Snow Queen* was renamed *Frozen* (Disney, 2013). Is this perhaps to encourage boys to see the film? Do the producers think boys will not go if they think it is a princess movie?

Frozen is based on the Hans Christian Anderson tale of *The Snow Queen*. In class, I would ask if anyone could explain a brief synopsis of the plot and the message of the film – essentially, what it is all about. You would be surprised how many older teenagers become excited talking about Disney.

Usually someone will retell the story, scene by scene, but we only want a brief overview. Answers tend to focus on the fact it is about sisterly love. When Anna needs true love's kiss, it is not a man that provides the lifesaving kiss, it is her sister. This is another point to notice; in the last few Disney princess movies they haven't got married at the end, which is traditional. But whilst these are all good answers, they are wrong. It might surprise you to realise but *Frozen* is actually all about grooming and sexual exploitation.

No, seriously… let me explain.

Anna and Elsa are princesses. It just so happens that Elsa has these magic ice powers. When they were little she accidentally *iced* her sister whilst playing and nearly killed her. To ensure it never happens again, Elsa locks herself away, in her room and simply ignores her sister in order to keep her safe.

However, this is unbeknown to Anna as she doesn't remember a thing. Instead, she has grown up knocking on the door, asking: 'Do you wanna build a snowman…?' and being completely ignored.

Time-lapse forward and it is the day of Elsa's coronation and Prince Hans turns up – the villain of the piece. Han picks up on her vulnerability and uses it to build a connection. He tells her he completely understands what it is like to grow up feeling isolated and lonely, as he had older brothers who used to bully him and ignore him. Suddenly everything clicks for Anna. She has finally met someone who understands her.

*Frozen* is the only Disney film in which the *goodie* and the *baddie* have a song together – and in this song Hans grooms Anna. He convinces her that he understands her like no one else as they sing of all the things they have in common. This is the epitome of grooming.

Grooming is the process of convincing someone that you are safe to be around and you understand and care for them like no one else. It is all about making a connection, finding what makes you vulnerable and exploiting the weakness. Importantly, we are all vulnerable in our own way. Some people crave attention like Anna because they are lonely, some people crave love or praise or perhaps to be treated like a grown-up. Some people are in need of material things that are out of their reach due to financial restriction (so be wary if a child suddenly turns up with expensive gifts without explanation). People often think that groomers and exploiters are monsters – they are not; they are charming and convincing, just like Prince Hans. In Frozen, Hans takes on the role of a boyfriend, but sometimes exploiters will take on the role of a friend or parent, or someone who has a caring role for the victim. Grooming can be a slow process, built over months and years, or can be as quick as it is for Anna. Be aware, young men can be groomed too – it is not just something that happens to girls.

The next step is to isolate the victim from their support networks.

Hans does this in one foul swoop as he proposes to Anna. Obviously, having her sister's best interests at heart Elsa refuses to marry her sister off to some strange man in Mickey Mouse gloves. This drives a wedge between the sisters, as Anna believes her sister is treating her like a child and stealing her happiness.

Ok… obviously this is not *sexual* exploitation as it is Disney – but it is '*Kingdom*' exploration. Hans grooms Anna because he wants her kingdom. When she needs true love's kiss, he rejects her and explains he is only in it to win the kingdom – like all exploiters he doesn't actually care for his victim.

Frozen is a really good example of how someone might pretend to care in order to win something for themselves. Whilst with smaller children, we would not use the language of Child Sexual Exploitation (CSE) and grooming, we can still talk through the model.

# Tale as old as time...

Next let's move on to *Beauty and the Beast*. We are going to focus mainly on the original Disney animation rather than the new one with Emma Watson, which is much better and has a more feminist retelling. We start the story with Prince Adam (yes, that was his name – his name was not just *Beast*), who is turned into a Beast by a fairy godmother. She has heard that he has grown up to be arrogant and selfish – some of those key qualities of toxic masculinity epitomised by Gaston – the real beast of the tale.

The fairy godmother turns Adam into a beast to reflect his bad behaviour and casts a spell over the castle. However, the point of tension in the story is how to break the spell. It is not he that has to improve how he behaves and learn how to love. The spell will only break if someone falls in love with him, despite his beastly ways. Essentially, the message is: *If you love him (enough), he will change* – which sounds a lot like a key component of domestic abuse.

Victims of relationship abuse[4] are often made to feel like they deserve their abuse; as if it is their fault. Perpetrators of abuse often blame their partners by saying things such as, 'If you didn't make me jealous...' or 'If you didn't make me angry...' as if this is an excuse for their bad behaviours. 'If only they love them more' it wouldn't happen – we call this gaslighting. To be clear, you are always responsible for your own behaviour and your own feelings. No one makes you behave badly, it is merely a sign you can't manage your feelings.

The 'if you love him, he will change' message feels a lot like gaslighting.

Consider the Beast's other behaviours. Essentially Belle is kidnapped, taken away from her home and told she can't leave. She is a prisoner in his castle. The Beast repeated shouts and screams at her as he has his temper tantrums, throwing furniture around and then blames his behaviour on her.

In the background we also have Gaston, the muscle-bound bundle of testosterone and toxic masculinity. He tells everyone he will *make* Belle his wife – in his mind, she doesn't have a choice. He reeks of entitlement and privilege as he refuses to recognise Belle's own right to sexual citizenship. Gaston even tries to manipulate and coerce Belle to acquiesce by threatening to have her father sectioned. And they say romance is dead.

No wonder Belle decides to stay with the Beast; at least he has a library of books.

# The make-over

Another classic adaptation from the Hans Christian Anderson tale is that of *The Little Mermaid* (Disney, 1989). Like many classic high-school teen flicks, *The Little Mermaid* needs a make-over in order to get her man. Ariel has to completely change her appearance in order for Eric to notice she exists. She gives up her fish tail for a pair of human legs.

Interestingly, in the original fairy tale, when Ariel takes a step on her new human legs, it feels like walking on broken glass. It is a painful process to pretend to be someone you are not. We all have had relationships, whether they be with friends, family members or with partners, where we feel like we are not enough, and so we have to put on a bit of an act in order to fit in. This is never a healthy option – if being yourself is not enough, then they are not really your friends – they should like you because you are your authentic self, because you are fantastic.

It is not only her fishy tail Ariel needs to sacrifice. She also has to give up her voice. This is a really symbolic gesture. If you have no voice in a relationship, you have no say and no control, and no power. This is demonstrated in the boat scene when the creatures, Sebastian and Flounder try to engineer the kiss, to break the spell. Ariel is powerless to seize control of the situation and either say what she wants or instigate the kiss for herself. Why does she have to wait for him to kiss her?

# Not so charming

The story of *Snow White* (Disney, 1937) starts off with the archetype of the evil stepmother. These days, families come in all shapes and sizes and it is not uncommon to have blended or extended families. Nevertheless, this is the story of the magic mirror and the evil queen, who is so obsessed with her appearance (she would literally be taking selfies all day long to post on Instagram). *Mirror, mirror on the wall who is the fittest of them all…* But then one day, the mirror replies, 'Y'alright luv? Whilst you're still pretty nice, Snow White is looking mighty fine!' The Queen, in a jealous rage, sends the Woodcutter to kill Snow White.

The Woodcutter takes pity on poor Snow White, who runs away to live in the forest with seven little hairy men, who make her cook and clean – and no one calls social care? There are definitely some safeguarding issues that need to be addressed here…

Meanwhile, the Queen goes to take another selfie, only to be told by the Mirror that Snow White has checked in on Facebook and is still alive. Here is a lesson about location settings on your mobile phone and the importance of who you allow to follow you on social media.

The Evil Queen disguises herself as an old crone, with a basket of poisoned apples. Now, if Snow White swallows the apple she will drop down dead. However, Snow White, being on the greedy side, takes a huge bite and according to the original tale, the chunk of apple gets stuck in her throat, making her fall into a death-like sleep.

The next point is essential to the plot: the seven dwarves, thinking she is dead, because none of them have done a first aid course, decide she is too beautiful to possibly bury in the ground; instead they decide to lay her in a glass coffin in the woods, so they can watch her rot, which is much better.

Now enter stage left, Prince Charming. Consider, at this point of the story Prince Charming – because that is his name – knows nothing of the Evil Queen, the magic mirror, or the seven little hairy men Snow White has been living with. He knows nothing of the poisoned apple, he doesn't even know anything about Snow White. He is simply riding by on his horse, when he stops and says to himself, 'Hey, look – there's a dead girl in the woods…' He then decides to lift the lid off her coffin, and kisses her so passionately, with his big lizard tongue, he somehow manages to dislodge the apple from her throat, thus waking her up.

If we think back to the chapter about consent: if you remember, there are three requirements we need in order to consent.

# Consent

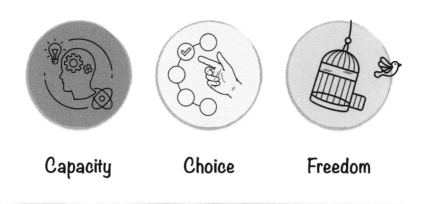

| Capacity | Choice | Freedom |

In this situation, does Snow White have capacity? *No, she was dead at the time.*

Does she have freedom? No, she is literally locked in a glass coffin.

Does she have any choice? *No, she is unconscious!*

It would seem Prince Charming isn't so charming.

At this point, there is always someone who argues that the prince saved her life – if he hadn't kissed her, she would have remained asleep/dead. This is an excellent point. If someone has had a heart attack, for example, and is unconscious, as a passer-by, we don't need to wait for permission, we can just start CPR, as their life is in danger. However, when you give the kiss of life, you do not stick your tongue down someone's throat.

In this case, the prince could have equally lifted the lid off the coffin, and said: 'Urgh, you've got something stuck in your gob,' and grabbed the chunk of apple out of her mouth. When she awoke, he could then have said, 'Do you want a cup of coffee…?' and got all flirty.

This is an awful example of consent, however the original story of sleeping beauty is even worse… but we are not going to go there. Instead, I am going to leave you with this fabulous cartoon by Chris Grady, better known as Lunarbaboon (Figure 13.1).[5]

**Figure 13.1** Remake, by Lunarbabon

# Lessons in consent from *Love Island*

When it comes to consent for kissing, Prince Charming could learn his lesson from the ITV2 show *Love Island*.[6] I think I am one of the very few people who can claim to watch the nightly show for 'work purposes'. Whilst *Love Island* has come in with its fair share of criticism, and a lot of it justified, whether we are talking about issues of lack of diversity, body image or the duty of care responsibilities of reality TV show production companies to their contestants. However, it is one of the only places you will ever get to see consent for a kiss done properly on TV.

Usually, when it is time for the big romantic kiss in the TV drama or Hollywood Romcom, there is *that moment*. The planets align as the moonlight shines flattering soft lights across the stars' face; the wind slowly picks up and their hair gently floats on the breeze; it starts to rain (but only in a romantic way, rather than a drowned rat sort of way), the music starts to play, softly at first as the couple look dreamily into each other's eyes, and grows in intensity as they slowly lean in… until it reaches a crescendo, as their lips meet…

You know what I mean – there is always this big moment. It is romantic, it is perfect, and everyone always knows what to do with their hands.

I regularly have the conversation with young people about how you negotiate a first kiss. How do you know the other person is interested? What are the signs? How do you make your move? And when is the perfect moment? But most importantly, why are we so afraid to ask for permission?

This is where *Love Island* comes in. Due to the nature of the show, with lots of singles coupled up (some by choice, other couples of convenience), to ensure there are no blurred lines or misread signals, the producers have put certain rules in place. Contestants must always ask permission before they kiss or touch in any intimate way.

This has created a novel situation we are not used to seeing on TV; a couple on a date, flirting and give-it-all-the-eye, and then the moment comes (the show adds the music after I assume), but rather than just leaning in, Dave the scaffolder from Grimsby, pipes up and says, 'I think your dead nice, you got have lovely eyes… err, can I have a kiss, babe?' and Danielle, the Beautician from the Wirral, smiles in reply, and says 'Go on then, but only cause you're a bit of me…' And consent is done. The kiss is on and they live happily ever after.

Yes, it is a little awkward, sometimes cringeworthy, but it is also a really important development in changing social script norms.

*Love Island* is far from perfect but it does offer unique opportunities to unpick healthy and unhealthy relationships, communication techniques and the rules of 'girl code', and 'boy code'.

# Normal people, intimacy co-ordinators

If we want to step things up and move from consensual kissing, to a full-blown consensual sexual encounter, then look no further than *Normal People* (BBC, 2020), which is currently still available on the BBC iPlayer. Based on the best-selling book of the same name by Sally Rooney, it tells the story of two high-school friends, Connell and Marianne, and their on–off love affair as they navigate adulthood at Trinity College.

As a sex educator, if I could write a perfect love scene from an RSE point of view, to encapsulate every key message you would hope for from a first sexual encounter, this would be it. It occurs in episode 2 and is the first time sixth formers Marianne and Connell have sex. The scene is a combination of sweet, intimate, awkward, reassuring, sex positive and most importantly joyful.

The display of consent is excellent, as is the communication between the pair. Marianne asks if they can get undressed; Connell asks if what he is doing feels good; Marianne reciprocates; they stumble as they get undressed; Marianne asks if he has a condom; Connell asks if she wants penetrative sex; Marianne is clear about what she wants; there is absolutely no coercion from either of the characters and they both push the encounter mutually forward. But the best bit by far is when Connell turns to Marianne as he puts his condom on and reassures her, 'We can stop, if you want – I promise it won't be weird.' The entire scene is a perfect example of consent, communication and that sex should be something done together.

It is not surprising to learn that behind the scenes was Ita O'Brien, intimacy co-ordinator. This is a fairly new role to production. It may be surprising to learn that, whilst there have always been fight co-ordinators on production teams, to risk assess, plan, manage and choreograph scenes of violence, a similar role for intimate scenes, from kissing to simulated sex, in the past was overlooked.

It is only since the #MeToo movement that more has been done to work with actors and plan the scenes properly (Witton, 2020). At one time, the actors were pretty much told to get on with it. Now intimate scenes are planned with the same meticulous precision as fight scenes. The actors decide what they are happy to do, how much flesh they are comfortable with showing, and how intimate they are happy to be with their co-stars. It removes the pressure of being regarded difficult if an actor refused to do something that made them uncomfortable (ibid.).

Ita O'Brien has worked on some of the most exciting dramas of the last few years, including: *Sex Education* (Netflix), *I will Destroy you* (BBC3), and *Gentleman Jack* (BBC). She is credited as creating supportive and safe environments, where actors' personal boundaries are respected, and they feel confident to perform acts of intimacy without pressure. It is good to know the same level of detail that has been put into preparing actors to perform scenes of violence on screen is now being put into creating scenes of sexual intimacy. Whilst some of the scenes may depict sex acts that are non-consensual, as part of the drama, you can now be sure, behind the camera, consent was at the forefront of every aspect of planning and production (Witton, 2020).

# Notes

1  Please do not do this, I am being facetious. It is a criminal offence under Section 12 of the Sexual Offences Act 2003 to facilitate a child to watch a sexual act (and that includes pornography).
2  In class, when I ask students to give me their abridged version of the tales, I insist they start their answer with: 'Once upon a time…' It makes everyone laugh, as they humour me.
3  *The Snow Queen* was an original fairy tale written by the Danish author Hans Christian Andersen, first published in 1844 in New Fairy Tales.
4  Again, language is important. When we refer to domestic abuse with young people, their impression is what happens to their parents or other adults. They tend not to associate domestic abuse with young people's relationships – despite its prevalence. This is why the term 'relationship abuse' is preferred when talking with young people. Relationship abuse can include violence, coercion, emotional abuse, financial abuse and sexual abuse, or a combination.

5  You can find Chris Lunababoon on twitter: @Lunarbaboon, or on Patreon: www.
   patreon.com/user?u=82761 His cartoons deal with themes of family life;
   parenting advice; mental health and *Star Wars*. I would strongly encourage you
   to check out his work and follow him on social media to genuinely brighten
   your days. He has kindly given permission to reproduce his work here.
6  ITV Studios and Motion Content.

# References

BBC (2020). Normal People, produced by Element Pictures for BBC3.

Dahl, R. (1982). *Revolting Rhymes*, Jonathan Cape, London.

Disney (1937). *Snow White and the Seven Dwarves*, Disney Studios.

Disney (1989). *The Little Mermaid*, Walt Disney Feature Animation and Silver Screen
   Partners.

Disney (1991). *Beauty and the Beast*, Walt Disney Feature Animation and Silver
   Screen Partners.

Disney (2010). *Tangled*, Disney Animation Studios.

Disney (2012). *Brave*, Pixar Animation Studios.

Disney (2013). *Frozen*, Disney Animation Studios.

The Police (1986). *Every breath you take*, Produced by The Police, Hugh Padham,
   Nigel Grey, and Laurie Latham, A&M.

Witton, H. (2020). Doing it podcast: The role of an intimacy coordinator in sex
   scenes with Ita O'Brien. Available at: https://podcasts.apple.com/gb/podcast/
   doing-it-with-hannah-witton/id1464870183?i=1000484987860.

# CHAPTER 14

# MOBILE PHONES AND LIFE ONLINE

## Do mobile phones make life easier or more challenging for kids growing up today?

It often feels as if mobile phones are the bane of our lives. This is especially true if you work in schools. There is always some drama or other around a mobile phone, or you are constantly having to tell kids to put them away. If you have teens at home, they are continually glued to their screens, like some sort of wi-fi zombie with their earphones in, ignorant to the world around them. If you have little ones, they are either stealing your phone so they can play some game or whining about when they can have their first phone.

On top of all that, as adults we are constantly worried of the dangers that lurk online: we worry what they might be looking at on the internet and who they might be talking to. We have heard all about online grooming, trolls and paedophiles who skulk around in chatrooms. We worry what apps our kids might be using, what content they are posting online and who can see it.

There is little surprise to hear young people say, often the only conversations they have with the adults in their lives concerning mobile

DOI: 10.4324/9781003122296-20

phones are inherently negative and concentrate on the dangers of being online (Phippen, 2017). Perhaps this is understandable, considering the majority of parents never grew up with a mobile phone.

Personally, I bought myself my first mobile phone when I was 18 – the classic Nokia 3210, the phone of phones, but it was nothing like a smart phone. You could call, text and play snakes, nothing else. Whereas a modern smart phone is a mini Tardis in your pocket. It is a phone, a wallet, a camera, a video camera (and editing studio); it can host your entire music collection; you can stream the latest movies and boxsets; game console, more powerful than my Sega Mega-drive ever was; you have full access to the internet; personal banking; SAT-NAV, and the full office experience with access to your emails, including your files, word-processor and you can design and run presentations too. It is insane.

However, this is the point: conversations about mobile phones are not simply about mobile phones. Young people use their phone as a digital gateway, a means to access the online world of games, apps and social media. Unfortunately, young people report the adults in their lives rarely talk to them about their online lives or show any interest in discussing the digital world generally (Katz and Asam, 2020; LGfL, 2018). This is a huge missed opportunity, as evidence shows, general engagement by parents in their teen's online life does help to protect them and keep them safe (ibid.).

This is further compounded by the online safety education young people are given at school, which often positions young people as passive consumers in need of protecting (Phippen, 2017), or instead focused on scare stories and 'harmful' apps, rather than building practical skills (Katz and Asam, 2020). In short, young people are dissatisfied by the support they are offered to prepare them for life online. Instead, they want practical advice to help them to deal with real-life situations (Katz and Asam, 2020; Setty 2020; McGeeney and Hanson, 2017; Phippen, 2017) and to focus on helpful competencies and the creative things they could do online (Katz and Asam, 2020). Developing a sense of digital competence is an essential skill all young people need. Ridiculously, this is not new information. The Byron Review, or 'Safer Children in a Digital World', commissioned back in 2007 by the then Prime Minister, Gordon Brown made the same recommendations,

> Having considered the evidence I believe we need to move from a discussion about the media 'causing' harm to one which focuses on

children and young people, what they bring to technology and how we can use our understanding of how they develop to empower them to manage the risks and make the digital world safer.

(Child Psychologist, Professor Tanya Byron, 2008)

Unfortunately, this approach has largely been ignored by politicians and policy makers due to media pressure and in exchange for a series of quick wins (Phippen, 2017). The clearly wrong direction of travel taken by the new Coalition Government was highlighted when Professor Tanya Byron, followed her 2008 report, in 2010 with a second: 'Do we have safer children in a digital world? A review in progress since the 2008' highlighting the areas which were being purposely ignored.

# Miscommunicating

The irony is, when it comes to devices specifically meant to help people communicate, we clearly are not talking or listening to each other. Young people overwhelmingly see the internet and social media as a positive thing, which offers personal freedoms and opens up possibilities (Katz and Asam, 2020). This is especially true for young people who identify as LGBTQ+, for whom the internet offers a lifeline and a space where they can be themselves (Katz and Asam, 2020; McGeeney and Hanson, 2017). Unfortunately, traditional online safety messages which focus on the dangers and the rules miss the mark. If you are a 15-year-old LGBTQ+ young person, who is literally *the only gay in the village*, how is the message of don't talk or meet strangers online going to help?[1]

There is a lack of trust on behalf of young people in adults' ability to help effectively when something goes wrong (Katz and Asam, 2020; LGfL, 2018; McGeeney and Hanson, 2017; Phippen, 2017); and a feeling that parents are simply out of touch and don't understand what life online is like for young people (Katz and Asam, 2020; LGfL, 2018; McGeeney and Hanson, 2017).

In school, young people fear reporting abuse received online as they assume they themselves will be told off, the response being, 'Well, what do you expect posting on Instagram' (Phippen, 2017). This is especially true of children under 13, who fear the focus will be instead be on their age rather than other's negative behaviours, being *too young to be on social media apps.*[2] This belief is what comes from education which focuses on risks, and painting apps as inherently harmful (Katz and Asam, 2020; LGfL, 2018; Phippen, 2017).

This is not only the message young people receive at school but also at home. Young people admit they often do not tell parents if they receive abuse or experience bullying whilst playing games online (Phippen, 2017). The most likely outcome they believe is parents confiscating the game and them being told they are not allowed to play anymore. Indeed, a 2018 survey by the London Grid for Learning discovered two in five young people have never told any adult the worst thing that happened to them online (LGfL, 2018).

This reflects my own experience of discussing mobile phones with young people too. I make a habit of asking young people if they would tell the adults in their life if they got in trouble on their mobile phone. The answer is always the same… 'No, they will take my phone off me'. Young people fail to ask for help from the safe adults around them, due to fear they would be punished for other's bad behaviours.

It seems it is time to change the conversation.

Rather than continuing to focus on the negative side of mobile phones and life online, can we instead switch the focus to some of the positives? As parents, it is literally our job to try and keep our young folk safe – clearly our approach has not been working. Instead, we need to start a new conversation, one that won't end in, 'I told you so', when things go wrong. Instead, conversations should focus on how we can build positive digital citizens who know how to behave, will treat others with respect and most importantly will know whom they can call on when things go wrong to help, not just take their phone off them.

# A phone is freedom

There are a number of key issues we need to get out of the way before we focus on the positives. There are certain behaviours we seem to spend all our time telling kids off for when it comes to their mobile phones. Things like the amount of time they spend distracted by their phone, doom scrolling on social media – just wasting time to no end? Or the fact they are glued to their screen all the time, not present during family time such as at the dinner table. They become so absorbed they ignore you or don't respond when spoken to? Or they sleep with their phone next to their bed, so the last thing they do (when they eventually tear themselves away from the warm glow of their phone in the darkness), before they go to sleep, and the first thing they do in the morning is scroll. The irony being these are all behaviours young people complain about their parents doing too. Young people see you distracted by your phone, checking social media when you could be engaging with them.

We are equally as guilty… pot, kettle, black and all that.

We seriously undermine our protests and anxieties about how our young folk manage their time with their phones, when it is one rule for one, and one rule for another. Young people can spot unfairness and inconsistency at a mile!

I recommend this exercise at home, although the results often don't make for pretty reading. Give everyone a piece of paper and take two minutes – no more – to write down the behaviours that wind you up when it comes to your phones. Have the kids write a list for the adults and you write a list of peeves for the kids. Often you will find you share the same frustrations. Now make rules for *all of you*, not just the young people – and be consistent. If the rule is no phones at the table during mealtimes, then fine – but when you justify needing to check your work email 'because it is important', don't be surprised if your teen needs to check their message from Molly which is equally important – *to them* (Molly has just split up which her boyfriend and it is all kicking off).

It might be interesting to know, the most frequently felt effects of being online are, 'helping me to relax after school' (84%) and 'preventing boredom' – reported by 87% (Katz and Asam, 2020). The internet is just the TV of the day.

Equally, one thing Covid-19 and life during lockdown has taught us is that not all screen time is equal or a waste of time. Suddenly, overnight having a mobile phone and access to the internet became an instant lifeline for everyone. The online world became the office, school and a connection to loved ones. No one had heard of Zoom a year ago, and certainly no one dreamed of doing meetings, lessons or interviews via a webcam.

Imagine if lockdown had taken place during our childhood? How would schooling have functioned? How would we have carried on working?

How would we have stayed in touch with friends and family? Now, the majority of young people[3] could still hang out online, play games, chat and generally be kids – even if they couldn't do it in the same room. We would have been stuck playing patience by ourselves with a battered deck of cards.

During lockdown, we got to see many of the positive sides of life online. Neighbourhoods were setting up WhatsApp or Facebook groups to offer help with shopping or emotional support to people in their street they had never even spoken to before. Marcus Rashford prevented millions of kids from going hungry with an online campaign holding ministers to account to provide free school meals. And you only have to spend 30 minutes on TikTok to see real joy and creativity from young and old folk alike. All these things helped to see us through the dark days.

# Teachable moments – opening up the dialogue

Most young people tend to get their first mobile phone ready for the move to high school. There's a transition from being the oldest in school to suddenly being the youngest, as they are thrown in with the big kids. Suddenly, children have more freedom, as they take bus rides to school or have to make their own way there. With the move to high school also comes the shift away from home emotionally too. The major influence on young people's lives now shifts from family to their peers. A mobile phone is often given to young people with the view to keep them safe, so they contact home if they miss their bus, get stuck, need help or simply to stay in contact with home.

I always recommend to the parents I speak to, to give children their first phone before they go to high school. Even if it is only six months before, but give them the opportunity to practise whilst they are still the big fish in the small pond. Primary school is a far smaller world than high school; any problems are much easier to manage when the peers around them are a much smaller circle of influence. Give them the chance to get things wrong, make mistakes and earn the responsibility of having a phone. Set the rules to keep them safe and drip feed extra rewards as they can prove they can be trusted. This might be in allowing them access to extra apps or games they want or the time they are allowed to spend online. But importantly, be prepared for the fireworks: they will fall out with friends, there will be issues, but you have an opportunity to set the tone for how these are managed.

When our daughter Izzy was given her first phone, it was a battered old iPhone, the oldest one we had in the house, for her 11th birthday in the February. This gave her five months left in school and the month of the school holidays for her to show she could be trusted. I had a newer iPhone 7 available (still second hand but in pristine condition and with a much bigger memory) – that was the carrot for her if she stuck to the rules we agreed.

We spoke openly about what apps Izzy could use and set her up with her own Apple ID that was connected to ours as a family. This meant before Iz could download any games or apps, she would have to put in a request to us that we would have to sign off. This created ongoing opportunities for dialogue, which is key, but these were kept positive in tone. She had the opportunity to put her case forward and explain why the game she wanted was *sooo cool*, which of her friends were playing it, and what it was about – but also, we had an opportunity to talk to her about the ploys games use to make you spend money and buy extras, about the ads in free apps, the data they might collect or how to keep her profile private. Yes, it is occasionally a pain, when she was desperate for a new app and we were busy and missed the notification (her sending it three times doesn't help the situation!), but there was ongoing opportunity to have a conversation.

As time moved on, we could ask her what she needed be aware of or why she thought the app was free (what did they get in return?), and we could help her keep herself safe. When she downloaded new apps, I would sit down and we would go through the privacy settings together and agree the boundaries of how each could be used. Not only were we far more aware of what apps or games she was using but also learning how they worked for ourselves. Rather than us telling her what she could or couldn't do, we instead came up with solution together – as she had a buy-in she was more likely to follow the rules, as she understood them and had made them herself.

Apps have their own privacy settings. Most social media platforms allow the user to choose who can and can't see their posts, plus allow you to lock your profile, meaning only those people you approve can have access and see the things you post. In the early days I tried to make a point, to revisit the new apps Iz was using, checking how she was getting on, who she was following and who she had allowed to follow her (it is amazing how many friends of friends people can collect very quickly in a quest to be popular). Again, this was an opportunity for her to critically reflect about who she let know her business, not an opportunity for me to dictate who she allows to follow her. But equally, this was an opportunity for her to show me all the stuff she liked, her favourite content or teach me how to play another game I would be crap at. You miss a trick if you don't think young people know more about mobile phones and shortcuts than you do…

## Strangers online

I am not a fan of the message, 'don't speak to strangers online' as a safety message. I don't think it is practical or particularly helpful. This is especially true for LGBTQ+ young people, who may need to speak to strangers to make connections with other LGBTQ+ people; or for older teens who may be using online dating apps. If we never spoke to people we don't know, we would never make new friends, or meet anyone new.

Instead, I use the analogy of the bus stop. If a young person is stood at the bus stop waiting for the next bus to come along, if someone asks you the time there is absolutely nothing wrong with being polite and replying. You may even go so far as a chat about the weather and to complain about the cut in funding for rural bus services… however, what you don't do is invite them to look through your handbag, read your diary and invite them home for tea.

There is a difference between interacting with someone in a public space (or platform) and being invited by a stranger to a private place.

The internet is just another huge public space. In that huge room, there are just normal people; yes in any public space there will be a few people who are looking to steal your wallet, or are looking for a fight – there may even be a few people with masks on, pretending to be someone they're not – but it is still just a huge public room. The rules are the same… make sure people know where you are, who you left with and you keep an eye out for your friends.

But most importantly the rule was (and still is in our house), if you come to us and ask for help when things have gone wrong – it doesn't matter what it is, if you see something you aren't sure of; someone sends you something rude, violent or offensive; someone sends weird messages, or contacts you and you don't know them; someone is being mean (even if you were mean first) – we will help you to manage the situation and you get to keep your phone. If we find out things are going on and you haven't told us, then you lose your phone.

Do I honestly think our daughter tells us everything that goes on? No, I'm not daft – I work with teenagers for a living… but she is more likely to come to us when things go properly wrong this way; the little things, I hope she now has the skills to deal with by herself.

I have another cheat up my sleeve due to my job – I regularly ask Izzy for advice: if she has heard about the latest app or game that someone has mentioned during sessions and I get her to explain it to me. Again, it is simply another excuse to start a conversation.

# Online communications

There is another bonus too. Social media apps give you another channel of communication with your teens. You can set up a shared board, or tag them in posts, or send them gifs or memes you have seen you think they might like, or simply to show them you are thinking about them.

As we talked about earlier, sometimes it is easier to say the things we struggle to say through a screen than it is face to face. Think back to our story of Jess, asking her mum to go with her to get the contraceptive pill (Chapter 7). I do this a lot with Izzy if we fall out; it gives me the opportunity to explain decisions, or highlight why someone might be upset or to apologise (we get things wrong too), and she can read it or respond when she is ready.

However, there is a darker side to this phenomenon too. Whilst it might be easier to say the things we struggle to say in person due to embarrassment, it is also true it seems easier to say the horrible things we would never say face to face as well: 'the online environment seems to provide a disconnect in empathy' (Phippen, 2017, p. 73). When you can't see the horror of the impact of your words it is easier to be cruel as there is less impact on you than there would be in person.

The abuse young people (and adults) experience online, the harassment, the inequalities are not unique to the internet, they are merely reflections of the same abuses and inequalities that exist in the real world, only amplified by echo-chambers of people who share your vision of the world (Katz and Asam, 2020; LGfL, 2018; McGeeney and Hanson, 2017; Phippen, 2017). However, there are things we can do.

You do not owe anyone the space to abuse you. Trolls need air to breathe. Mute, block and report those that misbehave or upset you. Your feed is your feed. Freedom of speech does not mean you can come into my home and hurl abuse at me. You can think what you like and say what you like under your own roof but there is no reason why I, or anyone else, has to listen. If you are blocked from a platform due to breaking their terms of use, it is not someone curtailing your right to free speech, it is the consequence of you being a dick. Freedom of speech is not freedom from consequence.

When someone is drunk and abusive in a bar, the bouncers politely show them to the door. They have not been cancelled. It is ridiculous. We need to stop treating the online world as something separate to the real world when it comes to acceptable behaviour. If you flash your genitals at a stranger in the street, it is a criminal offence – it is sexual harassment. Why should it be any different online?

At the end of the day, you get to choose who you follow, and who follows you. You can create and protect your own community online. If the people on your feed do not enrich your life, whether intellectually, emotionally or intimately, if they do not add creativity, inspiration and joy, why on earth are you following them? Just as in life, you can pick your tribe and the people you want to surround yourself with and give your time to. The same is true in the digital world.

The messages and conversation I have advocated all the way through this book are just as apt online as in the real world. The lessons are the same.

One final point… the beauty of a mobile phone is when you are surrounded by so much noise and people that you feel overwhelmed – all you have to do is plug your earphones in and you can have peace, quiet and solitude in a crowded space. Alternatively, when you are feeling lost, and alone in the darkness of your room, you can simply swipe your phone and fill your room with the warm light of screen and be surrounded by friends.

Mobile phones are all about connecting and communication. The irony is we don't always use them to talk.

## Notes

1  This is a reason that LGBTQ+ young people are more at risk online. This is especially true of young people who are not out to their family yet or do not have

their support. This raises the risk level, as LGBTQ+ young people are forced to behave in secret and have fewer places to turn if things go awry (Katz and Asam, 2020; LGfL, 2018; McGeeney and Hanson, 2017).

2 Most social media apps have age restriction of 13+ in order to make an account. This is not due to the content of the apps, or for safeguarding purposes. It is to do with legal requirements in the US, where consent is needed to collect the data of minors under 13 or to advertise to children. By having people sign up to confirm they are over 13, this removes their responsibility.

3 One of the starkest lessons of Covid-19 has been to highlight the pre-existing inequalities that are present in society – the number of children who do not have access to the internet due to the price of wi-fi, or lack of a device to use. Access to the internet is a human right when your education and mental health depend on being able to get online.

# References

Byron (2008). Safer Children in a Digital World, HMSO, London.

Byron (2010). Do we have safer children in a digital world? A review in progress since the 2008 Byron Review, HMSO, London.

Katz, A. and Asam, E.A. (2020). *The Cybersurvey: In their own words: The digital lives of schoolchildren*, Youthworks and Kingston University, London.

LGfL, London Grid for Learning (2018). Hopes and streams: LGfL DigiSafe report on the 2018 Pupil Online Safety Survey, *London Grid for Learning*. Available at: DigiSafe.lgfl.net.

Martin, G. (2020). They told me to change my clothes. I changed the law instead, *TEDxWarwick*, 27 October. Available at: www.youtube.com/watch?v=_K_n-x-W7pY&list=PLo3OAN5w6MGR7T0u6BMK_sb29X66VsPKC&index=14.

McGeeney, E. and Hanson, E. (2017). *Digital Romance: A research project exploring young people's use of technology in their romantic relationships and love lives*, National Crime Agency and Brook, London.

Phippen, A. (2017). *Children's Online Behaviours and Safety: Policy rights and challenges*, Palgrave Macmillan, London.

Setty, E (2020). *Risk and Harm in Youth Sexting Culture: Young people's perspectives*, Routledge.

# CHAPTER 15

# SHAME-LESS SEXTING: IS FLIRTING A CRIME?

**I**magine the situation... **we have two teenagers,** both 17. They are in some sort of a *relationship* and have been happily sexually active with each other for some time. They are mature, sensible and responsible. They have thought and talked about being safe and are taking precautions with the sex they are having. They treat each other with respect and everything they do is agreed and consensual. One day, they go back to one of their houses after school and have sex. They have a lovely time. Later that evening, when back in their separate homes, one of the teenagers picks up their phone and sends the following text with an image attached:

> I was just thinking about all the things we did together earlier naked... Wow, I love being naked with you... you look so good naked...
>
> here is a picture of me naked, to remind you of all the nakedness we did naked

DOI: 10.4324/9781003122296-21

These teens have just broken the law. Both of them have…

Whilst it is perfectly legal for these two young people to have sex: they can be naked in the same room, touch each other naked, look at each other naked – but if they share a picture, suddenly they could both be charged with a sexual offence. Even if the image was shared consensually, it is still illegal (despite the fact, an hour ago they were touching each other naked!) You can understand why this just doesn't seem to add up or make sense to young people. The offence they have committed is pretty serious stuff: distributing and/or being in possession of indecent images of a child.[1]

However, this was never the intention behind the implementation of these laws. These laws were intended to protect children from abuse, not to criminalise young people for flirting with each other. I would hope we would all agree these teenagers are not paedophiles or sex offenders, and whilst we may not be comfortable with or agree with them sharing naked images of themselves with each other, I am sure we do not think they should be needlessly criminalised for their behaviour. In this case, they are already having physical sex in person. Where is the harm? They can't get pregnant from sending a photo (assuming they are a heterosexual couple) or pass on an infection? So, what is the issue?

## Outcome 21

The outcome 21 code, was launched in 2016, and formalises the discretion available to the police when dealing with incidents of the sharing of nudes and semi-nudes.

Outcome 21 states:

*This means that even though a child or young person has broken the law and the police could provide evidence that they have done so, the police can record that they chose not to take further action as it was not in the public interest.*

This allows the police to record the incident but without any further action being taken. This means young people are not needlessly criminalised for incidents of consensual sharing that have been reported to the police.

It is worth noting, however, although the words: 'has come into contact with the police for sharing indecent images of children' appear on any future criminal records checks, it is possible for an incident of sharing nudes and semi-nudes recorded on police systems with outcome 21 to be disclosed on a DBS certificate.

However, information falling short of conviction or caution can only be included on a DBS certificate when an individual has applied for an Enhanced Criminal Records Check. In such cases, it would be for a chief officer to decide if the information is relevant for inclusion.

# Digital romance

If we are going to talk about young people's relationships, whether we like it or not, mobile phones need to be part of the discussion. Technology is an integral part of how young people *do* romance – and for good reason. Young people report, it is easier to flirt with someone you fancy, over messages without everyone watching and listening during break (McGeeney and Hanson, 2017). However, young people are well aware their messages will probably be seen by mates, or even shared, if they say anything too daft.

Interactions over text allow young people to craft their response, or think about what they are going to say as part of the conversation. It helps to remove the pressure of being on the spot – face to face – with the person you have a massive crush on and trying to talk, and maintain a visage of cool despite the fact your mouth has gone dry, your heart is in your throat, your tongue has got stuck, your pulse is racing and you are sweating profusely. Sitting quietly whilst you compose a message by yourself, or with the help of friends, sounds much better. Although, people report a text is now the most common way to break up too. It would seem it is easier to have all manner of difficult conversations via text rather than face to face (McGeeney and Hanson, 2017).

Young people like sending messages as a way to build intimacy and talk openly in ways that are difficult as you start to get to know someone new. This is a benefit but can also lead to oversharing information that in the wrong hands could make someone vulnerable (McGeeney and Hanson, 2017).

Sexting is a natural part of this digital landscape of dating. It makes perfect sense why two people who fancy each other might want to send each other explicit messages or pictures. This is not new behaviour; it is the whole reason Polaroid Cameras were invented back in the day. It is even older than that – history is littered with personal and explicit love letters;

## In class ethics: is it OK?

One of the things I do a lot of with young people is to give them ethical scenarios to explore.

How we use mobile phones in our relationships is no different. There are some very interesting discussions that can come from these sorts of questions, around healthy and unhealthy behaviours. It is a good way of promoting digital citizenship. Here are a few to consider...

### 'Is it OK to...'

- Check your partner's phone to read their messages?
- Look at your Ex's Instagram to see who they are hanging out with?
- Post photos of your friends on social media?
- Ask someone you fancy for a nude?
- Show your friend the nudes you've been sent?
- Pretend to be someone you're not on social media?

and you only have to wander around an art gallery to see pictures and sculptors of the artists' latest fancy – they are the artist equivalent of a sext – they just took much longer to send!

Sending someone a sext can be an effective way to discuss personal boundaries and consent. As we have said, it is much easier to have difficult conversations about what you like, what you are into, or what you might be ready to do via text messages rather than looking someone in the eye and telling them you are into sucking toes. Sexting offers a new way to be sexual with a partner, without the normal risks associated with sex or without the pressure to go further than you planned. You can turn your partner on but there is no pressure to go upstairs as things start to escalate, as you are in separate houses (Setty, 2020; McGeeney, and Hanson, 2017). Although young people are savvy enough to know they also need to be careful not to make promises in the heat of the moment as they send messages back and forth, as they worry, now their partner has it in writing, they may try to hold you to your word (McGeeney, and Hanson, 2017).[2]

The most common reason young people give for sharing explicit images is 'I was in a relationship and I wanted to' (Katz, and Asam, 2020). There is a lot of academic research into sexting behaviours which observe its positive role in relationship satisfaction (Walrave et al., 2018).

For the vast majority of young people, sexting is a positive experience: 78% said nothing bad happened after they sent the image/video/livestream (Katz and Asam, 2020). However, that does not mean that there aren't risks involved because there clearly are. I am often called into schools to help manage the fallout from incidents involving sexting; and you only have to pay attention to the news to hear of the latest celebrity, sports star or even politician who has had pictures leaked. There are clearly risks involved, and both adults and young people will fall foul of them on occasion. However, it is rarely the taking or the original sharing of the images that is the problem.

It is worth pointing out, *not all young people engage in sexting behaviours.* Although many schools will have incidents to deal with,[3] research suggests a significant number of young people aren't sending or receiving nudes (McGeeney, and Hanson, 2017):

- 26 per cent had sent a nude image to someone they were interested in;
- 48 per cent had received one of someone else, sent by that same person.

These figures will hopefully be reassuring. I am aware in a chapter about sexting, me regaling the benefits of sexting is most likely not what you want to hear. However, I am merely trying to set the scene and give you an objective view of these behaviours and why they happen. As parents, thinking of your teens sending or asking other for photos can be an uncomfortable notion to contemplate. However, there is a growing body of evidence that suggests that this is not only typical behaviour for teens (and adults) to engage in, but also the positive nature of sexting behaviours, especially amongst young people (Setty, 2020: Klettke et al., 2019;BPAS, 2018; McGeeney and Hanson, 2017; Crofts et al., 2015).

However uncomfortable it may be, it is a positive thing: young people have new means to building intimacy and trust within a relationship, whilst removing the pressure to actually have sex – as couples can be sexual with each other, without the need to actually have sex (Vanwesenbeek et al., 2018; McGeeney, and Hanson, 2017).[4] The British Pregnancy Advisory Service (BPAS), teenage pregnancy report (2018) highlighted sexting as a contributing factor to the drop in teenage pregnancy and a delay in sexual debut.

Instead, the risk and harm is caused by breeches in privacy or consent, rather than the production and exchange of personal sexualised images themselves (Setty, 2020; Klettke et al., 2019; Crofts et al., 2015). Unfortunately, there is no distinction in the law between consensual sharing and abusive behaviours of coercion or blackmail, and non-consensual sharing. This is also true for how we educate young people about sexting, both at home and school. The extent of education around sexting is often to remind pupils sexting 'is illegal and that if they engage in such practices they are breaking the law' (Phippen, 2017, p. 56).

Whilst this is true in sentiment, it can have drastic repercussions for young people who receive this message, as when things go wrong, they feel unable to report for fear of being blamed or criminalised themselves (Setty, 2020; Walrave, 2018; Phippen, 2017).

# Language – let's be sure we are all talking about the same things

Before we go any further, it is worth taking a moment to consider what we mean when we use the term 'sexting'. This is a term rarely used by young people themselves, and when it is used, refers mainly to rude or explicit text messages (including emojis: apparently 🍆 🍑 💦 🔞 is quite rude and does not refer to your grocery shopping list). This is a different usage than the adults and policy makers who prefer the term *sexting* are using it to mean (UKCIS, 2020). In the eyes of adults, sexting refers to the self-generation and distribution of sexually explicit images to one or more people (Phippen, 2017. Young people tend to refer to these as simply *nudes*. Indeed, the latest guidance from the UK Council for Internet Safety (UKCIS), reflects this more common use of language in the title of their updated guidance: *Sharing nudes, and semi-nudes: Advice for education settings working with children and young people, Responding to incidents and safeguarding children and young people* (2020). This replaces their previous guidance *'Sexting in schools and colleges: Responding to incidents and safeguarding young people* (2016).

Other terms include:

- **Youth produced sexual imagery** or self-generated sexual imagery (in terms of adults).
- **Indecent imagery**: this is the legal terminology used to define nudes or semi-nude images and videos of those under the age of 18.

- **'Child porn'**: as mentioned in Chapter 12 there is no such thing as child porn. They are either indecent images of children or images of child sexual abuse. It is important to use the correct language and not minimise the offence. This is a term used predominantly by the tabloid press. However, young people will often use this term to refer to the legal implications of sexting – 'you get done for kiddy porn.'
- **Image-based sexual abuse**: this term is often used when referring to the non-consensual sharing of nudes and semi-nudes.[5]

Language is important. However, when it comes to educating young people around sexting, as we have already mentioned, there is often no distinction made between consensual and non-consensual sharing of images. They are all lumped in together as if they are the same. It is positive to see the new UKCIS guidance includes the recommendations by Wolak and Finkelhor (2011), who make a clear distinction between 'developmentally-normative' youth sexting and what they refer to as 'aggravated sexting'. As we have discussed above, *developmental-normative* sexting conceptualises these behaviours as a typical part of adolescent courtship routines and a healthy development of bodily and sexual expression (Setty, 2020). In contrast, *aggravated* sexting is characterised by unwanted or coercive behaviours, peer pressure, harassment and potential unauthorised distribution with breeches of privacy and consent (ibid.).

This is an important distinction to make with young people when we discuss sexting practices. As a result of how sexting has been defined as inertly risky and a deviant behaviour, by both the media and educators regardless of the circumstances, there has been a tendency to blame the individual who sexts, rather than blaming the individual who has breached trust or engaged in those 'aggravated' behaviours (Walrave, 2018). For those who have been victims of coercion, abuse or had their pictures shared without their consent, they are often met with the attitude of, 'Well, what did you expect to happen, how could you have been so stupid?' It is often the victim of these breeches of trust who is publicly shamed as well as blamed.

This is especially true of young women. Sexting does not occur in a vacuum but is part of broader social gendered phenomenon, which firmly places female sexuality as either passive or problematic (Setty, 2020). Meanwhile, male sexuality is taken for granted, as young men accrue 'lad-points' for the nudes they can collect, boosting their ego and social standing. In contrast girls are slut shamed (ibid.). These messages are reinforced as schools attempt to deal with the fall-out of an incident.

One of the most consistent phone calls I receive is from schools calling and requesting support around issues of sexting. I am asked if I can come into school and deliver an assembly or a series of class workshops to the year in question. This in itself is not an issue; however, these phone calls with senior leaders often carries the tone of, 'Can you come in and tell the boys to stop pressuring the girls for pictures, and have a word to the girls, and say nice girls don't give in to that sort of thing…' This is not something I am comfortable in doing. I believe this message is counterproductive and only serves to reinforce those gendered stereotypes and has the opposite effect. The boys in the room, especially those that do not and never have pressured girls into sending nudes, hear the message, *this is what is expected of guys and what I should be doing instead*? And the girls in the room who have engaged in sexting, hear the age-old message that 'nice girls' don't sext, so those that do *must deserve everything they get.*

Much of the early discourse around sexting cultures centred on the notion of girls as victims of sexualisation. If only they could learn to be more resilient; engaging in sexing behaviours was considered a sign of low self-esteem and a lack of respect (Setty, 2020). Again, sexting is another example of how young women are not allowed to claim their own sexual agency or citizenship. Instead, it is seen as a failing of character, or a consequence of a sexualised culture rather than entertaining the notion young women might have an interest in sexual and bodily self-expression (Setty, 2020). In contrast, young men are afforded an unquestioned right to sexual citizenship. There is an expectation they will pursue girls by any means at their disposal and when some display inappropriate or harmful sexualised behaviours such as coercion, it is dismissed as 'boys will be boys'; instead, somehow it is still the girl who is held to blame for giving in (Setty, 2020).

Not only are these conceptualisations inherently heteronormative, raising the question, if young women only sext to please their male partners, why then do young women in same-sex relationships still engage in the behaviour? Indeed, if we continue with these messages framing young women as passive victims, without a sense of autonomy or their own desire, how can we expect them to ever take control of the sexual situations they find themselves in? If we continue to deny their right to sexual citizenship and bodily autonomy, how can they ever begin to explore and articulate what they do and don't want (Setty, 2020)? We need to stop framing sex as something *that happens* to women.

Incidentally, young women who do engage in sexting consensually do not see themselves as victims. They describe sexting as being about mutual pleasure, and a sign of respect in their relationships; they enjoy trusting and being trusted in return with the intimacy of an image (Nielsen et al., 2015). However, the constant messages of shame surrounding female sexuality only serves the purpose of creating a barrier to disclosures of non-consensual acts perpetrated against them (Vanwesenbeek et al., 2018; Walrave et al., 2018).

This has been acknowledged in the new UKCIS guidance (2020), where it states,

> Teaching should reflect best practice in delivering safe and effective education: **challenge victim-blaming attitudes.** Some children, young people and adults may express victim-blaming attitudes around the sharing of nudes and semi- nudes. These should be challenged in a constructive and supportive way that encourages them to think critically about the language they use.
>
> (UK Council for Internet Safety, 2020)

# Revenge porn

There needs to be a shift in focus to those who perpetrate aggravated sexting, instead of shaming their victims. Rather than condemning consensual sharing, messages of warning should be aimed at the harmful behaviours of coercion, pressure, blackmail harassment and sharing without consent. Unfortunately, too much of the focus 'is on the act, rather than the abuse a victim may receive as a result' (Phippen, 2017). Too many young people feel unable to ask for help when things go wrong, due to fear of being judged or blamed.

Even the language for non-consensual sharing carries an element of victim blaming, as we call it *Revenge Porn*. This is an awful term and campaigns are underway to review the legislation. First of all, privately produced sexual images are not porn. If we return to the definition we used for pornography in Chapter 12: porn is commercially produced with a view of being shared for financial gain. These are private images, intended for private use; therefore it is not porn. Furthermore, the use of the word *revenge* is troubling. You take revenge because you were slighted first, i.e. this implies the victim must have done something to warrant the attack in the first place.

Revenge porn was made a criminal offence under section 33 of the Criminal Justice and Courts Act 2015. Defined as the non-consensual sharing of private sexual images or videos with the intent to cause distress. However, as solicitor Honza Cervenka explains, this is another problem with the legislation, 'the problems is, how do you prove they did it to cause distress… it is very difficult?'[6] Many who readily admit to sharing images without consent, whilst they have confessed to the crime, they did not necessarily intend to cause distress. They did it in the moment, without thinking or for a laugh, to boost their ego, or impress their friends. In this regard, the legislation falls short.

To make matters worse, as revenge porn is prosecuted as a communications crime, and is not classified as a sexual offence, victims are not awarded anonymity. This has the unfortunate effect of making any images shared publicly potentially spread further, especially when the images are of a celebrity.

There is a current campaign to have the law amended to address these issues. This has come after the successful work of Gina Martin in securing *upskirting* be added to the Sexual Offences Act 2003. Gina Martin took to social media after being let down by the lack of response by the authorities when she reported an incident which took place at the British Summer Time Festival in 2017. A group of lads approached her, and one of them placed a phone between Gina's legs, and took photos just inches away from her crotch. He then shared them with his group of friends. Alerted to the incident Gina snatched his phone and ran to security. In the end there was nothing the police could do, as there was no protection under the law as it stood (because she was wearing underwear – they were not classed as indecent).

A two-year campaign followed, and finally in January 2019 the House of Lords signed off the new bill, adding the criminal offence of 'upskirting' under the Voyeurism Act 2019. This is a really important step forward, as a behaviour many viewed as a bit of a joke is now recognised for what it is, an act of image-based sexual abuse. Language is important. We need to call things what they are. The campaign continues to add revenge porn, cyber-flashing[7] and deepfake under the same banner of image-based sexual abuse.

We have a collective responsibility to challenge these behaviours. Unfortunately, whilst both men and women may enjoy engaging in consensual sexting, it seems to be predominantly men who push the boundaries and women who are shamed and intimidated by incidents of aggravated sexting. As Gina Martin says, in her very powerful TEDxtalk[8] about her experience, men have a responsibility to help solve these issues, as these crimes are predominantly perpetrated by men. Unfortunately, these calls to action are often met with the reply, 'Well, not all men…', and no it is not all men – however, as Gina Martin points out:

> Because maybe if they were, we'd be living in a society where when I talk to guys or male politicians about sexual violence, they want to solve it with me more than they want to prove that they're not the problem.
>
> (Gina Martin, TEDxWarwick, 27 October 2020)

We have a duty to do more as allies and to challenge those who are the problem and not to tolerate these behaviours.

## Shameless…

I am firmly of the belief that simply telling young people sexting is wrong, illegal, risky and something young people should not engage in is not the way forward. I know as a parent, we want to protect our teenagers from decisions that could cause them harm or may come back to haunt them in the future. However, from speaking to young people of all ages, the current approach and messages they receive at home and school, is not making them safer.

Whether we are comfortable with the behaviour is neither here nor there; for me, the point is what will help to keep teenagers who do engage in sexting safe. I believe the way forward is to instead reframe the message. This requires us to take communal action to shift the blame and what we identify as shameful: 'What if being known as "someone who gossips, and shares sexual images without consent" was the more shameful identity and was presented to young people as such?' (Albury 2017, p. 722). This would require acknowledgement and celebration of young people's right to self-expression and sexual citizenship (regardless of their gender). The damage would then be done to the reputation of those who violate other's rights by sharing non-consensual pictures.

By acknowledging a young person's right to sexual citizenship, to be respected and to be in control of their own boundaries, to engage in sexual practices without shame, only reinforces messages of consent, respect and treating each other with shared dignity. There is a moment in the Netflix's TV drama *Sex Education*, which highlights this communal shift.

# Spoiler alert

In episode five of series one, the plot centres around an image, a close-up of a girl's genitals, that has been shared around the school. The anonymous sender is threatening to reveal the identity of the person in the picture, who happens to belong to the bitchy girl, Ruby. Otis, our teenage sex counsellor, explains to Ruby, it is not her that should feel ashamed. The episode culminates in one of the most memorable scenes, as Mr Gruff, the head teacher, is predictably leading an assembly shaming the original sexter, for not only being stupid, but explaining they also could face legal consequences, whilst simultaneously ignoring the behaviour of the black-mailer. However, the students have another idea. They refuse to allow Ruby to be shamed and instead one of the girls stands up in a Spartacus-style moment, and shouts, 'That's my vagina.' One by one, more and more of the girls claim the picture as theirs: 'No, that's my vagina', even one of the boys claims allyship, as he stands and shouts, 'No, that's my vagina'. By their collective effort, the shame is moved from Ruby. It is a fabulous scene… except it's actually a vulva – not a vagina!

Shame less, and open doors for young people to ask for help when things go wrong.

One thing I tend to do in my sessions around sexting is to deliver some simple tips on *safe-sexting*. This is no way an encouragement, but merely some tips for harm-reduction. These may be useful points to talk through with your own teens…

# Safe sexting

**Keeping your phone safe**: this is a very basic point of phone safety. Have a key lock, pin, thumb print, face-scan – whatever, but make sure your phone is secure. A mobile these days has all of your personal details – not only your personal photos. Make sure no one else can access your data and pictures by ensuring your phone locks. This includes changing the settings so your phone locks as soon as you put it down and sleeps.

**Think about where you store your photos**: most apps now will instant store photos you are sent into your camera roll album. Which is fine, until you are showing grandma your holiday snaps, and the picture your partner sent you via WhatsApp late last night suddenly pops up in the feed... Grandma doesn't want to see your dick pics... (I assume?). Most apps allow you to turn off this feature, and also has hidden folders to keep 'personal' photos in. However, please be aware, having photos on your phone of anyone (including yourself) who is under 18 is a criminal offence even if they are consensually produced or shared.

**Think before you share**: one of the problems with mobile phones is everything is instant. It is so easy and quick to share a photo. Sometimes it is worth taking a moment, stepping away from your phone and thinking before you share. This goes for all types of photos, not just sexts. Sometimes we share funny photos of our friends, drunk, in compromising situations, or looking rough as a laugh – but before you post that picture, how would you feel if it were you? Show a bit of empathy. Is it your photo to share? Can you trust who you are sending it to? How likely is it to be kept private? Just take a moment...

**Keep your face and identifying features out of the picture**: if you are unsure, keep your face out of the shot – then there is no proof it is you. Sometime deniability can be a saving grace.

**Only do what you feel comfortable doing**: this is a general sexual health message – or life message. Only ever do what you feel is right and are comfortable with. If someone is pressuring you to send photos (or anything else), they clearly do not respect you, your feelings or boundaries. This is a massive red flag and should be a warning as to how much respect they will show to your private pictures too.

**Add a water mark**: most phones these days allow you to edit or write on the picture. Write on any image who you have sent them to, *'especially for Dave...'* Why would Dave share an image with his name on; everyone will know where it has come from and who is responsible for sharing the image without consent. Dave is now facing a criminal charge.

However, my final tip comes from a young person I had the pleasure of working with for a number of years, as part of a youth council project board. Her name was Danii. We were talking about sexting and gathering the group's views about the best ways to tackle the issue with other young people. Danii shared her story to make her point. I should say Danii was 18 at this point and just about to leave for University. Her view is we should teach young people how to flirt…

Danii explained, she was at home in the bath, and a lad she had been getting to know had text her: 'What you doin'?' She text back, she was in the bath… This tells you how bright this lad was, as his response was, 'Are you naked…?!' Danii being Danii said no, and described the imaginary outfit she was wearing – of course she was naked, she was in the bath! Predictably, this lad text back, 'Send me a picture.' So she did. She took a photo of her toes sticking up out through the bubbles at the end of the bath…

Disappointed, he text back, 'No, a proper photo…'

And this is the killer blow – rather than being pressured into doing something she didn't want to, Danii text her reply: 'you will have to imagine the rest 😉.'

Now that is not only really good flirting, but also Danii hasn't compromised herself in any way. She didn't really know or trust this lad, but equally was enjoying his attention and had fun messaging him. She flirted and teased, but she refused to put herself in a vulnerable position. If a photo of her toes gets out, who cares, she had her nails done.

Perhaps, if we instead acknowledged young people's right to explore and express their sexual desires with their partners, to flirt and have fun as they choose, we could better prepare them to do so in a way that will keep them safe. I agree with Danii, lessons in good flirting sound good to me.

# Notes

1 In the UK, successive acts of Parliament have prohibited the production, possession and distribution of images of children under the age of 18: The Protection of Children Act 1978 (s.1); The Criminal Justice Act 1988 (s.160); The Sexual Offences Act 2003 (s.45). These laws have all been applied to incidents of under-18s sexting.

The law criminalising indecent images of children was created with the aim of protecting children and young people from sexual abuse by adults. It was not devised or intended to be used to criminalise young people. The majority of these laws were also developed long before mobile phones (especially smart phones) become common place and the norm.

Nevertheless, young people who share nudes and semi-nudes of themselves, or peers, are breaking the law and can be prosecuted.

2 Saying in a sext you would like to do something is not consent. There is no obligation to perform whatever act you have agreed to via txt, it is not a contract and this is not how consent works. Consent is fluid. You have the right to change your mind, at any point. Although, this is a conversation I often have with young people who feel the pressure to keep their 'promises' they may have text.

3 In my experience, I am most often contacted by schools to deal with issues with younger teens – usually year 9 or 10s, rather than those that are actually fully sexually active in the older age groups. Year 9 tend to be that funny year, that all go a bit 'wibble'; they have been at the school long enough to feel like they are settled and cocky, unlike years 7 and 8 who are still finding their feet, yet they don't have the responsibility of years 10 and 11 who are working to their GCSEs and have purpose. In my experience, year 9 tend to be a bit rudderless, and desperate to be seen as grown-up which can be challenging (for me, this makes them the most fun to work with!). Older students seem to have more positive attitudes and be more streetwise when it comes to managing sexting, perhaps from learning from experience when something went wrong for someone in their year when they were in lower school.

4 It will be interesting to see how Covid-19 and lock-down has affected sexting behaviours when we get that data. However, I would assume, there has been some real positives in helping couples to maintain intimacy and a sexual relationship, even whilst they are kept apart and isolating from each other.

5 Terms to describe offences such as 'revenge porn' and 'upskirting' are also used to refer to specific incidents of nudes and semi-nudes being shared. However, these terms are more often used in the context of adult-to-adult abuse rather than in discussion of young people. Non-consensual image-sharing offences are outlined in the Criminal Justice and Courts Act 2015 (s.)33–5, Voyeurism (Offences) Act 2019 and (s.67A) The Sexual Offences Act 2003.

6 Honza Cervenka is a solicitor at McAllister Olivarius, focusing primarily on revenge porn cases. He was part of a panel discussion for the online newspaper: Tortoise ThinkIn: Life in the porn age: the discussion was chaired by: Nichi Hodgson, and panellists included: Paula Hall, sex addiction therapist; Charlotte Rose – sexpert and consultant; Misha Mayfair, porn actress; Jerry Barnett, Founder, Sex and Censorship Campaign and Honza Cervenka, solicitor at McAllister Olivarius, focusing primarily on revenge porn cases, www.youtube.com/watch?v=2Za58f7R0IM&list=WL&index=32&t=0s

7 Cyber-flashing refers to sending unsolicited sexual images to unsuspecting people using your mobile phone's wi-fi. On apple phones, it is using the Airdrop setting on a similar things can be done using Bluetooth on android. When you

click on a photo on your phone, you can share via airdrop – all of the devices with the setting switch in the vicinity will appear.

This can be particularly frightening when in a public space and you receive a dick-pic with a message saying 'hello beautiful', for example. You have no idea who has sent the message, other than the ID they have assigned their phone – which can be set to whatever you choose.

To prevent strangers from accessing your handset in this way you can change your settings, and either turn the feature off, or to only phones in your contacts.

8 They told me to change my clothes. I changed the law instead. | Gina Martin | TEDxWarwick 27 October 2020: www.youtube.com/watch?v=_K_n-x-W7pY

# References

BPAS (2018). British Pregnancy Advisory Service Report: Social media, SRE, and sensible drinking: Understanding the dramatic decline in teenage pregnancy, May.

Crofts, T., Lee, M., McGovern, A. and Milivojevic, S. (2015) *Sexting and Young People*, Palgrave Macmillan, Basingstoke.

Katz, A. and Asam, E.A. (2020). The Cybersurvey: In their own words: The digital lives of schoolchildren, Youthworks and Kingston University, London.

Klettke, B, Hallford, D.J., Clancy, E., Mellor, D.J. and Toumbourou, J.W. (2019). Sexting and psychological distress: The role of unwanted and coerced sexts, *Psychology, Behaviour and Social Networking*, 22(4), 237–42.

McGeeney, E. and Hanson, E. (2017). *Digital Romance: A research project exploring young people's use of technology in their romantic relationships and love lives*, National Crime Agency and Brook, London.

Neilsen, S., Paasonen, S. and Spisak, S. (2015). Pervy role-play and such: Girls' experiences of sexual messaging online, *Sex Education*, 15(5), 472–85.

Phippen, A. (2017). *Children's Online Behaviour and Safety: Policy and rights challenges: A case study of child online safety in the UK 2010–2015*, Palgrave Macmillan, Basingstoke.

Setty, E. (2020). *Risk and Harm in Youth Sexting Culture: Young people's perspectives*, Routledge.

UKCIS (2016). UK Council for Internet Safety, Sexting in schools and colleges: Responding to incidents and safeguarding young people', UKCIS in collaboration with the NPCC and Charlotte Aynsley, London.

UKCIS (2020). UK Council for Internet Safety, Sharing nudes, and semi-nudes: Advice for education settings working with children and young people Responding to incidents and safeguarding children and young people. Document produced in coordination by UK Council for Internet Safety's Education Working Group in partnership with the NPCC. Available at: www.gov.uk/government/organisations/uk-council-for-internet-safety.

Vanwesenbeek, I., Ponte, K., Walrave, M. and Van Ouytsel, J. (2018). Parents' role in adolescents' sexting behaviour, in M. Walrave, J. Van Ouytsel, K. Ponnet and J.R. Temple (eds), *Sexting*, Palgrave, Basingstoke.

Walrave, M., Van Ouytsel, J., Ponte, K. and Temple, J.R. (2018). 'Sharing and Caring? The role of social media and privacy in sexting behaviour', in M. Walrave, J. Van Ouytsel, K. Ponnet and J.R. Temple (eds), *Sexting*, Palgrave, Basingstoke.

Wollack, J. and Finkelhor, D (2011). *Sexting: A typology*. University of New Hampshire, Crimes against Children Research Centre, Durham.

# CONCLUSION: IT TAKES A VILLAGE...

**T**hank you for sticking with me – or for at least being the type of person who reads the last chapter first…

I am well aware some of the content of this book may have made you feel uncomfortable. However, it has not been my intention to try and be radical, or cause offence. My aim is, and always has been, to keep young people safe. Unfortunately, in my experience, many of the things we have been doing in the hope of keeping children safe, have often made things worse. I hope the topics we have explored and the stories I have told have at least been food for thought and challenged some of your thought processes?

When we are discussing sex and relationships, we are cutting down to the foundations of our beliefs, our values, and how we see the world. Sex has always been political. Nevertheless, as I say to young people at the start of every session – this is not a maths lesson, where there is always an obvious correct answer. You get to decide your own values and beliefs when it comes to sex – I am not here to try and convince you to follow mine.

My intention in this book has been to make sure that you are better informed of not only the issues and research in each topic – but most importantly, you get to hear the voice of young people and what they say when the adults are not around. Unfortunately, if we are not the ones

DOI: 10.4324/9781003122296-22

filling the gaps in young people's knowledge, answering their questions, and helping them to form positive attitudes to sex, relationships and their partners, they are left to search for answers elsewhere.

I know for some of you the thought of talking to young people about topics such as pornography, sexting or worst of all their sexual pleasure may be horrifying, regardless of whether you are a parent, teacher or social worker. However, I honestly believe it is the only way to bring about sexual equality and help young people to gain their sexual citizenship and the tools they need to help keep themselves and their partners safe. But equally I know it can be scary… and tempting to leave it up to someone else.

Years ago, back in the early days of working with young people, I was sent to a day-long event exploring working with young people around bereavement. It didn't just focus on death, but other forms of bereavement too, such as loss, separation and divorce as well. I can't remember anything about the day, except the plenary at the end of the event. I remember walking into the main hall, which was packed – it was a massive event for a couple of hundred people. And a guy put his hand up. He thanked the trainer for an amazing day that had really made him think about bereavement in a completely different way… and then he said, 'But no matter what you say, I really don't think I am the best person to talk to a young person about a death in their family… I know no matter how much training I have – I wouldn't know how to manage the situation, what to do or the right thing to say…'

I watched as the trainer nodded along as he spoke and looked back with empathy as she thanked him for being brave enough to speak up and be completely honest. And then the trainer said something that has stuck with me ever since…

She said, 'I don't give a shit…'

You could see the guy, along with everyone else in the room, look taken aback before she went on '… and neither do young people. Young people don't go to the most qualified person to talk to, the one with all the training – they go to the person they trust and think will listen. They don't want you to have all the answers – they just want you to listen.'

This is a story I retell all the time in my trainings with professionals, because If you are working with young people – teenagers especially – you need to be prepared for them to talk to you about their worries and concerns.

The trainer was right. Young people talk to who they trust – not the person with the counselling qualification. They go to who they like and have a relationship with. That means it could be you… this is true of talking about bereavement, it is also true of issues around sex and relationships. You don't need to have all the knowledge or be the *best person* to talk to – you just need to be able to listen.

To be honest, however uncomfortable the situation may be, or how horrifying the disclosure, at the end of the day it is a compliment – they are coming to you because they see something in you that makes them *think* you are the one who will listen. You must have been doing something right. It doesn't matter whether or not you think you have the right skills, or the right temperament, or the right words of wisdom to pull out of your top pocket. If we are working with young people, we have a duty to manage these situations and we should all be able to listen. And if we can't… why are we working with young people in the first place?

It doesn't matter if you have been reading this book as a parent, a carer, a teacher, a social worker, a youth worker or whatever – if you are living with, or working with children and young people, you are the right person to have these conversations. The truth is, you don't get to decide – whether you like it or not, the children in your life will be looking at you for answers, and to see how *you* manage your relationships. They are looking and listening to see how you react, what you say, and what your values and beliefs are in regard to sex and relationships. Children do not learn about sex and relationships only from formal lessons and planned conversations. They piece things together and absorb the world around them. It is our job to help them make sense of it and model the best examples we can as we go.

The problem: many of us are still working these things out too… and that is OK. Telling young people you do not have all the answers is OK – it is not only OK, it is preferable. Teenagers always think they should have all the answers – especially when they get to year nine!

Whilst this book was originally aimed at parents, it is just as important a read for those who work with children and young people too. Any safe adult who spends time with young people has a duty to be ready to help shape young people's views and attitudes in a positive way.

To be honest, most of us wear more than one hat anyway. As parents, many of us have jobs which bring us into contact with other people's children, making us the safe adults in the room. Teachers have kids themselves, social workers have nieces and nephews. Me, I wear a number of hats. I train professionals, work with parents as well as talking to children and young people; but I am also an uncle and a dad too. Whilst I have young people I have never met before telling me all their secrets – I don't assume for a moment I am always my own daughter's first choice of safe adult she chooses to talk to. However, I reason, the more young people I talk to and teach and the more safe adults I can help to answer her (and other kids) questions, the safer she will be.

Remember, we do this work not only so young people have the information and the tools to keep themselves safe, but also to instil the values and messages that will prevent them from causing harm to others and keep their partners safe. Whilst every victim of sexual assault is someone's child, so is every perpetrator.

They say it takes a village to raise a child. This is what they mean.

Whilst we may find it easier to be the professional managing other people's kids and their dramas, than managing the conflicts in our own home; or to find it easier to be the teacher at the front of the class answering questions, than talking to our own child. None of us are perfect. None of us have all the answers. All children need a village of safe adults around them, to help shape and reinforce positive messages and so they can pick and choose who *they* want to talk to.

There is another book I recommend to all of the professionals I work with, because it struck a chord with me. It is by Paul Dix. He has is a teacher, a teacher trainer and behaviour management specialist, who has spent his career working in and supporting some of the toughest pupils in schools and referral units. His book is called *When the Adults Change, Everything Changes* (Dix, 2017). As the title suggests, it is all about safe adults modelling positive behaviours. How can we expect young people to manage their feelings or relationships, if the adults around them can't lead by example. Behaviour management is not about intimidating children, shaming them, or using your power to bully them into toeing the line.

Whether we like it or not, in the eyes of young people we are on trial 24/7. They are watching us to not only see how they should behave and react to situations – but also for signs you are a safe person to talk to. As I have said constantly throughout these pages, we have to earn the right for young people to talk to us. We have to store up collateral for a rainy day when our teens world has come crashing down, if we want to be the one allowed to help tidy the mess.

You may have noticed there is no specific chapter on relationships or, more accurately, healthy relationships, as this has been a theme throughout the book. I have tried to highlight the important messages of how we should treat our partners with kindness, respect and empathy – it doesn't matter if they are a one night stand or the love of your life. They all deserve to be treated as an equal citizen. The reason I decided not to write a chapter exploring healthy relationships is we tend to repeat the patterns and behaviours we have learned. This is why I have tried to emphasise the importance of safe adults modelling these behaviours – rather than writing you a list of positive qualities. We all want a partner who is kind, caring, funny and thoughtful – but if it was that easy, why do sensible and intelligent people enter into abusive relationships?

If you want your child to choose healthy relationships, teach them how to manage their emotions. The psychotherapist and agony aunt Philippa Perry in her book, *The Book You Wish Your Parents Had Read (and your children will be glad that you did)*, suggests there are four key skills we need to teach our children:

These are:

1. Being able to tolerate frustration
2. Flexibility
3. Problem-solving skills
4. The ability to see and feel things from other people's point of view
(Perry, 2019, p.175)

Again, these are best taught through modelling, through how we respond to our child and how they see us behave towards others around us – especially during points of conflict.

None of these are one-off lessons – they are things we need to practise every day. Again, that is a key theme to the messages in this book. None of this can be done in a single sitting. The idea of sitting down with your child and having the talk is a ridiculous notion. These messages need to be drip-fed, and weaved into family life, and day-to-day interactions. Less of the talk and more of an ongoing conversation.

The greatest barrier I believe is shame. Shame slams doors and encourages secrets and silence. For so long we have used shame as a means to curtail and control sexuality, especially for young women. In every instance this serves the only purpose of making young people less safe, as they are too ashamed to ask for help. However, empathy is the antidote to shame. 'If you put shame in a petri-dish, it needs three things to grow exponentially: secrecy, silence and judgement. If you put the same amount of shame in a petri-dish and douse it in empathy it can't survive' (Brown, 2012).

In my opinion, our job as safe adults is to open as many doors as we can. We can do nothing more.

I suppose at this point, it is worth returning to the question I raised in the introduction: When it comes to our child's intimate relationships and their first sexual experience, what is it we want?

For me, this is still the essential question – it is the point of everything between these covers and everything we should all be working towards.

Throughout this book I have used the phrase *safe adult*. Regardless of your role or relationship. That means you.

# References

Brown, B. (2012). Listening to shame TED. Available at: www.youtube.com/watch?v=psN1DORYYV0.

Dix, P. (2017). *When the Adults Change, Everything Changes: Seismic shifts in school behaviour*, Independent Thinking Press, Carmarthen.

Perry, P. (2019). *The Book You Wish Your Parents Had Read (and your children will be glad that you did)*, Penguin Books, Milton Keynes.

# QUIZ ANSWERS

## General knowledge

1. Heterosexual: 16; between men: 16; between women: 16
2. There are no age restrictions, access is governed by the Fraser Guidelines and Gillik Competency. See pages 227–8.
3. Same as above: see pages 227–8.
4. There are no official age restrictions on buying condoms, but individual retailers may have their own policies in place.
5. 16–17 (various surveys put age of sexual debut between 16–17 years old).
6. 1.3% according to figures from BPAS (2018) Social media, SRE, and sensible drinking: understanding the dramatic decline in teenage pregnancy.
7. 16–19 followed by 20–25. This is why we prefer to use the term 'relationship abuse', as 'domestic abuse' is often assumed to be associated with older age groups.
8. Section 28 prohibited the promotion of homosexuality as a legitimate lifestyle/family in schools and other local authority settings such as libraries (books were banned). It was essentially a ban on acknowledging or talking to young people about the existence of gay people in society.
9. 2003 in England and Wales, Scotland revoked section 28 in 2000.
10. For nudes or semi-nudes you have to be over 18 years old: see Chapter 15.
11. How their vagina smelt. These are needless worries caused by shame.
12. Pluck their mistress's pubic hair. Removing all pubic hair has not come from the influence of porn – it has been going on for a long time.

# Sexual health

1. It implies you would need to take it first thing the next day with your cornflakes – this is not true. You have up to 3–5 days for emergency contraception to be effective. See pages 224–5 for more details.
2. There is no age limit – sexual health treatment comes under the Fraser Guidelines and Gillik Competency. See pages 227–8 for more details.
3. Chlamydia is still the most common, mainly due to it often being asymptomatic.
4. Parasites such as crabs and scabies can be passed on through close body to body contact, as can genital warts. Hepatitis and HIV can also have other routes of transmission. To find out more about STIs, check out Chapter 9.
5. i. urine sample. ii. swab test iii. blood test iv. visual examination
6. Up to 24 weeks.
7. Studies show that shaving and waxing, as it can damage the sensitive skin around the genital, can increase the likelihood of passing on STIs.
8. These both allow young people under the age of consent (16) to access sexual health services, including contraception services, STI screening and abortion services. See pages 227–8 for more details.
9. 1855.
10. 1 December every year. People wear red ribbons to raise awareness.
11. Stealthing is the practice of removing a condom during sex or pretending to wear one. This is a criminal offence as it nullifies consent. Your partner only consented to sex with a condom; this changes the perimeters of the encounter.
12. A merkin is a pubic wig. They became popular to hide the signs of having secondary stage syphilis. Often those infected would develop a rash across their body, but also one of the other occasional symptoms of syphilis can be loss of hair, including pubic hair. But more commonly loss of hair was due to the treatment of giving patients mercury – this certainly did cause hair loss. Merkins were used to hide these symptoms (especially by sex workers, who would simply pull up their skirts in alleyways rather than get undressed in a room).

# Contraception grid (with answers)

| Hormonal | Barrier | Other |
|---|---|---|
| Combined pill | Condom | IUD |
| Minipill | Femidom | IUS |
| Implant | Diaphragm (not STI) | Withdrawal* |
| Patch | | Rhythm* |
| Injection | | *not reliable or |
| Nuva-ring | | recommended |

| Emergency | Permanent | LARC |
|---|---|---|
| EHC – morning after | Vasectomy | IUS |
| Ellal | Sterilisation | Implant |
| IUD | | |

# Sex media

1. Actually there is no law to say how old you have to be to watch porn. It could, however, be illegal to watch porn with someone who is under 18, even if you are under 18 too. It is illegal to sell or facilitate watching porn to anyone under 18.
2. There are no official restrictions – if it can be sold in a petrol station or paper shop, it is not porn. However, individual retailers may introduce their own guidance.
3. See above. Books (even erotic fiction) are not classed as porn.
4. The watershed marks the time programmes that are aimed at adults began on television – 9pm. However, it is kind of a moot point now that everyone watches digital TV and rarely watches programmes live.
5. If you can imagine it, there is porn of it.
6. Penguin books for publishing the banned D.H. Lawrence novel, *Lady Chatterley's Lover* in 1960.
7. A woman with pubic hair. Before this all women had the classical figure – hairless.
8. Allows the police to record an incident of no further action, when a young person comes in contact with the police for (consensual) sexting offences, rather than criminalising them needlessly. See pages 295–6 for more details.

You may have come across the following terms in the media, but what are they?

9. Deepfake: is a fake image or film produced using A.I. See page 258 for a proper explanation.

10 Upskirting: as it says, taking non-consensual images under a person's clothes. It became a criminal offence in 2019 under the Voyeurism Act 2019. See page 303 for a proper explanation.

11. NoFap: is an online group who promote the 'health benefits' of not ejaculating. The idea is based on pseudo-science and is linked to misogynistic groups and conspiracy theories, such as the red pill. See page 261 for more details.

12. Cyber-flashing: using an open wi-fi connection through blue tooth or airdrop to send unsolicited sexual images to strangers in a public place. See page 303 for more details.

# INDEX